THE LITERARY MASTERPIECE CALLED THE *Book* OF *Mormon*

THE LITERARY MASTERPIECE CALLED THE *Book* OF *Mormon*

JAMES T. DUKE

CFI
Springville, Utah

Paperback ISBN13: **978-1-4621-4816-5**

Published by Cedar Fort, Inc.
925 N. Main Springville, Ut., 84663
www.cedarfort.com

Distributed by:

Cover design by **Shawnda Craig**

Printed in the United States of America
10 9 8 7 6 5 4 3 2 1
Printed on acid-free paper

Library of Congress Cataloging-in-Publication Data

Duke, James T., 1933-
The literary masterpiece called the book of Mormon / James T. Duke.
p. cm.
ISBN 1-55517-711-5
1. Book of Mormon--Criticism, interpretation, etc. I. Title.
BX8627.D85 2003
289.3'22--dc22
2003015136

PREFACE

The Book of Mormon is my favorite book and I love it with all my heart. I had the wonderful opportunity to teach classes in the Book of Mormon at BYU, and learned much from my teaching and preparation.[1] I had read articles by John Welch concerning chiasmus and found that my students were very interested in this literary form. I even found a couple of these myself, which was a great thrill.[2]

I'll never forget my excitement when I started reading *The Book of Mormon Text Reformatted according to Parallelistic Patterns* by Donald Parry.[3] Suddenly I saw things with new eyes. Here was the Book of Mormon, but Brother Parry had organized it in such a way that I could see how many parallels were present, such as chiasms, alternates, and antitheticals. I was amazed at the things Parry had discovered. I read Parry's two introductory essays, read through the Book of Mormon several times quickly, and then began to read very slowly, studying each word and sentence. This led me to more discoveries, more research, and more reading about Biblical poetry and parallelism over six or seven years. The result is this book.

I believe anyone who teaches classes concerning the Book of Mormon needs to read Parry's reformatted version of the Book of Mormon. The influence of this book on my own study of the Book of Mormon has been extensive,[4] and I will never be able to repay him for this great treasure. It has increased my understanding of the doctrines of the book and my testimony of it as well.

Much of this present book is the result of my own research and thinking. However, much of it relies on the scholarship of many individuals who have studied the Book of Mormon over many years. One of my goals in writing this book is to make the writings of these scholars more accessible and to bring together in one place the many strands of research concerning the literary structure of the Book of Mormon. I have done this in order to "make the case" that the book is a literary masterpiece, and I have tried to be very careful to distinguish the contributions of others to the analysis of the literary structure of the Book of Mormon.

While my testimony of the Book of Mormon was developed many years ago, and has grown through the decades, I now know with greater certainty that it is a book of ancient date and could only have been translated through the gift and power of God. It is my sincere prayer that this present work will help the reader to understand and appreciate the Book of Mormon more fully, and to love it as I love it.

NOTES

1. John W. Welch, "Chiasmus in the Book of Mormon," *BYU Studies* 10/1 (Autumn 1969): 69-84.
2. James T. Duke, "The Literary Structure and Doctrinal Significance of Alma 13:1-9," *Journal of Book of Mormon Studies* 5/1 (Spring 1996): 103-118.
3. Donald W. Parry, *The Book of Mormon Text Reformatted according to Parallelistic Patterns*. Provo: FARMS, 1992.
4. See especially chapters 9-10, 15, 17, 19-22. In these chapters, and occasionally elsewhere, I have followed Parry's methods of presenting parallels, such as his numbering and lettering formats. These are quite different from those originally used by Welch.

CONTENTS

CHAPTER ONE

INTRODUCTION

The Book of Mormon is a literary masterpiece! It contains a wealth of literary forms and figures of speech, with dozens of literary patterns. Its language is poetic, symbolic, magisterial and beautiful. It encompasses a treasure of literary gems, such as metaphors and similes, idioms, aphorisms, maxims, and quotable phrases. Its text is memorable and stirring, stimulating both spiritual and emotional sentiment and also intellectual thought and reflection. Many of its teachings have great depth of meaning, and this meaning is communicated at many different levels.

Any literary work must be judged by the standards of its time and place. The greatness of the Book of Mormon should be judged by reference to Hebrew language and culture, not by the standards of nineteenth-century America or those of literature departments of twenty-first-century American universities. As we will show, the Book of Mormon has many links to Hebrew literature and culture, such as the use of parallelism and chiasmus. There is also much historical and interpersonal conflict, which often is the standard of great literature. Granted, there is some use of repetition, but such repetition is used to create parallelism, which is the standard of Hebrew literature. However, the repetition used is relatively minimal, and the style is never boring, dull, or monotonous. Some frequently used expressions such as "behold" and "and it came to pass" are standard expressions in Hebrew culture. Thus, to call the Book of Mormon a literary masterpiece is not hyperbole but rather justified acknowledgment.

While the spiritual aspects of the scriptures are always the most important matters to which the reader should pay attention, the literary aspects are not simply "accidental by-products" or "felicitous embellishments."[1] According to Robert Alter, "Literary art [in the scriptures] is neither intermittent in its exercise nor merely ancillary to the writer's purposes."[2] Rather, literary forms are essential features of scripture. Indeed, God speaks to his human children in literary speech and style. The aim of this book is to analyze the literary features of the Book of Mormon as a means of helping us to read the book with "new eyes" by giving us a new appreciation for this monumental masterpiece.

The Book of Mormon is a record of several entire societies. It chronicles the creation of two competing societies, the Nephites and the Lamanites, and their conflicts and wars for more than a thousand years, resulting in the annihilation of the Nephites. It also chronicles the history of the Jaredite society, the sweep of its history for perhaps sixteen hundred years, and its eventual destruction through civil war.

The Book of Mormon covers such important historical processes as sea voyages, movements of large numbers of people, wanderings in the wilderness, wars and revolutions, assassinations, the intrigues of rulers and kings, the preaching of prophets and the fulfillment of their prophecies, and the societal processes of changes in languages, governments, religion, and social institutions. It reports alterations of culture and the conflicts of socioeconomic classes. It also documents the lives both of people of great achievement and intellect and people of more modest existence, as well as the machinations of people seeking power and privilege.

What makes a literary work a masterpiece? First, the language is often luxuriant and poetic.

> Since poetry is our best human model of intricately rich communication, not only solemn, weighty, and forceful but also densely woven with complex internal connections, meanings, and implications, it makes sense that divine speech should be represented as poetry.[3]

Literary works are full of metaphors and similes, of carefully chosen words and phrases, of notable sayings and aphorisms. Great literature also has a monumental theme and subject matter, and while referring to a particular time and place, has universal appeal and application.

This great work of scripture reflects the writings of a number of authors, most of whom were men of great learning and intellect and who were leaders of their people. These authors struggled with many challenges and sought to do God's will. As they wrote, they made use of a remarkable series of literary patterns and styles, including dozens of literary devices. Ethelbert W. Bullinger, one of the great analysts of the literary style of the Bible, called these simply "figures of speech."[4] He noted that the Greeks and Romans identified approximately two hundred different figures of speech. However, the Middle Ages brought a decline in the usage of these figures and an almost total neglect of literary analysis.[5] Bullinger tried to rectify this with a definition and classification of Biblical figures of speech. He "catalogued over 200 distinct figures, several of them with from 30 to 40 varieties. Many figures have duplicate names which brings up the total number of names to more than 500."[6] Much of the nomenclature used to identify these figures of speech is from either Greek or Latin, whereas we have tried to give English titles to many of these figures of speech. The use by Biblical and Book of Mormon authors of many and varied literary figures of speech is "exceedingly" unusual and remarkable, and illustrates the extraordinary literary abilities of the authors.

Joseph Smith had no knowledge of these figures of speech and no literary training, but these literary forms are as readily found in the Book of Mormon as they are in the Bible. God speaks to human beings not in dull and monotonous speech, but in literate and distinctive speech that catches the attention of the reader and causes deep reflection and solemn pondering.

As Adele Berlin has said, "it is relatively easy to make a cake if you have the recipe. It is somewhat trickier to start with the cake and from that figure out how it is made."[7] Our desire is to start with the cake, the text of the Book of Mormon, and to identify the recipe used by its authors, that is, the literary means by which it was accomplished.

Two other things are remarkable about The Book of Mormon. The first is that this literary masterpiece appeals so strikingly to ordinary readers who find in it meaning and inspiration, but who would find the literary masterpieces of their society, such as the writings of Shakespeare, Milton, Goethe, or Dumas, too daunting and intimidating. In many respects it is similar to the Holy Bible, which also is a literary masterpiece and which has great appeal to the masses and to people with limited literary skills.

The second remarkable thing about the Book of Mormon is that, unlike the Bible, its brilliance has never fully been appreciated by its readers. Even people who have been recognized as experts in the study of the Book of Mormon, such as Sidney Sperry, have sometimes been embarrassed by what they considered to be peculiar and unusual literary conventions, such as its "boring" repetition and its tendency to use quaint words and phrases such as "behold," "yea," and "it came to pass" much too frequently for the literary tastes of such experts. Sperry labeled the Book of Mormon "translation literature" which, he said, uses "simple literary forms."[8]

Some critics, therefore, have had what they thought was a field-day in criticizing some aspects of the Book of Mormon text without themselves recognizing the intricacies of its literary structure, the beauty of its language, the remarkable aptness of its metaphors, the Hebraic nature of its contents, or the poetry of many of its passages. They made the mistake of using the criteria and conventions of 19th Century English literarture rather than those of ancient Hebrew literature.

With regard to my own qualifications, I agree with the sentiment of G. B. Caird, who said of his own work:

> This is a book by an amateur, written for amateurs. Only an amateur could undertake to write on such a subject, since one lifetime is too short for anyone to become expert on [such a subject]. . . . I am . . . a walker on the common. . . . I offer to other wayfarers on the same paths this guide to the things that may catch their eye or their ear."[9]

Universities and colleges have long had a tradition of teaching one or more courses in "The Bible as Literature."[10] Such courses are usually found in the English Department. However, to my knowledge no university has yet offered a course in "The Book of Mormon as Literature." My fondest wish would be that the present book would advance the recognition of the greatness of the literature found in the Book of Mormon.

NOTES

1. Alter, *World of Biblical Literature,* 26.
2. Alter, *World of Biblical Literature,* 63. According to Alter, "For a reader to attend to these elements of literary art is not merely an exercise in 'appreciation' but a discipline of understanding: the literary vehicle is so much the necessary medium through which the Hebrew [and Nephite] writers realized their meanings that we will grasp the meanings at best imperfectly if we ignore their fine articulations as literature" (63–64).
3. Alter, *Art of Biblical Poetry,* 141.
4. Bullinger, *Figures of Speech.*
5. Bullinger, *Figures of Speech,* v.
6. Bullinger, *Figures of Speech,* ix.
7. Berlin, *Poetics and Interpretation of Biblical Narrative,* 15.
8. Sperry, "What the Book of Mormon Is," 1.
9. Caird, *Language and Imagery of the Bible,* vii.
10. Baker, *Bible as Literature.*

CHAPTER TWO

STORIES IN THE BOOK OF MORMON

One of the distinguishing characteristics of the organization of the Book of Mormon is the alternation of stories and sermons. The book presents a historical narrative concerning Lehi and his descendants, but also includes information concerning the Jaredites and the Mulekites. The narrative is generally chronological but occasionally becomes quite complex as it records the major events in the experiences of several groups of people on the American continent. The history of the Nephites is told in extensive detail, while the histories of the Lamanites, the Jaredites, and the Mulekites are told is less detail.

Interwoven in the historical narrative are sermons, revelations, and gospel instruction. In a sense, the narrative ceases and time stands still while these teachings and sermons are given. These doctrinal elements are interwoven with the narrative in a seamless fabric in such stories as Abinadi's forceful sermon to King Noah and his court, Alma and Amulek's orations to the people of Ammonihah, Alma and Amulek's missionary sermons to the Zoramites, and King Benjamin's address to his people. Thus the distinction between history and sermons is somewhat artificial because the sermons and revelations are an integral part of the history. With regard to the New Testament, Sands distinguished between the "acts" of Jesus and the "sayings" of Jesus, and the two are interwoven in the Gospels.[1] The Book of Mormon has the same basic format.

Stories tell an incident in the lives of people and place this incident in the broader context not only of the history of the people, but of the life of the individuals whose stories are told. These stories frequently involve both an individual who is the center of attention, sometimes called a "protagonist" by literary authorities, and an adversary, also called an "antagonist." Examples include Nephi against Laman, Abinadi confronting King Noah, Alma judging Korihor, and Alma and Amulek opposing Zeezrom. In many of the stories, the protagonist, usually a prophet, is placed in a situation fraught with danger and the threat of attack or death. Nephi was in great danger when he confronted Laban concerning the plates of brass, and Abinadi was threatened and eventually killed in his confrontation with King Noah. In most cases, there is a conflict between good and evil as well as a conflict of wills between the protagonist and the antagonist, with an ultimate winner and loser.

Most stories have an eventual outcome. In most cases, this is the triumph of the protagonist over the antagonist, but in some cases the result is the physical death or the tribulations of the protagonist, who is the representative of good. Even when the result is death or defeat, however, the result ultimately results in the triumph of good, as when King Noah burns Abinadi by fire, but Alma the Elder is converted and Noah is eventually burned at the stake himself.

In scriptural stories, the hand of God is always present, either unseen or directly experienced. In many stories, the readers are left to draw their own inferences concerning the application of each story to their own lives. But the Book of Mormon writers often openly and specifically point out to the reader what he or she should learn from the story. This frequently is done with the phrase "and thus we see" (to be discussed in chapter 19), but may also be accomplished in other ways as well.

According to Adele Berlin, "It is ironic that, although telling is so important in the biblical tradition, there is no word for story [in the Hebrew language]. . . . Yet the Bible abounds in narrative—vibrant and vivid narrative that has an ongoing power to affect those who hear or read it."[2] The same may be said of the stories in the Book of Mormon. The stories here are complex, stirring, exhilarating, and inspirational.

Narrative is an extremely important element of literature, and we have neither the expertise nor the space to address the topic of narrative except very briefly. Narrative involves many important elements, including plot, character, motifs, narrator, and point of view. The narrator, who in the Book of Mormon is a prophet such as Mormon, Alma, or Nephi, chooses to tell a story in his own style and for his own (and God's) purposes. Some characters are seen as well-rounded individuals, and we can learn of their attitudes and motives by what the narrator tells us about both their thought processes and about their behavior. Other characters are "flat" and we come to know very little about them, even if they are named or identified.[3] For example, Nephi's wife and children are never given names, and they play very little role in the stories of Nephi.

According to Robert Alter, the essential elements of a narrative are (1) the choice of words, (2) actions, which frequently involve recurring incidents that often contain an analogy, (3) dialogue, and (4) the combination of omniscience and inobtrusiveness in the narrative.[4] Much narrative in both the Bible and Book of Mormon is given through direct speech or dialogue quoted by the prophetic narrator. One analyst of the Old Testament argued that there are four characteristics of stories told in that scripture. These are (1) "simplicity and vivid picturesqueness," (2) "realism and concreteness," (3) "absence of elaboration and of descriptive details of character, scenery, dress," and (4) "dramatic power, due to their rapidity, use of dialogue, [and] climaxes."[5] The stories in the Book of Mormon also possess these literary characteristics, and demonstrate a wonderful symmetry and harmony between the Old Testament and the Book of Mormon.

Below we have listed most of the important stories told in the Book of Mormon. However, there are other minor stories and many subplots of the stories listed. The reader might consider how well he or she could tell each story, and what gospel principles these stories illustrate.

MAJOR STORIES IN THE BOOK OF MORMON

Lehi leaves his home and possessions and takes his family into the wilderness to obey a commandment of God (1 Ne. 1–2).

Nephi and his brothers travel back to Jerusalem. Nephi slays Laban to obtain the plates of brass (1 Ne. 3–4).

Laman and Lemuel bind Nephi, but his bands are loosed by the power of God (1 Ne. 7).

Lehi has a dream, which he narrates to his family. Nephi prays and sees the same dream, and then receives the interpretation of the dream (1 Ne. 8-15).

The Liahona is found and guides the way in the wilderness (1 Ne. 16).

Nephi breaks his steel bow and Lehi's family experience hunger. Nephi then constructs a bow from wood, consults Lehi where to hunt, and obtains food for the family (1 Ne. 16).

Nephi builds a ship with inspiration from God (1 Ne. 17–18).

The Lehi colony enters the ship and begins their voyage. On the ship, Nephi is bound by Laman and Lemuel. A great storm ensues and Laman and Lemuel are forced to free Nephi. The people of the Lehi colony arrive in the promised land.

Lehi blesses his sons (2 Ne. 3–4).

Nephi takes those who will follow him and they separate themselves from the Lamanites (2 Ne. 5).

The Nephites desire to have many wives, and they seek gold and silver (Jacob 1).

Sherem contends with Jacob concerning what he calls a false belief in Christ. He demands a sign, is smitten of God, and dies (Jacob 7).

Enos goes to hunt animals in the wilderness, spends the day in prayer, and obtains promises from God (Enos 1).

Led by Mosiah, the Nephites leave the land of Nephi and join the people of Zarahemla (Omni 1).

King Benjamin addresses his people. They are humbled, repent, and receive a remission of their sins (Mosiah 2–5).

Ammon leads an expedition to the land of Lehi-Nephi to search for the lost colony of Zeniff. He is imprisoned by King Limhi, and learns of the tribulations of the Zeniff colony (Mosiah 7).

Ammon learns of the discovery of twenty-four gold plates and of the remains of the Jaredites' civilization (Mosiah 8).

Zeniff leads of a band of people who seek to reclaim their land of inheritance in the land of Nephi. King Laman allows them to live in the land of Lehi-Nephi, but they are eventually conquered and oppressed by the Lamanites (Mosiah 9–10).

King Noah causes his people to become wicked (Mosiah 11).

Abinadi confronts King Noah, preaches the gospel, calls the people to repentance, and is burned at the stake by King Noah (Mosiah 11–17).

One of King Noah's priests, Alma, is converted by Abinadi's words. He flees from King Noah and establishes a group of saints near the waters of Mormon (Mosiah 17–18).

Gideon fights with King Noah. The Lamanites invade, the men put their wives and children in front of them to placate the Lamanites, and the priests of Noah flee into the wilderness (Mosiah 19).

The priests of King Noah abduct the daughters of the Lamanites and the Lamanites attack the Nephites (Mosiah 20).

Limhi's people are oppressed by the Lamanites, are found by explorers led by Ammon, and escape to Zarahemla (Mosiah 21–22).

Alma's followers are found by the Lamanites, oppressed by Amulon, and then are aided by God to escape to Zarahemla (Mosiah 23–24).

Alma organizes the church in Zarahemla (Mosiah 25).

Alma the Younger and the sons of Mosiah seek to destroy the church. They are visited by an angel. Alma is struck dumb but is restored through the prayer and faith of his father Alma (Mosiah 27).

The sons of Mosiah leave on a mission to preach to the Lamanites (Mosiah 28).

King Mosiah proposes a new government organization led by judges, and the affairs of the Nephites are newly arranged (Mosiah 29).

Nehor teaches false doctrines, kills Gideon, and is executed (Alma 1).

Amlici rebels and is made a king by his followers. The Amlicites are defeated by the Nephites (Alma 2–3).

Alma embarks on the Great Reform Movement by preaching in the cities of Zarahemla, Gideon, and Melek (Alma 4–8).

Alma and Amulek preach in Ammonihah. They are challenged by Zeezrom, imprisoned, and many believers are burned. Alma and Amulek are delivered as the prison walls fall on their persecutors (Alma 8–14).

Alma heals and baptizes the repentant Zeezrom (Alma 15).

The Lamanites destroy the city of Ammonihah (Alma 16).

Ammon defends the sheep of King Lamoni against the Lamanites who attempt to scatter the sheep (Alma 17).

King Lamoni and his household are converted by Ammon (Alma 18–19).

Ammon and Lamoni meet Lamoni's father, who is king over all the Lamanites. The king fights with Ammon and is defeated, and Ammon spares his life. Aaron and the other missionaries are freed from prison (Alma 20).

Aaron preaches to the king of the Lamanites, who experiences a remarkable conversion (Alma 21–22).

The Anti-Nephi-Lehis are persecuted, they refuse to take up their swords, and over a thousand are slain. Many Lamanites are converted (Alma 23–24).

The Anti-Nephi-Lehis seek safety among the Nephites, are renamed the people of Ammon, and are given the land of Jershon (Alma 27).

Korihor the anti-Christ preaches false doctrine. He is taken before the chief priest Alma (the younger). and debates Alma. Korihor is struck dumb, cast out, and dies an ignominious death (Alma 30).

Alma leads a mission to the Zoramites. Many poor Zoramites are converted and join the people of Ammon in Jershon (Alma 31–35).

Alma teaches and blesses his sons Helaman, Shiblon, and Corianton (Alma 36– 42).

The Lamanites begin a series of wars. Moroni arms the Nephites and raises the title of liberty to his people (Alma 43–46).

Amalickiah becomes king of the Lamanites through treachery, murder, and conspiracy (Alma 47–51).

The king-men oppose the freemen and establish a king. The king-men are defeated (Alma 51).

The stripling warriors are valiant in battle and cannot be killed (Alma 56–58).

Rebellions in Zarahemla weaken the war effort, and Moroni and Pahoran exchange letters. The rebels and then the Lamanites are defeated (Alma 59–62).

King Pahoran is murdered by Kishkumen, who in turn is killed by Helaman's servant. Kishkumen and Gadianton form a rebellious band (Hel. 1–2).

The Lamanites invade the land of Zarahemla and capture much territory. Nephi gives up the judgement seat to Cezoram and preaches to the Lamanites with his brother Lehi in the land of Nephi. Both are put in prison, but are miraculously freed. Most of the Lamanites are converted, and they yield to the Nephites the land they had captured (Hel. 4–5).

Cezoram and his successor are murdered and the Gadianton robbers seize control of the government (Hel. 6).

Nephi prays from the garden tower, attracts a multitude, and prophesies the murder of the chief judge (Hel. 7–9).

Nephi calls down a famine on the land because of wickedness. The people repent, and the famine is stopped (Hel. 11).

Samuel the Lamanite preaches on the walls of Zarahemla and prophesies the coming of Christ. The people of Zarahemla attempt to kill him, but he escapes by jumping from the wall (Hel. 13–16).

The wicked Nephites plan to kill those who believe in the coming of Christ. Nephi prays and is comforted. That night the signs of Christ's birth appear (3 Ne. 1).

The Nephite people return to their wickedness. Lachoneus (leader of the Nephites), and Giddianhi (leader of the Gadianton band), exchange epistles. The robbers are defeated and their leaders slain (3 Ne. 2–4).

The Nephites repent and forsake their sins (3 Ne. 5).

The Nephites prosper, degenerate into sin, and are divided into classes (3 Ne. 6).

The chief judge is murdered and the people are divided into tribes. Nephi preaches with great power but little success (3 Ne. 7).

At the death of Christ in Jerusalem, great destruction and three days of darkness occur among the Nephites. Only the more righteous are spared (3 Ne. 8–9).

Christ visits the people at the temple at Bountiful, chooses twelve disciples, and teaches the people many doctrines (3 Ne. 11–16).

Christ heals the sick, blesses the children, and angels descend from heaven and encircle the children (3 Ne. 17).

Christ institutes the Sacrament and departs (3 Ne. 18).

The Twelve teach and baptize the people. Christ returns, provides the Sacrament again, prays with the people, and expounds all things (3 Ne. 19–26).

Christ appears to the Twelve and teaches them the name of the church. Three disciples wish to remain on the earth, their wish is granted by Christ, and a change is wrought in their bodies (3 Ne. 27–28).

After Christ departs, all the people are converted and a long period of peace and righteousness ensues. Eventually the people become wicked and are divided again into Nephites and Lamanites (4 Ne. 1).

Mormon leads the Nephites in many battles against the superior forces of the Lamanites. He abridges the plates and creates the record of The Book of Mormon (Morm. 1–5).

The Lamanites exterminate the Nephites in the final battle, and only Moroni escapes (Morm. 6).

Moroni finishes the record of his father and remains on the earth thirty-seven more years (Morm. 7–9).

The language of the people is confounded at the tower of Babel. Jared and the brother of Jared receive the blessing that their own language is not confounded. They take their families and journey toward the promised land (Ether 1–2).

The brother of Jared prepares 16 stones, sees the finger of the Lord, and is eventually able to see the spirit body of Christ. He is taught marvelous things by the Lord (Ether 3).

The Jaredite barges cross the sea to the promised land (Ether 6).

Jared, the son of King Omer, overthrows his father but is then deposed. To aid her father, the daughter of Jared dances for Akish. Akish forms a secret combination and they overthrow King Omer again (Ether 8–9).

The Jaredites are divided into two factions. In many battles, the Jaredites are almost all destroyed. Coriantumr refuses to restore peace (Ether 10–12).

In the final battle in which all the Jaredites are destroyed, Coriantumr kills Shiz. Ether lives to witness the destruction of the Jaredites (Ether 13–15).

Moroni writes final instructions upon the plates, closes the record, and leaves his testimony (Moro. 1–10).

CONCLUSION

These marvelous stories are filled with intrigue, adventure, good and evil, murder, political assassination, ethnic and cultural conflict, warfare, miracles, great missionaries labors, and prophetic leadership. The underlying theme in virtually all these stories is the conflict between good and evil, between prophets and strong and influential evil leaders. There are many splendid prophets, including Lehi, Nephi I, Mosiah I and II, King Benjamin, Abinadi, Alma I and II, Amulek, Samuel the Lamanite, Nephi II, Mormon, Moroni, the brother of Jared, and Ether. Great military leaders, many of whom were prophets, include Captain Moroni, Mormon, King Benjamin, and Helaman and his stripling warriors.

Influential and charismatic evil personalities abound, including Laman, Laban, Sherem, King Noah, Nehor, Korihor, Amalickiah, Kishkumen, Gadianton, and Coriantumr. Great missionary labors are performed by Ammon and Aaron, and by Alma, Amulek, and the people who accompanied them. Sexual desire, while treated very carefully, is exhibited in the craving of the Nephites to have many wives and concubines, in the abduction of the twenty-four daughters of the Lamanites by the priests of King Noah, the abuse of women by soldiers during the last days of the Nephites, and the so-called "Dancing Princess" incident (Ether 8).

There are stories of repentance and reformation, including Alma the Younger, Zeezrom, King Lamoni and his father, and the Anti-Nephi-Lehis. There are long stretches of continual warfare, but also a long period of peace and righteousness. And above all, there is the surpassing and transcendent visit of Jesus the Christ to the people in Bountiful. Any author who could create such memorable characters and such extraordinary events in his or her entire literary career would be justified in any plaudits received.

For a young and uneducated man like Joseph Smith to have written such stories in about three months is beyond comprehension, and is unequaled in the history of great literature. The Book of Mormon is truly a literary masterpiece.

NOTES

1. Sands, *Literary Genius of the New Testament,* 1.
2. Berlin, *Poetics and Interpretation of Biblical Narrative,* 11.
3. Berlin, *Poetics and Interpretation of Biblical Narrative,* 31–32.
4. Alter, *Art of Biblical Narrative,* 178-85.
5. Sands, *Literary Genius of the Old Testament,* 22.

CHAPTER THREE

SERMONS IN THE BOOK OF MORMON

In addition to the fascinating stories in the Book of Mormon, the book contains at least forty-seven full sermons. Many other doctrinal teachings are presented in other formats, including letters, debates, dreams, visions, psalms, quotations of scriptures, blessings, and direct revelations.

Sermons are usually verbal expositions concerning doctrines and principles of the gospel. They explain God's plan, His commandments, and His will concerning His children. The sermons in the Book of Mormon cover an extremely broad spectrum of gospel subjects, but Jesus Christ and His gospel are at the center of almost all of them. These sermons, taken together, give a comprehensive and virtually complete summary of the principles of Christ's gospel. Of special note is the number of sermons devoted to the life of Christ, the atonement, what is called "the doctrine of Christ," and other aspects of Christ's life and works.

While God did not reveal a few doctrines until the dispensation of the fulness of times, such as the doctrine of the three degrees of glory, virtually every other gospel principle is found in the Book of Mormon. The prophets who gave these sermons taught the doctrines of Christ with directness, simplicity, and plainness. Thus, these sermons help the reader gain an understanding of the doctrines of Christ that is more complete and thorough than can be obtained by reading the Bible.

In the pages that follow, I have listed and categorized

the sermons and doctrinal teachings found in the Book of Mormon. Using such a list will help the gospel student gain an understanding of the complete and comprehensive nature of the doctrines taught in the book.

SERMONS AND DOCTRINAL EXPOSITIONS

REFERENCE	TYPE	SPEAKER	AUDIENCE	SUBJECT
1 Ne. 8	Dream	Lehi	His Family	Lehi's dream
1 Ne. 10	Sermon	Lehi	His family	Scattering of Israel, John the Baptist
1 Ne. 11–14	Vision	Angel	Nephi	Meaning of Lehi's dream, Christ's appearance to Nephites, Nephite history, Gentiles, Jews, Lamanites, last days
1 Ne. 15	Sermon	Nephi	His brethren	Interprets Lehi's dream
1 Ne. 19	Sermon	Nephi	My people (upon plates)	Coming of Christ, House of Israel
1 Ne. 20–21	Biblical Prophecy	Quoted by Nephi	My people (upon plates)	Isaiah 48–49

REFERENCE	TYPE	SPEAKER	AUDIENCE	SUBJECT
1 Ne. 22	Sermon	Nephi	His brethren	Prophecies of Isaiah 48–49 explained
2 Ne. 1–2	Sermon	Lehi	His family	Destruction of Jerusalem, promised land, last days; opposition, Adam and Eve, free agency, coming of the Messiah
2 Ne. 3	Sermon	Lehi	Joseph	Calling and mission of Joseph Smith
2 Ne. 4	Psalm	Nephi	His children	Oh wretched man, desire to be righteous
2 Ne. 6–8	Sermon	Quoted by Jacob	People of Nephi	Prophecies of Isaiah 49–51
2 Ne. 9–10	Sermon	Jacob	My brethren	Atonement, plan of salvation, call to righteousness, no kings upon land
2 Ne. 11	Record	Nephi	His people	Testimony of Christ
2 Ne. 12–24	Biblical prophecies	Quoted by Nephi	His people	Prophecies of Isaiah 2–14

REFERENCE	TYPE	SPEAKER	AUDIENCE	SUBJECT
2 Ne. 25–33	Sermon	Nephi	His people	Christ, history of House of Israel, sealed book, latter-day conditions, Satan's plan, bible, baptism of Jesus, Holy Ghost, his testimony
Jacob 2–6	Sermon	Jacob	People of Nephi	Riches, polygamy, fidelity in marriage, revelation, scriptures, atonement, allegory of olive tree and House of Israel
Enos	Revelation	Voice of Christ	Enos	Repentance, welfare of Nephites and Lamanites, record to be preserved
Mosiah 2–4	Sermon	King Benjamin	People of Zarahemla	Service, atonement, repentance, salvation, the poor
Mosiah 11	Sermon	Abinadi	People of Zeniff	Call to repentance
Mosiah 12–16	Sermon	Abinadi	King Noah and his priests	Law of Moses, Ten Commandments, life and crucifixion of Christ, resurrection, judgment

REFERENCE	TYPE	SPEAKER	AUDIENCE	SUBJECT
Mosiah 26	Revelation	Voice of the Lord	Alma the Elder	Eternal life promised, obedience to commandments, repentance
Mosiah 27	Sermon	Alma Younger	Multitude in Zarahemla	Alma's conversion and visitation of angel
Mosiah 29	Letter	King Mosiah	People of Zarahemla	Discourse on kingcraft, representative government
Alma 5	Sermon	Alma Younger	City of Zarahemla	Reform of church, history of his people, exhorts to righteousness, judgment, his own revelation
Alma 7	Sermon	Alma Younger	City of Gideon	Testimony of Christ's coming and his atonement, exhorts to righteousness
Alma 9	Sermon	Alma Younger	City of Ammonihah	God's goodness, Lamanites and Nephites, traditions, exhorts to righteousness
Alma 10	Sermon	Amulek	City of Ammonihah	Amulek's conversion and testimony, call to repentance

REFERENCE	TYPE	SPEAKER	AUDIENCE	SUBJECT
Alma 11	Debate	Amulek	Zeezrom	Christ's coming, temporal death, resurrection
Alma 12–13	Sermon	Alma Younger	Zeezrom and Ammonihah	Plan of adversary, judged by works, spiritual death, fall of Adam, plan of redemption, priesthood, angels, call to repentance
Alma 18	Sermon	Ammon	King Lamoni	Teaches him about the "Great Spirit"
Alma 22	Sermon	Aaron	King of the Land of Nephi	Teaches him about God, plan of salvation
Alma 26	Dialogue	Ammon	His brethren	Glories in the Lord, their missionary work and blessings
Alma 29	Sermon	Alma Younger	Every soul (upon plates)	Yearning desire to preach repentance, blessings of God
Alma 32–33	Sermon	Alma Younger	Poor Zoramites	True humility, faith, perfect knowledge, true worship, prophetic testimonies of Christ

REFERENCE	TYPE	SPEAKER	AUDIENCE	SUBJECT
Alma 34	Sermon	Amulek	Poor Zoramites	The Son of God, great and last sacrifice, mercy and justice, prayer, time to repent
Alma 36–37	Blessing & Sermon	Alma Younger	Helaman	Alma's conversion, his mission, records, blessings for keeping commandments, exhorts to teach righteousness, Liahona
Alma 38	Blessing & Sermon	Alma Younger	Shiblon	Praise for missionary service, exhorts to meekness
Alma 39–42	Sermon	Alma Younger	Corianton	Corianton's sinful conduct, spirit world, resurrection, people judged by works and desires, restoration, tree of life, spiritual and temporal death, law, Atonement
Alma 45	Sermon	Alma Younger	Helaman	Prophecy concerning destruction of Nephites, blessings to sons and the church
Hel. 7–8	Sermon	Nephi	People from garden tower	Great sin among people, pride, call to repentance, prophetic testimonies of Christ

REFERENCE	TYPE	SPEAKER	AUDIENCE	SUBJECT
Hel. 10	Revelation	Voice of the Lord	Nephi	Nephi commended for prophetic work, Nephi given power
Hel. 12	Sermon	Mormon	Readers	Human frailty, cycle of prosperity and wickedness, power of God
Hel. 13–15	Sermon	Samuel, the Lamanite	People of Zarahemla	Wickedness of Nephites, sign of Christ's birth, repentance of Lamanites, extinction of Nephites, remnant to be saved
3 Ne. 9–10	Voice	Voice of Christ	All inhabitants	Destruction, declares himself Christ, law of Moses fulfilled, sacrifice of broken heart, how oft would I gather thee
3 Ne. 11	Sermon	Christ	Multitude in Bountiful	Declares himself Christ, shows marks in body, gives power to Nephi and disciples, baptism
3 Ne. 12–14	Sermon	Christ	Multitude	Calling of Twelve, Sermon on the Mount

REFERENCE	TYPE	SPEAKER	AUDIENCE	SUBJECT
3 Ne. 15–18	Sermon	Christ	Multitude	Law of Moses fulfilled, other sheep, House of Israel, gospel to Gentiles, healing of sick and blessing of children, Sacrament instituted, prayer, power to confer Holy Ghost given
3 Ne. 19	Prayer	Christ	Multitude	Commands to pray, thanks Father and prayer for his people
3 Ne. 20–21	Sermon	Christ	Multitude	Sacrament given second time, remnant of Jacob, Gentiles, House of Israel, last days, Gentiles, condemnation of impenitent, New Jerusalem
3 Ne. 22	Biblical prophecies	Christ	Multitude	Quotes Isaiah 54, blessings in last days
3 Ne. 23	Sermon	Christ	Multitude	Search scriptures, prophecies of Samuel the Lamanite added to record
3 Ne. 24–25	Biblical prophecies	Christ	Multitude	Quotes Malachi 3–4

REFERENCE	TYPE	SPEAKER	AUDIENCE	SUBJECT
3 Ne. 26	Sermon	Christ	Multitude	All things from beginning to end expounded, great things spoken by children
3 Ne. 27–28	Sermon	Christ	Disciples	Name of church given, gospel explained, baptism, repentance, enduring to end, revelation promised, each of Twelve granted his desire, blessings to Three Nephites
3 Ne. 29–30	Sermon	Mormon	Readers	Warning to those who spurn revelations, calls the Gentiles to repentance
Morm. 7	Sermon	Mormon	Lamanites (upon plates)	Lamanites are of House of Israel, call to repentance
Morm. 8–9	Sermon	Moroni	Readers	Record to be brought to light, don't judge this record, pride and riches, judgements upon unrighteous, exhortation, Moroni's testimony of Christ
Ether 2–3	Revelation	Christ (as Spirit)	Brother of Jared	Faith, Christ's future coming, men created in image of Christ

REFERENCE	TYPE	SPEAKER	AUDIENCE	SUBJECT
Ether 4	Voice	Christ	Moroni	Revelations to go forth among God's people, blessings for adherence to revelations
Ether 5	Instruction	Moroni	Translator of Book of Mormon	Three witnesses, Book of Mormon stands as a testimony to the world
Ether 12	Sermon	Moroni	Readers	Sermon on faith, weaknesses build strength, Moroni's farewell
Ether 13	Sermon	Ether	Jaredites	New Jerusalem
Moro. 2	Blessing	Christ	Twelve Disciples	Bestowal of Holy Ghost
Moro. 3–6	Instruction	Moroni	Readers	Ordination of Priests and Teachers, administration of Sacrament, conditions and mode of baptism, church discipline
Moro. 7	Sermon	Mormon	in synagogue	Good and evil works, good cometh from God, warning regarding false judgment, miracles, faith, hope, and charity

REFERENCE	TYPE	SPEAKER	AUDIENCE	SUBJECT
Moro. 8	Epistle	Mormon	Moroni	Little children need no repentance or baptism
Moro. 9	Epistle	Mormon	Moroni	Atrocities of Lamanites, Mormon's farewell
Moro. 10	Sermon	Moroni	Lamanites (upon plates)	Testimony of Book of Mormon, gifts of spirit, faith, hope, charity, exhortation to remember commandments and come unto Christ, farewell

CHAPTER FOUR

THEMES IN THE BOOK OF MORMON

Many themes and motifs are emphasized throughout the Book of Mormon. A theme is a special topic or subject that recurs throughout the book, and which is deemed to be important by both the authors and the readers. Most of these themes are doctrinal topics that are discussed with both great simplicity and great depth. When I read the Book of Mormon, two themes stand out to me in beautiful prominence. These are (1) the doctrine of Christ, and (2) the House of Israel. These and many other doctrines are treated in a more complete and comprehensible way than in the Bible, perhaps because many plain and precious doctrines have been lost from the Bible because of the wickedness or incompetence of translators (1 Ne. 13:26). These doctrinal topics—such as repentance, faith, moral agency, the plan of salvation, the spirit world following death, the judgment, justice and mercy, and many others—have been discussed with great insight by many prophets and other inspired leaders, and will not be discussed further in this book.

Other themes and motifs in the Book of Mormon are of a different type. Many of them involve the insights gained by the prophets in observing the social and political conditions of the people with whom they live. They have drawn morals, principles, and precepts from their own and other's experiences. I cannot make a full exposition of these themes in this chapter, but will briefly identify some of these themes and some of the insights that are expressed in the Book of

Mormon. I will not make a complete summary of all scriptures related to each theme, but will instead identify each theme briefly and give a few examples of the circumstances in the Book of Mormon in which they are presented.

The delineation of themes is a matter of individual interpretation and emphasis. Richard Rust identified six "principal archetypes" in the Book of Mormon: (1) fire, (2) light and darkness, (3) captivity and deliverance, (4) wilderness and wandering, (5) trees and waters of life, and (6) dust.[1] Six other "image clusters" discussed by Rust are (1) sleeping and waking, (2) heights and depths, (3) temples, tents and palaces, (4) clothes, (5) wholeness and rending, and (6) swords and other weapons.[2]

In this chapter I will discuss some other themes that are presented by the prophets in the Book of Mormon, and which deserve the study of all interested scholars.

THE LAW OF AMERICA: BLESSINGS THROUGH OBEDIENCE TO THE COMMANDMENTS

What some scholars call "The Law of America" is perhaps particularly applicable to the western hemisphere and to the people who were led by God to this part of the world. It is stated in several different ways throughout the Book of Mormon, and typically it is introduced by the word "inasmuch."

> Inasmuch as ye shall keep my commandments ye shall prosper in the land; but inasmuch as ye will not keep my commandments ye shall be cut off from my presence. (2 Ne. 1:20)

This "law" or principle is simple yet profound. All people who keep the commandments of God will be prospered and blessed, whereas those who are wicked and break the commandments will be rejected by God and eventually "cut off."

We should ponder and pray concerning the meanings of the phrases "prospered" and "cut off." To prosper usually means to people today to gain wealth and to become comfortable financially. But it also means much more, including obtaining peace because God softens the hearts of their enemies and does "all things for the welfare and happiness of his people" (Hel. 12:2). "Cut off" may mean many things, including being cut off from membership in His church, receiving a lesser portion of the Spirit, and perhaps losing one's life as well as one's peace and prosperity.

This law is stated at least thirty-one times in the Book of Mormon in different ways and in a great variety of circumstances. For example, Alma included it in his blessings to his sons Helaman (Alma 36:1; 36:30; 37:13, 43) and Shiblon (Alma 38:1). Sometimes the emphasis is on obedience and prosperity, and other times the emphasis is on disobedience and its consequences.[3]

Obedience in keeping the commandments is emphasized in other ways as well:

> for thou hast been faithful in keeping the commandments of God from the time which thou receivedst thy first message from him. (Alma 8:15)

Many other verses teach the principle of obedience to God's commandments.[4]

WARS AND CONTENTIONS

Wars are a common feature of the history of both the Jaredites and the descendants of Lehi, and the Book of Mormon often depicts military strategy and acts of heroism.[5]

> And it came to pass that I beheld multitudes gathered together to battle, one again the other; and I beheld wars, and rumors of wars, and great slaughters with the sword among my people.
>
> And it came to pass that I beheld many generations pass away, after the manner of wars and contentions in the land. (1 Ne. 12:2–3)

Wars occur because of sin and because people lose the spirit and follow Satan.

> For it has been their quarrelings and their contentions, yea, their murderings, and their plunderings, their idolatry, their whoredoms, and their abominations which were among themselves, which brought upon them their wars and their destructions. (Alma 50:21)

The Book of Mormon teaches that war is justified to protect one's family, religion, and right to freedom (Alma 43:48–49; 46:12–16; 50:34; 3 Ne. 2:12). However, only defensive wars are justified (Alma 35:14; 43:30, 47), and offensive wars, even to punish one's enemies, are not permitted by God (Alma 48:14; D&C 98:33–36).

PRIDE

President Ezra Taft Benson warned the members of the Church in our day against the evils of pride, taking his focus from the Book of Mormon.[6] The word "pride" appears fifty-seven times in the Book of Mormon, and there are also other terms that signify the same idea, such as "puffed up." The humble followers of Christ are exhorted and admonished not to be puffed up in pride, but to be humble and teachable, never thinking of themselves as superior to others. We are counseled to love and to serve, rather than to be concerned with our own wealth and power.

Pride is a typical accompaniment of wealth and power. People who have more of this world's goods seem to be much more likely to develop a sense of pride than those who are poor as to worldly wealth. Wealthy people seem not to believe that they need God and his blessings, since they are comfortable with life as they are presently experiencing it.

> And it was because of the pride of their hearts, because of their exceeding riches, yea, it was because of their oppression to the poor, withholding their food from the

> hungry, withholding their clothing from the naked, and smiting their humble brethren upon the cheek, making a mock of that which was sacred, denying the spirit of prophecy, and of revelation, murdering, plundering, lying, stealing, committing adultery, rising up in great contentions, and deserting away into the land of Nephi, among the Lamanites—
>
> And because of this their great wickedness, and their boasting in their own strength, they were left in their own strength; therefore they did not prosper, but were afflicted and smitten, and driven before the Lamanites, until they had lost possession of almost all their lands. (Hel. 4:12–13)

Other ideas and principles to be learned from studying about pride in the Book of Mormon include the following:

The "great and spacious building" seen in Lehi's dream represented the pride of the world (1 Ne. 11:36)

One of the major causes of the destruction of the Nephites by the Lamanites was their pride (1 Ne. 12:19; Moro. 8:27).

The Gentiles in the last days are warned against pride (2 Ne. 26:20; Morm. 8:28–36). The churches of the Gentiles are especially susceptible to pride (2 Ne. 28:12–15).

Jacob delivered a great sermon concerning pride (Jacob 2:13–22).

The pride of the Nephites in Zarahemla motivated Alma to leave the position of chief judge and begin what is called "the great reform movement" by preaching in the cities of the Nephites (Alma 4:19; see also Alma 5:28, 53; 6:3; and 7:6).

One of the major sins of the king-men was pride (Alma 51:17–21), which weakened the Nephites and made their wars with the Lamanites much more difficult.

In Mormon's "Great Editorial," he identified pride as a major causes of the rise and fall of Nephite and Jaredite power and achievement (Hel. 12:1–5).

Pride in their riches was a major cause of the destruction of many Nephite cities at the death of Christ (3 Ne. 6:10–15).

After more than a century and a half of peace following the visit of Christ, the Nephites returned to their feelings of pride, which led to a rapid deterioration of their civilization (4 Ne. 1:24).

The saints in the latter days were warned by Christ to avoid pride, lest the fulness of the gospel be taken from them (3 Ne. 16:10).

LAND OF PROMISE

Both the Jaredites and the Lehi colony were promised that they would be led to a promised land that was "choice above all other lands" (1 Nephi 2:20; Ether 2:10). The people who live upon this land are commanded to obey Christ and to love and serve Him. As long as they are righteous, they will be able to maintain their freedom upon this land and have no kings to rule them–the voice of the people will be the source of political order.

> Wherefore, I, Lehi, prophesy according to the working of the Spirit which is in me, that there shall none come into this land save they shall be brought by the hand of the Lord.
>
> Wherefore, this land is consecrated unto him whom he shall bring. And if it so be that they shall serve him according to the commandments which he hath given, it shall be a land of liberty unto them; wherefore, they shall never be brought down into captivity; if so, it shall be because of iniquity; for if iniquity shall abound cursed shall be the land for their sakes, but unto the righteous it shall be blessed forever. (2 Ne. 1:6–7; see vv. 5–12)
>
> And now, we can behold the decrees of God concerning this land, that it is a land of promise; and whatsoever nation shall possess it shall serve God, or they shall be swept off when the fulness of his wrath shall come upon them. And the fulness of his wrath cometh upon them when they are ripened in iniquity (Ether 2:9).

VOICE OF THE LORD

Throughout the Book of Mormon, God speaks to his people, both directly and through His prophets. Such revelation is often referred to as "the voice of the Lord," although it may come in a variety of ways and through many different types of manifestations.

> And it came to pass that after I, Nephi, had been in the land of Bountiful for the space of many days, the voice of the Lord came unto me, saying: Arise, and get thee into the mountain (1 Ne. 17:7).

The voice of the Lord is heard by both prophets and by large groups of people. Prophets who received the voice of the Lord included: Lehi (1 Ne. 16:9, 25–26, 39), Nephi (1 Ne. 17:7), Jacob (Jacob 7:5), Enos (Enos 1:10), Mosiah (Omni 1:12), Alma the Elder (Mosiah 26:14), Ammon (Alma 20:2), Samuel the Lamanite (Hel. 13:3), Nephi (3 Ne. 1:12; 7:15), and Mormon (Morm. 3:14).

FLEE

American tradition, which has come to us from the events of the American Revolution,[7] and which is expressed in countless stories and movies, is that people who are faced with superior force should be courageous and stand up against their powerful enemy and defeat that enemy. However, in the Book of Mormon, the typical tactic used against a powerful enemy is to flee. Those who believe that the Book of Mormon expresses nineteenth-century American values should contemplate the many times the strategy of flight is used in the Book of Mormon.

The Lehi colony fled Jerusalem to avoid capture by the Babylonians (1 Ne. 3:18).

Threatened by murder, Nephi took those who would go with him and fled from Laman and Lemuel (2 Ne. 5:5).

Mosiah fled from the land of Nephi, taking his followers to the land of Zarahemla and joining the Mulekites (Omni 1:12).

The Limhi colony escaped from the Lamanites and fled to Zarahemla (Mosiah 22:11–13).

Alma the Elder's small band of followers fled from Amulon and the Lamanites and arrived safely in Zarahemla (Mosiah 24:20–25).

The Anti-Nephi-Lehis fled from their brethren the Lamanites and joined the Nephites, living in the land of Jershon (Alma 27:5–14).

Many armies in battle fled from defeat (Alma 58:30; 62:38).

NAME

The name that people are called is an extremely important source of identity and individuality. It often signifies both their present character and future potential. The names of Jesus Christ, and of all the terms that are applied to Him, signify His central role as Savior and Redeemer, the God of this world, and the Son of God the Father. Helaman gave his two sons the names of Nephi and Lehi so that they would remember their forbears and follow their example. King Benjamin gave a special name, "the children of Christ," to his people to help them remember the spiritual experiences they had while listening to his sermon (Mosiah 1:11; 5:7).

PRESERVE

One of the common themes in the Book of Mormon is that God will preserve His people if they will be faithful in serving him. Life is often threatening, and this seems to have been especially true of the times and the peoples who are the center of attention in the Book of Mormon. Life was often short, death was ever-present, and the threats of war, famine, sickness, and contention were constant. Yet God was watching over his people and intervened to protect and preserve them in their times of need and distress (1 Ne. 22:17, Mosiah 1:13, 3 Ne. 5:29).

God's power is used to preserve people and things that might otherwise be destroyed, either physically or spiritually. The Book of Mormon shows that God's power has preserved the following:

the scriptures and records (1 Ne. 3:20; Jacob 1:3; Enos 1:13–16; Alma 37:14)

the interpreters (Alma 37:21)

the seed of the Lamanites (2 Ne. 3:16)

the liberty of the people (Alma 46:24)

SERVICE

If people live gospel principles, they will become different people and cultivate personality traits that are different from the characteristics of those who do not follow God. One of these fruits of the gospel is that people become more gentle and kind, more loving and patient, more willing to serve, care for, and minister to others. The humble followers of Christ are concerned for the welfare of others and are willing to put forth the time and effort needed to help others in ways that will truly benefit them and lead them to more happy and peaceful lives.

> And behold, I tell you these things that ye may learn wisdom; that ye may learn that when ye are in the service of your fellow beings ye are only in the service of your God. (Mosiah 2:17; see also Mosiah 2:11–12, 16–19)

The Book of Mormon instructs people to serve their fellow human beings (Mosiah 4:15), as well as to serve God. And of course service to God is linked to service to one's fellow sisters and brothers (2 Ne. 1:7; 2:3; Mosiah 18:10-13; Alma 42:4; Morm. 9:28; Ether 2:8–12; Moro. 6:3).

LEADERS

The Book of Mormon gives many examples of both good and evil leaders from which we may draw important conclusions concerning the influence of leaders and the importance of selecting and following righteous leaders.

Righteous leaders are found throughout the Book of Mormon, and include Lehi, Nephi, Captain Moroni, Teancum, Alma the Elder and his son Alma the Younger, King Benjamin, King Mosiah, and Mormon. They often led their people in battle against their enemies (Alma 43:44).

On the other hand, evil leaders also abound in the Book of Mormon, and include Laman, King Noah, Kishkumen, Amulon, Amalickiah, Sherem, and Korihor. These men were evil and proud, but they possessed much charisma and were able to gain many followers.

One of the great principles taught concerning leadership is that leaders are responsible for teaching their followers the principles of truth.

> And we did magnify our office unto the Lord, taking upon us the responsibility, answering the sins of the people upon our own heads if we did not teach them the word of God with all diligence; wherefore, by laboring with our might their blood might not come upon our garments; otherwise their blood would come upon our garments, and we would not be found spotless at the last day (Jacob 1:19).

REJOICE

The gospel of Jesus Christ is a gospel of joy and rejoicing. When we truly understand the nature of God, the purpose of this mortal life, and the joy which can come from keeping the commandments, we will naturally rejoice and find comfort and peace in the blessings of our God. God wants us to rejoice and be happy, and He knows that we will find the most happiness by keeping gospel standards and following the promptings of the Spirit. The ultimate reward of righteous living is exaltation in the Celestial Kingdom, where we will find rest from all our labors, where we will be relieved of temptation and tribulation, and where the solemnities of God will rest upon our minds continually. In the mortal world, we will constantly be faced with temptation and trials, so in this world our happiness will not be full (D&C 101:36). But we can rest assured that these trials will pass and that we will be able to face and overcome them by exercising faith and obedience.

> But behold, the righteous, the saints of the Holy One of Israel, they who have endured the crosses of the world, and despised the shame of it, they shall inherit the kingdom of God, which was prepared for them from the foundation of the world, and their joy shall be full forever. (2 Ne. 9:18)

Lehi (1 Ne. 1:15) and Nephi (2 Ne. 4:30) rejoiced in the revelations they received. The followers of Christ rejoiced in His coming (Alma 13:25; 37:9; Hel. 8:17) and in their God (Mosiah 28:2). They rejoiced in the remission of their sins (Mosiah 3:13; 4:12). They rejoiced in the scriptures (2 Ne. 11:8), in the promise of immortality (Enos 1:27; Alma 28:12), in their knowledge (Alma 7:26), in the fruits of their missionary labors (Alma 25:17; 26:1), and in the privileges of their church (Alma 61:14). In essence, the gospel of Jesus Christ is a gospel of joy and rejoicing, of happiness and peace, even in the midst of afflictions.

REMEMBER

"Remember" and "remembrance" are words that occur frequently in the Book of Mormon. It appears that we mortals tend to forget quickly, and that we need to be reminded constantly of our blessings. God's children frequently forget him, perhaps because of sin or because of present concerns. We forget to pray, to read the scriptures, to love and serve others. We forget the lessons we have learned from our own experiences as well as the experiences of others. We forget principles of truth that we have previously learned, and quickly slide into bad habits and old ways.

The peoples of the Book of Mormon were admonished to remember God (1 Ne. 19:18), His covenants (1 Ne. 19:15), His laws (2 Ne. 1:16), His words (2 Ne. 9:52), and the scriptures God has given us (Jacob 1:5; Alma 33:3). These peoples were also admonished many times to remember their past history and the things, both positive and negative, that resulted from their actions (2 Ne.29:4; Mosiah 23:9; 25:16; 27:16; Alma 9:9; 29:11).

TRADITIONS

One of the interesting themes of the Book of Mormon is the influence of traditions on the religious behavior of the people. Traditions are cultural beliefs, values, norms, and customs that are accepted by the people as acceptable ways of believing and behaving.[8] Social scientists are very aware of the influence of cultural traditions on the lives of the people of any society. One who has grown up in Poland and has learned the customs of that society is far different than a person who has grown up in Japan, or Thailand, or Nigeria, or Bolivia. The people of each society come to believe that their way of life, their values and traditions, are normal and "the best." We call this attitude "ethnocentrism." It is an attitude that pervades the societies of the Nephites and the Lamanites.

Some traditions foster righteousness and some foster unrighteousness. A tradition of chastity before marriage is in keeping with the commandments of God, whereas a tradition that fosters premarital intimacy, cohabitation, or pornography is likely to corrupt the people and lead to the degeneracy of the society. The Doctrine and Covenants says this beautifully:

> And that wicked one cometh and taketh away light and truth, through disobedience, from the children of men, and because of the tradition of their fathers. (D&C 93:39)

Traditions that foster righteousness identified in the Book of Mormon were generally Nephite traditions, although not all Nephite traditions were righteous (Alma 23:5; 3 Ne. 1:9). Lamanite traditions were often identified as false, incorrect, or corrupt, either because they misinterpreted the way things really had happened, or because they fostered war, murder, plunder, and other unrighteous acts (Mosiah 1:5; Alma 3:8; 9:16–17; 17:9; 19:14; 21:17; 23:3; 24:7; 26:24; 47:36; Hel. 5:19; 15:7). However, in the time of Samuel the Lamanite, the traditions of the Lamanites were more righteous than those of the Nephites (Helaman 13:1).

When individuals or societies became evil in Book of Mormon history, they frequently criticized the prophets and the true followers of Christ as teaching and accepting "foolish traditions." The most notable examples of this response are found among the people of Ammonihah (Alma 8:11), the Amalekites (Alma 21:8), and in the teaching of Korihor the Anti-Christ (Alma 30:14).

VISITATION OF ANGELS

Elder Jeffrey R. Holland pointed out the many times that the visitation of angels occurred, which is another notable theme that is found frequently in the Book of Mormon record.[9]

> Yea, and the voice of the Lord, by the mouth of angels, doth declare it unto all nations. (Alma 13:22)

> And now, he imparteth his word by angels unto men, yea, not only men but women also. Now this is not all; little children do have words given unto them many times which confound the wise and the learned. (Alma 32:23)

Angels appeared to Nephi (1 Ne. 11–15; 2 Ne. 4:24), King Benjamin (Mosiah 3:2), Alma and the sons of Mosiah (Mosiah 27:11), Alma near Ammonihah (Alma 8:14), Amulek (Alma 10:7), Samuel the Lamanite (Hel. 13:7), Nephi (3 Ne. 7:18), and to the children blessed by Christ (3 Ne. 17:24).

In addition, Lehi received a vision in which he saw numberless concourses of angels (1 Ne. 1:8), and both Lehi and Nephi saw the heavens open and angels descend to earth (1 Ne. 11:18).

> And behold, many [Lamanites in the court of King Lamoni] did declare unto the people that they had seen angels and had conversed with them. And thus they had told them things of God, and of his righteousness. (Alma 19:34)

We also need to point out that the evil spirits that followed Satan are referred to as "the devil and his angels," and Korihor said that the devil appeared to him in the form of an angel (Alma 30:53).

CONCLUSION

In addition to many doctrinal expositions, the Book of Mormon expresses a number of themes concerning the relationship of the gospel to the lives of the people. Rather than a single exposition of a doctrine or theme in one place in the scriptures, God instead gives us many themes scattered throughout the scriptures so that our minds might come back to them repeatedly. This repetition and reaffirmation of thematic principles is a wonderful device to help us learn, remember and retain the principles learned.

NOTES

1. Rust, *Feasting on the Word,* 172–82.
2. Rust, *Feasting on the Word,* 182–91.
3. 1 Nephi 2:20; 4:14; 2 Nephi 1:9; 4:4; Jarom 1:9; Omni 1:6; Mosiah 1:7; 2:22, 31; 7:29; 23:18–19; 26:37; Alma 1:31; 9:13; 45:7–8; 48:25; 50:20; 62:45–48; Helaman 3:20; 4:13–15; 11:15–20; 12:1–3; 4 Nephi 1:1–7; Ether 7:26.
4. 1 Nephi 15:25; 17:3; 22:30–31; 2 Nephi 2:3; 5:31; 30:1; 31:7–14; Jacob 2:29; Mosiah 2:22, 41; 5:5; 6:6; 12:33; 15:26; 18:10; 21:31; Alma 30:3; 58:40; Helaman 5:6; 3 Nephi 6:14; 12:20; 15:10; 18:14; Moroni 4:3.
5. Hamblin, "Importance of Warfare," 523–43. See also Ricks and Hamblin, eds., *Warfare in the Book of Mormon.*
6. Benson, "Beware of Pride," 4–7.
7. Bushman, "Book of Mormon and the American Revolution," 189–212.
8. Duke, "Traditions of Their Fathers," 39–41.
9. Holland, "For a Wise Purpose," 12–19. See also Alma 13:22.

CHAPTER FIVE

POETRY OR PROSE? PARALLELISM IN THE BOOK OF MORMON

A substantial part of the Bible is written in parallelistic patterns. *Parallelism is defined as "a similarity of construction of adjacent word groups equivalent, complimentary, or antithetic in sense, [used] especially for rhetorical effect or rhythm."*[1] Typically, parallelism involves two or more words or statements arranged so that they look alike or correspond in fundamental details. Parallelism involves likeness, correspondence, similarity, resemblance, matching, and syntactic equivalence.[2] It is generally acknowledged that parallelism represents the classical method of creating poetry among the Hebrews, and there are literally dozens of types of parallelism found in the Bible.[3]

The people whose lives are chronicled in the Book of Mormon had Hebrew roots, and much of the Book of Mormon is also written in parallelistic patterns, as we will validate throughout this book. Accordingly, the writings of Nephite prophets should also be adjudged as poetry, and much of the Book of Mormon should be recognized as being poetic in style and substance.

Adele Berlin noted:

> It has been recognized since ancient times that the Hebrew Bible contains poetry, but the definition of what constitutes biblical poetry, the description of poetic features, and the identification of poetic passages have varied greatly over the centuries.[4]

Many volumes have been written about Hebrew poetry. One accepted conclusion is that in many books of the Bible, poetry and prose are often intertwined in complex patterns.[5] According to Watson,

> In some translations of the Bible and even in some printed editions of Hebrew text there is no indication that much of the Old Testament is in verse. While the Psalms have always been considered to be poetry, as has Proverbs, it is now evident that nearly all the prophetic books are also in verse. This includes most of Isaiah, large sections of Jeremiah and Ezekiel, almost all of Hosea . . . Now that our models are not classical Greek and Latin verse but the poetic traditions of the ancient Near East, the debate . . . has been resolved.[6]

Gradually, scholars of the Book of Mormon are coming to realize that it also contains a great deal of poetry.[7] This poetry is written in a variety of forms, many of which are types of parallelism.[8] However, there is still substantial discussion as to the nature of literary or poetic expressions in Nephite literature, and little understanding of what constitutes poetry in this wonderful volume. Indeed, we should recognize that few scholars today would admit that the Book of Mormon contains any poetry, except perhaps the Psalm of Nephi (2 Ne. 4:17–34).[9] However, I believe that in a day not far distant, scholars will recognize the Book of Mormon as one of the world's great works of literature, comparable in many respects to the Bible.

Remarkable strides have been made in recent years in identifying chiasms, alternates, antitheses, metaphors, similes, and many other literary features found in the Book of Mormon,[10] and which will be discussed in this volume. Now may be an appropriate time to discuss the existence and nature of poetry in the Book of Mormon.

The Book of Mormon itself does not identify certain passages as poetic and others as prose, whereas some books of the Bible are specifically classified as poetic. The arrangement of the text into lines and verses in the English translation of the Book of Mormon does not deal with the text as anything but prose. Nor are there any discourses found therein that would enable us to understand the thinking or purposes of Nephi, Mormon, or other authors concerning the literary implications of the book.

Wilfred Watson, one of the most respected scholars of Biblical poetry, stated nineteen criteria by which to judge whether a biblical passage is poetic.[11] These criteria include (1) line forms, (2) verb gapping (the first line contains a verb, the second line leaves the verb out), (3) unusual vocabulary, (4) conciseness, (5) unusual word-order, (6) archaisms, (7) use of metre, (8) regularity and symmetry, (9) parallelism, (10) word pairs, (11) chiastic patterns, (12) envelope figures (the same word or phrase is used both at the beginning and the end of a poetic passage), (13) break up of stereotype phrases, (14) repetition, (15) gender-matched parallelism, (16) tricolon[12] (three parallel statements), (17) rhyme, usually end-rhyme, (18) other sound patterns, such as alliteration, and (19) absence or rarity of prose elements. Many but certainly not all of these criteria apply favorably to many passages in the Book of Mormon, although it would take a much longer treatise to discuss these criteria adequately.

I believe that many of these criteria are met in passages from the Book of Mormon, with the exception of gender-matched parallelism, metre, rhyme, and sound patterns such as alliteration. However, I believe it is distinctly probable that if we had access to the original language in which the Book of Mormon was written, we would find passages with metre, rhyme, gender-matched parallelism, and alliteration.

We will discuss both rhyme and metre more fully below, but can say at this point that rhyme is not present in the English translation but may have been present in the Nephite language. Formal metre, such as is present in LDS hymns, is also not found in either the Book of Mormon or most Biblical poetry, but there are clear patterns of rhythm and regularity of expression. In both metre and rhyme, the Book of Mormon and the Bible demonstrate comparable patterns, and both are quite different from English poetry. However, the Book of Mormon contains much poetry that is representative of the Hebrew people.

We must understand Book of Mormon poetry on its own terms, rather than applying modern English standards to it. Book of Mormon poetry, we must assume, is based on the literary traditions of the Nephite people, which presumably were closely related to the literary traditions of the Hebrews. Thus, we can learn much about Nephite poetry by studying biblical poetry and the poetic traditions of the Hebrew people. While it is beyond the scope of this chapter (and beyond the expertise of this author) to summarize and evaluate all aspects of Hebrew literature, we can begin that process by making some preliminary generalizations concerning Hebrew and Nephite literature.

EXTENT OF POETRY

Much of the Book of Mormon is written as poetry if by poetry we mean parallelistic expressions. However, much is also written as prose. The same is true of the Bible. The so-called "poetic" books of the Old Testament—Job, Psalms, Proverbs, Ecclesiastes, and Song of Songs—are almost exclusively poetic—that is, parallelistic. But much of Isaiah is also poetic, as are Jeremiah, Ezekiel, and Hosea. Further, many lines in other books contain poetic expressions.[13] While non-biblical poetry in the English language is usually characterized by formal structures, rhyme, and meter, Hebrew and Nephite poetry are characterized by parallelism, intensification of meaning, repetition of elements, and terseness—every word and phrase is "loaded with meaning."[14]

RELIGIOUS ORIENTATION

Both Nephite and Old Testament poetry are at their essence religious and spiritual. The deepest feelings and beliefs of the prophetic authors are expressed in poetic form. Sanford Yoder summarized the Old Testament attitude this way:

> To the Hebrew the universe was aglow and radiant with the presence of God. Everything moved at the impulse of His divine will . . . Some of this poetry teems with history; most of it is lyrical; a few of the great compositions contain elements of the drama. All of it springs from the heart of those who wrote, or spoke, or sang about their own inner experience.[15]

Further, according to Yoder, biblical writers

> deal with sublime and majestic materials. They had great ideas, lofty ideals, and immense concepts which they expressed with an artlessness and earnestness that are in contrast with the deliberative and conscious efforts of other [people].[16]

Those of us who love the Book of Mormon would also apply the above sentiments to what we read in that great book. Robert Alter expressed the connection between poetry and prophecy beautifully when he said:

> Since poetry is our best human model of intricately rich communication, not only solemn, weighty, and forceful but also densely woven with complex internal connections, meanings, and implications, it makes sense that divine speech should be represented as poetry.[17]

The Book of Mormon writers also expressed their ideas in "solemn, weighty, and forceful" ways, and their writings are sublime, majestic, and poetic.

PARALLELISM

Parallelism "has emerged as the predominant feature

of biblical poetry,"[18] and parallelism is also the predominant feature of Book of Mormon writing.[19] Parallelistic writing involves a first statement followed by another statement that mirrors or parallels the first. These two statements are usually referred to as a couplet. One expression in the Book of Mormon perhaps captures this idea best: "being on a *parallel,* the one on the one hand and the other on the other hand" (3 Ne. 26:5). Many recent works have discussed parallelism, and understanding parallelistic linguistic structures adds significantly to our understanding of all scriptures.[20]

TYPES OF PARALLELISMS

Biblical parallelism has traditionally been divided into three types: synonymous, antithetical, and synthetic, following the original categories established by Bishop Robert Lowth, who is credited with discovering biblical parallelism.[21] There are many more types of parallelisms in the Book of Mormon, most of which will be discussed in this volume.[22]

Concerning Hebrew poetry, Adele Berlin concluded that "there are infinite ways to activate linguistic equivalences, and hence there are infinite ways to construct a parallelism."[23] While some parallelism involves identical words or phrases, most parallel constructions are more creative. Robert Alter argues that we should recognize "that literary expression abhors complete parallelism, just as language resists true synonymity, usage always introducing small wedges of difference between closely akin terms."[24]

LACK OF FORMAL VERSES

Neither Hebrew nor Nephite poetry is arranged in formal poetic verses, as is English poetry.[25] The division of the text of the Book of Mormon into scriptural verses does not always follow the patterns of parallelism found in the text, presumably because Orson Pratt, who divided the original text into verses, was not familiar with parallelistic patterns.

LACK OF PATTERNS AND RHYME

Both Hebrew and Nephite parallelisms have "no fixed number of lines or types of patterning"[26] as is typical of English poetry. Rhyme is not present in the English translation of the Book of Mormon text, although it may have been present in the language of the Nephites.

RHYTHM INSTEAD OF METER

To most readers of nonreligious English poetry, rhyme and meter are the distinguishing marks of poetry. Meter is not present in its typical form in the Bible or Book of Mormon. However, there is a kind of rhythm present in many sentences in both the Bible and Book of Mormon. This is usually achieved through the use of equal-length phrases or sentences.[27] Such rhythm "sets up a regular pattern" but also "implies the unusual" and forces the author to "break away from stock expressions, everyday vocabulary and normal syntax."[28]

WORD-PAIRS

Parallel word pairs, such as "silver and gold," or "cold and hot," which are typical of Ugaritic and Hebrew poetry,[29] are also typical of Book of Mormon writing (see chapter 13), although Book of Mormon parallel words are much more extensive and free-form.[30]

LEVELS OF PARALLELISM

Parallelism may operate at the level of the word, the line, the verse, the chapter, or larger portions. Some parallel statements contain only two phrases or sentences (couplets), while many have three (tricola) or more elements. One of the newest discoveries of Hebrew poetry is what is called "internal" or "half-line" parallelism,[31] in which the first part of a sentence is matched or paralleled in the second part of the sentence (see chapter 11).

Some parallelistic expressions are short and others involve long and involved phrases. Many parallel phrases are included in chiasms or alternates, but others are found in diverse literary forms. Some parallels involve the repetition of a word or phrase. Some are found in phrases of unequal length. But still they are unmistakably written as parallel statements, and those who regularly read the Book of Mormon usually acquire a feeling for the parallelistic mode of expression that characterizes much of the book.

Noel Reynolds first demonstrated that the book of First Nephi is composed of two parallel units (chapters 1–9, chapters 10–22).[32] Clay Gorton showed quite conclusively that the book of First Nephi contains four levels of parallelism, including an extensive parallel structure composed of 165 parallel words or phrases.[33] Gorton's book deserves investigation by many who are interested in the literary structure of the Book of Mormon.

Donald Parry made a monumental contribution to the study of parallelism in the Book of Mormon when he arranged the whole text of the book into parallelistic patterns.[34] One simply cannot study parallelism in the Book of Mormon without reference to Parry's work. My own study has been immeasurably influenced by the arrangement of the Book of Mormon text into parallelistic patterns by Parry.

My good friend and fellow missionary Elder Hugh Pinnock, before his untimely death, published a marvelous study of ancient literary forms found in the Book of Mormon.[35] Many of these were identified first by Parry, but Pinnock also included many other literary forms not discussed by other authors (see chapter 24). I recommend this book to anyone who desires to study the literary forms contained in the Book of Mormon.

IMAGERY AND FIGURES OF SPEECH

Both the Bible and the Book of Mormon are rich in imagery.[36] They contain many similes and metaphors, aphorisms and memorable phrases, as well as personification, allusion, apostrophe, reverse reasoning, hyperbole, understatement, rhetorical questions, and other figures of speech. Hebrew and Nephite literature both contain many motifs and themes, as discussed in chapter 4.[37]

ORAL TRADITION

The prophets who wrote the Bible and the Book of Mormon were highly educated and literate individuals, and they urged their people to study the scriptures. However, it is probable that many of the people in both societies could not read. Their culture and traditions, instead, depended on oral expressions. The prophets and teachers were probably very skilled at expressing their teachings orally in a way that the people could understand and remember, and the people probably were very skilled at listening and remembering. Like Hebrew poetry, Book of Mormon poetry is perhaps best identified and appreciated when it is read aloud.

These comparisons between Hebrew and Nephite literature demonstrate many similarities, which leads to the conclusion that the Book of Mormon writers were steeped in the grand tradition of Hebrew literature. This in itself is a significant evidence of the truthfulness and authenticity of the Book of Mormon.

POETIC PARALLELS

In the remainder of this chapter, I will discuss several examples of poetic parallelism found in the Book of

Mormon. These are statements created by the author in parallel fashion to comply with the typical Hebrew ideal that true literature is found in expressions that parallel each other.

Hugh Nibley[38] argued that the best example of Hebrew poetic expression and parallelism found in the Book of Mormon, and an essential proof that the Nephites were descendants of the Hebrews, is found in 1 Nephi 2:9–10:

> And when my father saw that the waters of the river emptied into the fountain of the Red Sea, he spake unto Laman, saying: O that thou mightest be like unto this river, continually running into the fountain of all righteousness!
>
> And he also spake unto Lemuel: O that thou mightest be like unto this valley, firm and steadfast, and immovable in keeping the commandments of the Lord!

Nibley says that this little poem is in the form of what the Hebrews called a *saj*`.

> The proudest boast of the desert poet is, "I utter a verse and after it its brother," for the consummation of the poetic art was to have two verses perfectly parallel in form and content.[39]

Further, Nibley concludes that "nowhere could one find a more perfect illustration" of Hebrew poetry than this couplet.[40]

Another classic example of poetic expression occurred when God the Father introduced his son Jesus Christ to the surviving Nephites.

> Behold my Beloved Son,
> in whom I am well pleased,
> in whom I have glorified my name—
> hear ye him (3 Ne. 11:7)

This passage fulfills many criteria of scriptural poetry, such as conciseness, rhythm, regularity, symmetry, and repetition. The first three lines are of equal length, whereas the fourth and concluding line is shorter and more emphatic, and also breaks up the symmetrical pattern with a new and creative expression. Parry classifies this passage as anabasis,[41] and Gorton thinks it is a chiasm.[42] It certainly is poetic in its expression and form.

An unappreciated literary gem in the Book of Mormon is the wonderful poem found in 3 Nephi 29, composed by Mormon, which follows directly after the report of the ministry of the Savior at the temple in the land of Bountiful. This chapter is a model of the use of parallel sentences to present a strongly worded literary masterpiece of warning and promise. I have diagramed the whole chapter as follows:

THIRD NEPHI, CHAPTER 29

And now behold, I say unto you that when the Lord shall see fit, in his wisdom,

A that <u>these sayings shall come</u> unto the Gentiles according to his word,

B then <u>ye may know</u> that the covenant which the Father hath made with the children of Israel, concerning their restoration to the lands of their inheritance, is already beginning to be fulfilled.

B And <u>ye may know</u> that the words of the Lord, which have been spoken by the holy prophets, shall all be fulfilled;

C and <u>ye need not</u> say that the Lord delays his coming unto the children of Israel.

C And <u>ye need not</u> imagine in your hearts that the words which have been spoken are vain,

D for behold, the Lord will remember his <u>covenant which he hath made unto his people of the house of Israel</u>.

A And when ye shall see <u>these sayings coming forth</u> among you,

E then ye need not any longer <u>spurn at the doings of the Lord</u>, for the sword of his justice is in his right hand;

E and behold, at that day, if ye shall <u>spurn at his doings</u> he will cause that it shall soon overtake you.

E <u>Wo unto him</u> that <u>spurneth at the doings of the Lord</u>;

F yea, wo unto him that shall deny the Christ and his works!

F Yea, wo unto him that shall deny the revelations of the Lord,

G and that shall say the Lord no longer worketh
by revelation,
or by prophecy,
or by gifts,
or by tongues,
or by healings,
or by the power of the Holy Ghost![43]

G Yea, and wo unto him that shall say at that day, to get gain, that there can be no miracle wrought by Jesus Christ;

H for he that doeth this shall become like unto the son of perdition,

H for whom there was no mercy, according to the word of Christ![44]

I Yea, and ye need not any longer hiss, nor spurn, nor make game of the Jews, nor any of the remnant of the house of Israel;

J for behold, the Lord remembereth his covenant unto them,

J and he will do unto them according to that which he hath sworn.

I Therefore ye need not suppose that ye can turn the right hand of the Lord unto the left,

D that he may not execute judgment unto the fulfilling of the covenant which he hath made unto the house of Israel.

Most of the parallelisms expressed in this poem contain identical words or phrases, and most are truly parallel in that the second or parallel line follows directly after the first line of the parallelism. However, the (A) and (D) parallels are separated but are obvious intended to be parallel elements. The different parallels within the passage are of substantially different length, but each separate couplet is composed of two lines with roughly equal length. Parallels (E) and (F) are linked by the word "wo," which is again repeated in the conclusion of (G). The word "spurn," which is a central element in (E), is picked up again and repeated in (I). Further, the passage contains an extended synonymia (or a literary list) of six elements presented in (G).

Another familiar example of parallelism in the Bible and Book of Mormon is found in the beatitudes, with their repetition of sentences that each begins with the word "blessed." This is an example of anaphora, or "like sentence beginnings," to be discussed in chapter 22. Jesus Christ began his most memorable sermon with this classic use of parallelism, which would have been especially appreciated by both Hebrew and Nephite listeners.

CONCLUSION

Our conclusion is that the Book of Mormon is poetic at its very heart, and that much of the book is expressed in poetic and literary forms. The more one reads and studies this great volume, the more one appreciates the richness of its language, the brilliance of its spirituality, and the inspiration that is to be obtained from it. In the rest of this book, I hope to be able to elucidate many other forms of parallelistic patterns found in the Book of Mormon, and to do so in such a way that the average reader, and I include myself in this category, will be able to understand and appreciate the literary forms contained therein. I hope we all can read the Book of Mormon with "new eyes."

NOTES

1. *Webster's Third New International Unabridged Dictionary,* s.v. "parallelism."
2. See the excellent discussion in Watson, *Classical Hebrew Poetry,* 114–59. See also Bullinger, *Figures of Speech,* 349–93.
3. Parry, *Book of Mormon Text Reformatted,* i–iii.
4. Berlin, "Introduction to Hebrew Poetry," 4:301.
5. Freedman, "Another Look at Biblical Hebrew Poetry," 11–28.
6. Watson, *Traditional Techniques in Classical Hebrew Verse,* 15.
7. Watson, *Traditional Techniques in Classical Hebrew Verse,* 27. Pages 32–44 note that American Indian and Meso-American literature demonstrate many aspects of parallelism that are similar to Hebrew poetry.
8. Parry, *Book of Mormon Text Reformatted;* Nibley, *Lehi in the Desert,* 98.
9. Sperry, "Literature in the Book of Mormon: Epistles," 77.
10. Parry, *Book of Mormon Text Reformatted;* Gorton, *New Witness for Christ.*
11. Watson, *Classical Hebrew Poetry,* 46–55.
12. Watson, *Classical Hebrew Poetry,* 177–85.
13. Bullock, *Introduction to the Old Testament Poetic Books;* Kugel, *Idea of Biblical Poetry,* 59; Watson, *Traditional Techniques in Classical Hebrew Verse,* 15.
14. Berlin, "Introduction to Hebrew Poetry," 4:303.
15. Yoder, *Poetry of the Old Testament,* 4.
16. Yoder, *Poetry of the Old Testament,* 23.
17. Alter, *Art of Biblical Poetry,* 141.
18. Berlin, "Introduction to Hebrew Poetry," 304.
19. Parry, *Book of Mormon Text Reformatted.*
20. Welch, "Chiasmus," 69–84; Parry, *Book of Mormon Text Reformatted;* Gorton, *New Witness for Christ;* Duke, "Literary Structure and Doctrinal Significance of Alma 13:1–9," 103–18.
21. Lowth, *Lectures on the Sacred Poetry of the Hebrews.*
22. Parry, *Book of Mormon Text Reformatted,* i–li.
23. Berlin, "Introduction to Hebrew Poetry," 308.
24. Alter, *Art of Biblical Poetry,* 10.
25. O'Connor, *Hebrew Verse Structure,* 54–78.
26. Berlin, "Introduction to Hebrew Poetry," 302–3.
27. Yoder, *Poetry of the Old Testament,* 12–13; Berlin, "Introduction to Hebrew Poetry," 308–9; Watson, *Traditional Techniques in Classical Hebrew Verse,* 87–113.
28. Watson, *Classical Hebrew Poetry*, 112–13.
29. Watson, *Traditional Techniques*, 17-21. See also Watson, *Classical Hebrew Poetry,* 128–44.

30. See chapter 13
31. An extensive discussion of this technique is found in Watson, *Traditional Techniques in Classical Hebrew Verse,* 28-30, 83-85. Watson admits that his earlier volume, *Classical Hebrew Poetry,* which does not discuss this technique, would have to be almost entirely rewritten today.
32. Reynolds, *Book of Mormon Authorship,* 58.
33. Gorton, *New Witness for Christ,* 23-33.
34. Parry, *Book of Mormon Text Reformatted.*
35. Pinnock, *Finding Biblical Hebrew and Other Ancient Literary Forms.*
36. Yoder, *Poetry of the Old Testament,* 9-10.
37. Rust, *Feasting on the Word.*
38. Nibley, *Lehi in the Desert,* 97–106.
39. Nibley, *Lehi in the Desert,* 101.
40. Nibley, *Lehi in the Desert,* 99.
41. Parry, *Book of Mormon Text Reformatted,* 398.
42. Gorton, *New Witness for Christ,* 34-35.
43. This is an instance of what I have called a "literary list" (see chapter 13) and what Parry, *Book of Mormon Text Reformatted,* refers to as synonymia.
44. These two lines (H) and the two lines found in (J) are examples of synthetic parallelism, in which the second line completes the thought of or adds to the information contained in the first line.

CHAPTER SIX

PSALMS, ALLEGORIES, SIGNS AND WONDERS, TYPES AND SHADOWS

We now turn to a discussion of many of the literary forms and patterns used by Mormon, Nephi, Alma, and other authors of the Book of Mormon. There are dozens of literary forms utilized by these authors, and they are all replete with symbolism and meaning. In a book originally published in 1898, Ethelbert W. Bullinger called these "figures of speech."[1] More recently, the great Biblical scholar Wilfred G. E. Watson called these "literary devices."[2] Donald Parry refers to these literary devices as "forms of poetic parallelisms."[3] All of these terms are meaningful and acceptable, but we prefer the term "literary forms."

Literary forms not only make the scriptural text more interesting and add to its significance and relevance, but they also give weight to the claims by Joseph Smith that he translated the text from ancient records. It is manifestly impossible for a man with the limited education and youthful inexperience of Joseph Smith to have produced such a complex literary text in the short time in which the translation was completed. Many of these literary forms are linked to Hebrew literature and Mid-Eastern culture, a knowledge of which was very limited at the time of Joseph Smith.

We need to appreciate these literary forms for what they contribute to the Book of Mormon text, for their beauty and charm, and for their magnificence and significance. Throughout the rest of this book, we will be discussing numerous literary forms. These are forms of expression in both oral and written discourse that communicate in a literate and poetic manner. However, the real significance of the Book of Mormon is that it communicates spiritual truth to its readers, whether these readers understand anything about literary forms, Hebrew poetry, or other aspects we will discuss here. Personally, I love the Book of Mormon, and learned great spiritual truths from it long before I learned anything about literary forms. The Book of Mormon speaks to all of us, whether we are young or old, rich or poor, learned in the ways of the world or not. The book attracts and instructs new converts as well as people who have been members for many years. I believe that all of us have yet much to learn about the truths taught by the Book of Mormon. It is my hope that those who learn about the literary forms used by the authors of the Book of Mormon will be able to read it with new insights–or, to use a metaphor, to read it with new eyes.

PSALMS

A psalm is a sacred hymn or song, a passage of scripture that reads like a song or a sacred poem. Many psalms are found throughout the Bible, especially in the Book of Psalms. Such sacred songs are typical of Hebrew expression and written literature, so it would be expected that the descendants of the Lehi colony, who were Israelites, would also express themselves in this way.

THE PSALM OF NEPHI

The most notable example of a psalm in the Book of Mormon is what Sidney Sperry called "The Psalm of Nephi," found in 2 Nephi 4:16–35.[4] This beautiful poetic expression by Nephi is emotional and spiritual, expressing Nephi's struggle with his own temptations, but also demonstrating his strength of will to overcome these temptations and to remain righteous and faithful to his calling as a prophet.

Nephi's emotion, his pains as well as his triumph, are marvelously expressed in this psalm. He also demonstrates that an effective method of overcoming temptation is to express one's gratitude for one's blessings and to remember the great blessings received from God. Nephi praises God and sings his commitment in a series of remarkable poetic phrases that may represent the pinnacle of literary expression in the Book of Mormon. Those who love great literature should read the Psalm of Nephi frequently, both for its literary value and for its spiritual message.

> O wretched man that I am!
> Yea, my heart sorroweth because of my flesh;
> My soul grieveth because of mine iniquities
> I am encompassed about,
> Because of the temptations and the sins which do so easily beset me.
> And when I desire to rejoice, my heart groaneth because of my sins;
>
> Nevertheless, I know in whom I have trusted.
> My God hath been my support;
> He hath led me through mine afflictions in the wilderness;
> And he hath preserved me upon the waters of the great deep.
> He hath filled me with his love,
> Even unto the consuming of my flesh.
> He hath confounded mine enemies,
> Unto the causing of them to quake before me.
> Behold, he hath heard my cry by day,
> And he hath given me knowledge by visions in the night-time.
> And by day have I waxed bold in mighty prayer before him;
> Yea, my voice have I sent up on high;
> And angels came down and ministered unto me.
> And upon the wings of his Spirit
> Hath my body been carried away upon exceedingly high mountains.

And mine eyes have beheld great things,
Yea, even too great for man;
Therefore I was bidden that I should not write them.

O then, if I have seen so great things,
If the Lord in his condescension unto the children of men
Hath visited men in so much mercy,
Why should my heart weep and my soul linger in the valley
of sorrow,
And my flesh waste away, and my strength slacken
Because of mine afflictions?
And why should I yield to sin, because of my flesh?
Yea, why should I give way to temptations,
That the evil one have place in my heart
To destroy my peace and afflict my soul?
Why am I angry because of mine enemy?

Awake, my soul!
No longer droop in sin.
Rejoice, O my heart,
And give place no more for the enemy of my soul.
Do not anger again because of mine enemies.
Do not slacken my strength because of mine afflictions.
Rejoice, O my heart,
And cry unto the Lord, and say:

O Lord, I will praise thee forever;
Yea, my soul will rejoice in thee,
My God and the rock of my salvation.
O Lord, wilt thou redeem my soul?
Wilt thou deliver me out of the hands of mine enemies?
Wilt thou make me that I may shake at the appearance of
sin?
May the gates of hell be shut continually before me,
Because that my heart is broken and my spirit is contrite!
O Lord, wilt thou not shut the gates of thy righteousness
before me,
That I may walk in the path of the low valley,
That I may be strict in the plain road.

O Lord, wilt thou encircle me around in the robe of thy righteousness!
O Lord, wilt thou make a way for mine escape before mine enemies!
Wilt thou make my path straight before me!
Wilt thou not place a stumbling block in my way–
But that thou wouldst clear my way before me,
And hedge not up my way,
But the ways of mine enemy.

O Lord, I have trusted in thee,
And I will trust in thee forever.
I will not put my trust in the arm of flesh;
For I know that cursed is he that putteth his trust in the arm of flesh.
Yea, cursed is he that putteth his trust in man or maketh flesh his arm.
Yea, I know that God will give liberally to him that asketh.
Yea, my God will give me, if I ask not amiss;
Therefore I will lift up my voice unto thee;
Yea, I will cry unto thee,
My God, the rock of my righteousness.
Behold, my voice shall forever ascend up unto thee,
My rock and mine everlasting God. Amen. (2 Ne. 4:17–35)

THE PSALM OF ISAIAH

Another beautiful psalm, although not original to the Book of Mormon, is a psalm of Isaiah (Isa. 52:8–10) quoted by Abinadi to the court of King Noah.

Yea, Lord, thy watchmen shall lift up their voice;
With the voice together shall they sing;
For they shall see eye to eye,
When the Lord shall bring again Zion.

Break forth into joy,
Sing together, ye waste placed of Jerusalem:
For the Lord hath comforted his people,
He hath redeemed Jerusalem.

The Lord hath made bare his holy arm
In the eyes of all the nations;
And all the ends of the earth
shall see the salvation of our God. (Mosiah 15:29–31)

ALLEGORY

An allegory is a story in which characters and incidents symbolically represent principles, conditions, or historical events.[5] According to the Merriam-Webster's Collegiate Dictionary, an allegory is "an expression by means of symbolic fictional figures and actions of truth or generalizations about human existence."[6] The Book of Mormon contains several important allegories.

THE ALLEGORY OF THE TAME AND WILD OLIVE TREES

The classic example of an allegory in the Book of Mormon is found in Jacob 5. This is called the allegory of the tame and wild olive trees, and is quoted by Jacob from the prophet Zenos, whose writings were included in the brass plates brought from Jerusalem by Nephi and his brothers, but which are not found in the present corpus of the Old Testament.

This allegory has been the subject of much analysis,[7] so we will not make a full examination here. The Lord of the Vineyard visited the vineyard and found that the olive tree was decaying. He instructed his servant to pluck off the main branches and burn them, and to cut off many of the young and tender branches and graft them into other trees in the vineyard. He also instructed his servant to take branches from a wild olive tree and graft them into the tame tree. On his second visit, the master found that the wild branches that had been grafted into the tame olive tree were growing and bearing fruit. He then went to the nethermost parts of the vineyard and found that the branches from the tame olive tree were thriving in even the poorest parts of the vineyard. After a long time, the Lord of the Vineyard made a third visit, and found that the wild branches now cumbered the tame olive tree and none of the fruit was good. In the nethermost parts of the vineyard, the fruit had also become corrupted and the wild fruit had overcome the good part of the tree. After counseling with his servant, and asking what he could have done more for his vineyard, the master instructed his servant to take the natural branches and graft them in again to the tame olive tree, and to cut off and burn the decayed branches.

This allegory is extremely complex and obviously has many meanings and symbols. Here are some of the symbolic references and possible interpretations of the allegory of Zenos.[8]

Symbol	Possible Interpretation
First Visit	Old Testament times
Second Visit	New Testament times
Third Visit	Latter days
Vineyard	World
Tame Olive Tree	House of Israel
Master of the Vineyard	Jesus Christ
Servant	Prophet(s)
Wild Olive Tree	Gentiles
Branches	Groups of people who belong to the House of Israel
Graft in	Come to knowledge of Messiah (1 Ne. 10:14)
Decay	Apostasy
Good spot	American continent
Poor spot	Another area of the world
Poorer spot	Another area of the world
Good fruit	Righteous followers of Christ (Nephites)
Wild fruit	Those who have fallen away (Lamanites)
Prune, dig, nourish	Teach the gospel
Transplant natural branches	Scattering of Israel (and restoration)
Root gained strength	Church (Israel) grew and strengthened

Wild branches cumbered tree	Many denominations of Christianity
Nethermost part	Far off lands, including American continent
Cut down branches that cumbered good spot	Jaredites destroyed
Branches burned	Groups destroyed and judged
Last time	Second gathering of Israel
Servants sent forth	Missionary labors
Fruits equal	Both Gentiles and Israelites equally righteous
Lay up fruit for a long time	Millennium
Evil fruits come again	Satan loosed for a little season after the Millennium
Whole vineyard burned	Earth cleansed by fire at the end of the world

In addition to these symbols, there are many other important ideas presented in the allegory, such as the separate visits of the Lord of the Vineyard, which represent different periods of time in the history of God's dealings with His children. The Lord several times asks the rhetorical question "What more could I have done?" Further, at one point the wild fruit had overcome the good fruit, which probably symbolizes the destruction of the Nephites by the Lamanites.

This allegory carries much information that can only be acquired by careful study and prayer. The whole history of the House of Israel is represented, both past and future. Perhaps it is presented in allegorical form so that only the righteous will comprehend its meaning and the deeper significance will be impenetrable to less righteous people.

THE DREAM OF LEHI

The Dream of Lehi, and Nephi's interpretation of that dream, is another wonderful example of an allegory (1 Nephi 8-15). This remarkable vision of the tree of life presents many symbols, and most of the interpretations of these symbols are given in the text. What is also notable but seems to be less observed by readers of the Book of Mormon is that the symbols of the dream are closely connected with many events in the history of the world. In the following list of symbols and their possible meanings, taken primarily from the work of Daniel Ludlow,[9] the scriptural verses all apply to the book of First Nephi.

Symbol	Interpretation
Dark and dreary waste (8:7)	
Large and spacious field (8:9)	The world (8:20)
Great and spacious building (8:26)	Pride of the world (11:36)
Tree of Life (11:25)	Love of God (11:21–22)
Fountain of living waters (11:25)	Love of God (11:25)
Fruit of the tree (8:11–12)	Love of God (11:25)
River of water (8:13) (also called fountain of filthy water) (12:16)	Hell and depths thereof (12:16)
Rod of iron (8:19)	Word of God (11:25)
Mists of darkness (12:17)	Temptations of the devil (12:17)

Among the historical events covered by the dream are the following:[10]

The condescension of Christ in becoming mortal

The wars among the groups of people living on the American continent

Peace following the visit of Christ

The destruction of the Nephites by the Lamanites

The discovery of the American continent by Columbus

The great and abominable church among the Gentiles

A great free nation is established by the Gentiles

The Bible is preached among the Gentiles

The Book of Mormon is restored to the earth

The Gentiles who accept the gospel are numbered with the House of Israel.

As with the allegory of Zenos, the vision of Lehi is a remarkable symbolic scripture with many layers of meaning and many possible interpretations. It requires much study, contemplation, and prayer to understand it and appreciate it fully. My hope is that the few keys to the interpretation of this vision presented above will lead the student of the scriptures to more complete commentaries and a deeper appreciation for this wonderful allegory.

THE SHEPHERD AND THE WOLVES

A third and much shorter allegory is the allegory of the shepherd and the wolves.

> For what shepherd is there among you having many sheep doth not watch over them, that the wolves enter not and devour his flock? And behold, if a wolf enter his flock doth he not drive him out? Yea, and at the last, if he can, he will destroy him.
>
> And now I say unto you that the good shepherd doth call after you; and if you will hearken unto his voice he will bring you into his fold, and ye are his sheep, and he commandeth you that ye suffer no ravenous wolf to enter among you, that ye may not be destroyed. (Alma 5:59–60)

This allegory is included in Alma's great sermon to the people of Zarahemla in the first stop of his Great Reform Movement, after resigning as the chief judge to devote himself to the work of the ministry. The sheep are the humble followers of God, the wolves are evil people who seek to corrupt the sheep, the Good Shepherd is the Savior, and other shepherds are missionaries and leaders whose calling is to protect the flock.

SIGNS AND WONDERS AND TYPES AND SHADOWS

The Book of Mormon contains many "types"[11] that illustrate gospel principles and warn people concerning the consequences of their actions and of things to come. These "signs, and wonders, and types, and shadows" (Mosiah 3:15) are used by God and his prophets to warn the people, to illustrate gospel principles, and to communicate information concerning Christ and his gospel.

One type was the brazen serpent, that is, a serpent made of brass, on a pole that was raised by Moses when the children of Israel were being bitten by poisonous serpents. If they looked upon the brazen serpent with faith, they were saved and the poison did not harm them. But if they refused to look to the brazen serpent, they died.

> Yea, did he [Moses] not bear record that the Son of God should come? And as he lifted up the brazen serpent in the wilderness, even so shall he be lifted up who should come.
>
> And as many as should look upon that serpent should live, even so as many as should look upon the Son of God with faith, having a contrite spirit, might live, even unto that life which is eternal. (Hel. 8:14–15; see also Numbers 21:8-9; Alma 33:19)

Christ applied this type to himself when he told Nicodemus:

> And as Moses lifted up the serpent in the wilderness, even so must the Son of man be lifted up.
>
> That whosoever believeth in him should not perish, but have eternal life. (John 3:14–15)

Another type used in the scriptures is the Hebrew sacrifices, which signified the atonement of Christ and his crucifixion. The sacrifice of a lamb symbolized the sacrifice of the Lamb of God: the sacrifice must be a male lamb, the first born, without spot or blemish, and with no broken bones. The law of Moses contained many other typifications of the coming of the Messiah and of specific events in the life of Christ.[12]

> Therefore there was a law given them, yea, a law of performances and of ordinances, a law which they were to observe strictly from day to day, to keep them in remembrance of God and their duty towards him.
>
> But behold, I say unto you, that all these things were types of things to come. (Mosiah 13:30–31)
>
> Therefore, if ye teach the law of Moses, also teach that it is a shadow of those things which are to come. (Mosiah 16:14)
>
> Yea, and they did keep the law of Moses; for it was expedient that they should keep the law of Moses as yet, for it was not all fulfilled. But notwithstanding the law of Moses, they did look forward to the coming of Christ, considering that the law of Moses was a type of his coming. (Alma 25:15; see also Alma 13:14–16)

The Liahona, also called the ball and directors, was also considered to be a type used to illustrate gospel principles to the Nephites. Alma explained this type in the following words:

> And now, my son, I would that ye should understand that these things are not without a shadow [type]; for as our fathers were slothful to give heed to this compass (now these things were temporal) they did not prosper; even so it is with things which are spiritual.
>
> For behold, it is as easy to give heed to the word of Christ, which will point to you a straight course to eternal bliss, as it was for our fathers to give heed to this compass, which would point unto them a straight course to the promised land.

> And now I say, is there not a type in this thing? For just as surely as this director did bring our fathers, by following its course, to the promised land, shall the words of Christ, if we follow their course, carry us beyond this vale of sorrow into a far better land of promise. (Alma 37:43–45)

CONCLUSION

The Book of Mormon contains beautiful poetry expressed as psalms and allegories, and also contains a number of symbols, or what the Book of Mormon calls signs and wonders, types and shadows. These all have symbolic import and add to both the beauty and significance of the Book of Mormon text.

NOTES

1. Bullinger, *Figures of Speech.*
2. Watson, *Classical Hebrew Poetry,* see especially 273–348.
3. Parry, *Book of Mormon Text Reformatted,* iii.
4. Sperry, "Literature in the Book of Mormon: Epistles," 77.
5. Bullinger, *Figures of Speech,* 748–50.
6. Merriam-Webster Online, http://www.m-w.com/, s.v. "allegory."
7. Sperry, *Book of Mormon Compendium,* 262–65; Sperry, "Literature in the Book of Mormon: Allegories," 106–8.
8. Church Education System, *Book of Mormon (Religion 121–122),* 140.
9. Ludlow, *Companion to Your Study,* 101.
10. CES, *Book of Mormon (Religion 121–122),* 32-33.
11. Bullinger, *Figures of Speech,* 768, notes that the word *type* is used in the Bible in several senses, including example, pattern, form, and figure. The word *shadow* is also used in the New Testament, especially in Hebrews 10:1.
12. "Sacrifices," *Bible Dictionary,* 765-767.

CHAPTER SEVEN

METAPHORS

Imagery is the essence, the heart and soul, of both poetry and scripture. Metaphors and similes are the most significant aspects of imagery. "Metaphor belongs to the stuff of poetry, so that to understand poetry involves coming to grips with metaphor and metaphorical expressions."[1] It seems that all scriptures are replete with metaphors and similes. Without exaggeration, it might be said that metaphors are an essential aspect of all scripture, and that God speaks to His children through metaphors.

Both metaphors and similes draw comparisons between a subject addressed by the prophet and some aspect of life known to the reader or listener. Most comparisons are to things that are familiar to the average person. Fig trees, sheep and shepherds, wars and conflicts, birth and death were all aspects of life well understood by the Hebrew and Nephite people.

Because metaphors and similes are familiar, the person is more likely to understand and appreciate the comparison. But the metaphor or simile forces the individual to think about the gospel principle in a new and more comprehensive way. Further, the brilliance and relevance of the metaphor catches the person's mind and heart and makes it more likely that the person will remember it and ponder its meaning. For example, rather than just referring each time to the Savior by the name of Jesus Christ, the use of a metaphor such as "the lamb of God" carries special meaning to the hearts and souls of people, especially those who are fully familiar with flocks and lambs and sacrifices.

A metaphor is a figure of speech in which a phrase that denotes one thing is used to describe another thing. This is done to suggest a comparison between the two. A classic example is the comparison between the spirit and fire. A metaphor sometimes draws a comparison by asserting that one thing *is* another thing, such as "God is love" or "The Lord is my shepherd." With similes, the comparison is made more directly by using words such as *like* or *as* so that the comparison is made obvious. Then the reader can more clearly recognize that the comparison is not "real" or perfect. For example, the brother of Jared's boats were not really dishes, but were tight "like a dish" (Ether 2:17).

> Simile and metaphor overlap . . . the simile is more obvious than metaphor. This is either because it is more *explicit*, or because the *ground of comparison* is actually stated. By contrast, metaphor is more concise and at the same time, more vague.[2]

The interpretation of a metaphor or simile is often very complex and involves a range of meanings, clarifications, and explanations. Caird notes that there are two major reasons why metaphors and similes may be misunderstood. The first occurs if the reader is not familiar with the specifics of a comparison, for example, if a modern reader who lives in the city is not familiar with the care and characteristics of farm animals who are alluded to in the metaphor. The second reason is that for any metaphorical comparison, "when two things are compared, they are not to be considered like in all respects. There is an intended point of comparison on which we are being asked to concentrate to the exclusion of [other] irrelevant fact."[3]

Often the interpretation of such imagery requires prayerful and thoughtful contemplation to understand the full meaning of the comparison. For example, the comparison of hell as being "a lake of fire and brimstone" may be taken literally by some people who believe evil people will spend eternity actually being burned in such a lake of fire. Other revelations in modern times lead us to believe that this expression is rather a metaphor, and that it applies specifically to those who become the sons of perdition (D&C 76:32–36). Most evil people, after a sufficient period of suffering for their sins, will be released from their suffering and consigned to one of the three degrees of glory (D&C 76:38–39).

It is possible to make two opposite kinds of errors. The first error is to treat as literally true something that is meant to be symbolic. The opposite error is to treat an idea as metaphorical when it is literally true. One of the great challenges in reading and understanding the scriptures is to distinguish what is symbolic and what is genuinely true.

Some metaphors are so involved as to be classified as allegories, such as the allegory of the tame and wild olive trees (Jacob 5) and Lehi's dream (1 Nephi 8–15), as previously discussed in chapter 5.

In the examples that follow, we have not used Biblical passages from Isaiah or Malachi that are quoted in the Book of Mormon, even though there are numerous instances of metaphors in these chapters. However, we have used a few of the metaphors used by the Savior in the Sermon on the Mount and repeated in the Sermon at the Temple during the Redeemer's visit to the people in the land of Bountiful.

One of the most beautiful and notable metaphors in all scripture is the Sacrament. The partaking of bread in remembrance of Christ's body, and drinking wine or water in remembrance of his blood, is a metaphor of surpassing significance.

We begin with two long and involved metaphors that are especially notable.

THE WORD IS A SEED

> Now we will compare the word unto a seed. Now, if ye give place, that a seed may be planted in your heart, behold,

> if it be a true seed, or a good seed, if ye do not cast it out by your unbelief, that ye will resist the Spirit of the Lord, behold, it will begin to swell within your breasts; and when you feel these swelling motions, ye will begin to say within yourselves—It must needs be that this is a good seed, or that the word if good, for it beginneth to enlarge my soul; yea, it beginneth to enlighten my understanding, yea, it beginneth to be delicious to me. (Read the full metaphor in Alma 32:28–43)

THE FIELD IS RIPE

> Behold, the field was ripe, and blessed are ye, for ye did thrust in the sickle, and did reap with your might, yea, all the day long did ye labor, and behold the number of your sheaves! And they shall be gathered into the garners, that they are not wasted. Yea, they shall not be beaten down by the storm at the last day; yea, neither shall they be harrowed up by the whirlwinds; but when the storm cometh they shall be gathered together in their place, that the storm cannot penetrate to them; yea, neither shall they be driven with fierce winds whithersoever the enemy listeth to carry them. But behold, they are in the hands of the Lord of the harvest, and they are his; and he will raise them up at the last day. (Alma 26:6–7)

In the pages that follow, we will list many of the metaphors found in the Book of Mormon in the order of their appearance. Other readers will find other metaphors, or may feel that some of the ones we have listed are not true metaphors. The extensive listing demonstrates the penchant of the authors of the Book of Mormon to use metaphors for literary effect, and the significance of metaphors in teaching the principles of the gospel to those who seek wisdom and learning.

METAPHORS IN THE ORDER OF THEIR APPEARANCE

their brightness did exceed that of the stars in the firmament (1 Ne. 1:10)

judgment-seat of God (1 Ne. 10:21)

Messiah is the Lamb of God (1 Ne. 12:18)

out of captivity (1 Ne. 13:16)

mother Gentiles (1 Ne. 13:17)

mother of harlots (1 Ne. 13:34)

captivity of the devil (1 Ne. 14:4)

the fold of God (1 Ne. 15:15)

like unto the brightness of a flaming fire (1 Ne. 15:30)

that great church, which is the mother of abominations (1 Ne. 14:10)

this earth is his footstool (1 Ne. 17:39)

unto the consuming of my flesh (1 Ne. 17:48)

furnace of affliction (1 Ne. 20:10)

they shall be nursed by the Gentiles, and the Lord has lifted up his hand upon the Gentiles and set them up for a standard, and their children have been carried in their arms, and their daughters have been carried upon their shoulders. (1 Ne. 22:6; see v. 8)

that great and abominable church, which is the whore of all the earth (1 Ne. 22:13)

And every nation that shall war against thee, O house of Israel, shall be turned one against another, and they shall fall into the pit which they digged to ensnare the people of the Lord (1 Ne. 22:14)

the kingdom of the devil (1 Ne. 22:23)

they are those who must be brought low in the dust; they are those who must be consumed as stubble (1 Ne. 22:23)

And he gathereth his children from the four quarters of the earth; and he numbereth his sheep, and they know him; and there shall be one fold, and one shepherd; and he shall feed his sheep, and in him they shall find pasture. (1 Ne. 22:25)

gulf of misery and woe (2 Ne. 1:13)

I am encircled about eternally in the arms of his love (2 Ne. 1:15)

Awake, my sons; put on the armor of righteousness. Shake off the chains with which ye are bound, and come forth out of obscurity, and arise from the dust (2 Ne. 1:23, also v. 13)

instruments in the hands of God (2 Ne. 1:24; Alma 26:3; Mosiah 27:36)

Wherefore, he is the first-fruits unto God (2 Ne. 2:9)

the wilderness of mine afflictions (2 Ne. 3:3)

thou art the fruit of my loins (2 Ne. 3:5)

cried unto them from the dust (2 Ne. 3:20)

the consuming of my flesh (2 Ne. 4:21)

upon the wings of his spirit (2 Ne. 4:25)

my soul linger in the valley of sorrow (2 Ne. 4:26)

my heart is broken (2 Ne. 4:32)

Oh Lord, wilt thou not shut the gates of thy righteousness before me (2 Ne. 4:32)

gates of hell (2 Ne. 4:32)

encircle me around in the robe of thy righteousness (2 Ne. 4:33)

arm of flesh (2 Ne. 4:34)

that I may walk in the path of the low valley, that I may be strict in the plain road (2 Ne. 4:32)

God, the rock of my righteousness (2 Ne. 4:35)

they that fight against Zion and the covenant people of the Lord shall lick up the dust of their feet (2 Ne. 6:13)

we become devils, angels to a devil (2 Ne. 9:9)

transformeth himself nigh unto an angel of light (2 Ne. 9:9)

that monster, death and hell (2 Ne. 9:10)

and the keeper of the gate is the Holy One of Israel (2 Ne. 9:41)

God who is the rock of your salvation (2 Ne. 9:45)

the Lord has made the sea our path (2 Ne. 10:20)

the weapons of his indignation (2 Ne. 23:5)

the deadness of the law (2 Ne. 25:27)

the cry of the blood of the saints shall ascend up to God from the ground against them (2 Ne. 26:3)

the fire of the anger of the Lord shall be kindled against them (2 Ne. 26:6)

they sell themselves for naught (2 Ne. 26:10)

after the Lord God shall have camped against them round about, and shall have laid siege against them with a mount, and raised forts against them (2 Ne. 26:15)

those who shall be destroyed shall speak unto them out of the ground, and their speech shall be low out of the dust (2 Ne. 26:16)

their stumbling block (2 Ne. 26:20)

grind upon the faces of the poor (2 Ne. 26:20)

he leadeth them by the neck with a flaxen cord, until he bindeth them with his strong cords forever (2 Ne. 26:22)

buy milk and honey, without money and without price (2 Ne. 26:25; see also 2 Ne. 9:50)

ye shall be drunken but not with wine, ye shall stagger but not with strong drink (2 Ne. 27:4) he grasps them with his awful chains (2 Ne. 28:22)

For behold, he that is built upon the rock receiveth it with gladness; and he that is built upon a sandy foundation trembleth lest he shall fall (2 Ne. 28:28)

and their scales of darkness shall begin to fall from their eyes (2 Ne. 30:6)

righteousness shall be the girdle of his loins, and faithfulness the girdle of his reins (2 Ne. 30:11)

And then shall the wolf dwell with the lamb; and the leopard shall lie down with the kid, and the calf and the young lion, and the fatling together (2 Ne. 30:12–14)

the straightness of the path, and the narrowness of the gate, by which they should enter (2 Ne. 31:9)

then cometh the baptism of fire and of the Holy Ghost; and then can ye speak with the tongue of angels (2 Ne. 31:13)

feasting upon the word of Christ (2 Ne. 31:20)

suffer his cross and bear the shame of the world (Jacob 1:8)

their blood would come upon our garments (Jacob 1:19)

the hand of providence hath smiled upon you (Jacob 2:13)

raise up unto me a righteous branch from the fruit of the loins of Joseph (Jacob 2:25)

feast upon his love (Jacob 3:2)

awake from the slumber of death (Jacob 3:11)

and be presented as the first-fruits of Christ unto God (Jacob 4:11)

looking beyond the mark (Jacob 4:14)

that by the stumbling of the Jews they will reject the stone upon which they might build and have safe foundation (Jacob 4:15; see also Jacob 4:17)

I shall meet you before the pleasing bar of God (Jacob 6:13)

And I will tell you of the wrestle which I had before God (Enos 1:2)

my soul hungered (Enos 1:4)

there is a place prepared for you in the mansions of my Father (Enos 1:27)

led by the power of his arm (Omni 1:13)

offer your whole souls as an offering unto him (Omni 1:26)

my immortal spirit may join the choirs above in singing the praises of a just God (Mosiah 2:28)

guilt, and pain, and anguish, which is like an unquenchable fire (Mosiah 2:38)

they have drunk out of the cup of the wrath of God (Mosiah 3:26)

and they viewed themselves in their own carnal state, even less than the dust of the earth (Mosiah 4:2)

For behold, are we not all beggars? (Mosiah 4:19–20)

he should be diligent, that thereby he might win the prize (Mosiah 4:27)

garment in a furnace of fire (Mosiah 12:10)

it cuts you to your hearts (Mosiah 13:7)

the commandments of God . . . are not written in your hearts (Mosiah 13:11)

he hath poured out his soul unto death (Mosiah 14:12)

as a sheep before the shearer is dumb, so he opened not his mouth (Mosiah 15:6)

the Lord hath made bare his holy arm in the eyes of all the nations (Mosiah 15:31)

that old serpent that did beguile our first parents (Mosiah 16:3)

being an enemy to God; and also is the devil an enemy to God (Mosiah 16:5)

And if Christ had not risen from the dead, or have broken the bands of death that the grave should have no victory, and that death should have no sting (Mosiah 16:7)

for the arms of his mercy were extended towards them (Mosiah 16:12)

both Alma and Helam were buried in the water (Mosiah 18:14)

hearts knit together in unity and in love (Mosiah 18:21)

therefore ye were bound with the bands of iniquity (Mosiah 23:12–13)

he that will hear my voice shall be my sheep (Mosiah 26:21)

the Lord in mercy hath seen fit to snatch me out of an everlasting burning, and I am born of God (Mosiah 27:28; Alma 36:24)

bring fruit unto repentance (Alma 4:30)

image of God engraven upon your countenances (Alma 5:19)

for there can no man be saved except his garments are washed white; yea, his garments must be purified until they are cleansed from all stain, through the blood of him of whom it has been spoken by our fathers (Alma 5:21)

sheep having no shepherd (Alma 5:37, see vv. 38 and 39)

[a wicked person] must receive his wages of him; therefore, for his wages he receiveth death, as to things pertaining unto righteousness, being dead unto all good works (Alma 5:42)

the ax is laid at the root of the tree (Alma 5:52)

all ye that will persist in your wickedness, I say unto you that these are they who shall be hewn down and cast into the fire except they speedily repent (Alma 5:56)

For what shepherd is there among you having many sheep doth not watch over them, that the wolves enter not and devour his flock? (Alma 5:59–60)

he will come among us at the time of his dwelling in his mortal tabernacle (Alma 7:8) for I perceive that ye are in the paths of righteousness (Alma 7:19)

he cannot walk in crooked paths (Alma 7:20)

he doth not dwell in unholy temples (Alma 7:21)

having your garments spotless (Alma 7:25)

wrestling with God in mighty prayer (Alma 8:10)

weighed down with sorrow, wading through much tribulation and anguish of soul (Alma 8:14)

yield yourselves unto him that he may have power over you, to blind your eyes (Alma 10:25)

this man is a child of the devil (Alma 10:28; see also Alma 11:23)

loosing of the bands of death (Alma 11:41)

that he might encircle you about with his chains, that he might chain you down to everlasting destruction (Alma 12:6; see also Alma 12:11)

we would fain be glad if we could command the rocks and the mountains to fall upon us to hid us from his presence (Alma 12:14)

wanderers in a strange land (Alma 13:23)

he began to be encircled about by the pains of hell (Alma 14:6)

but that they might receive the word with joy, and as a branch be grafted into the true vine, that they might enter into the rest of the Lord their God (Alma 16:17)

even as a sheep having no shepherd is driven and slain by wild beasts (Alma 25:12)

encircled about with the matchless bounty of his love (Alma 26:15)

over that everlasting gulf of death and misery (Alma 26:20)

then cometh the night of darkness where there can be no labor performed (Alma 34:33) they drink the dregs of a bitter cup (Alma 40:26)

the sword of justice doth hang over you (Alma 60:29; Hel.13:5; Alma 26:19; Ether 8:23)

whosoever will may lay hold upon the word of God, which is quick and powerful, which shall divide asunder all the cunning and the snares and the wiles of the devil, and lead the man of Christ in a strait and narrow course across that everlasting gulf of misery which is prepared to engulf the wicked (Hel. 3:29–30)

when the devil shall send forth his mighty winds, yea, his shafts in the whirlwind, yea, when all his hail and his mighty storm shall beat upon (Hel. 5:12)

they were overshadowed with a cloud of darkness (Hel. 5:28)

they were encircled about, yea every soul, by a pillar of fire (Hel. 5:43)

he is the author of all sin (Hel. 6:30)

insomuch that they did trample under their feet and smite and rend and turn their backs upon the poor and the needy, and the humble followers of God (Hel. 6:39)

ripe for destruction (Hel. 13:14)

led by foolish and blind guides (Hel. 13:29)

we are surrounded by demons, yea, we are encircled about by the angels of him who hath sought to destroy our souls (Hel. 13:37)

the sword of destruction did hang over them (3 Ne. 2:19)

The teachings and sermons of Jesus Christ are especially filled with metaphors that carry special meaning and strike the mind with awe and wonder.

I am the light and the life of the world (3 Ne. 11:11; 15:9)

I will baptize you with fire and with the Holy Ghost (3 Ne. 12:1)

Verily, verily, I say unto you, I give unto you to be the salt of the earth; but if the salt shall lose its savor wherewith shall the earth be salted? The salt shall be thenceforth good for nothing, but to be cast out and to be trodden under foot of men. Verily, verily, I say unto you, I give unto you to be the light of this people. A city that is set on a hill cannot be hid. Behold, do men light a candle and put it under a bushel? Nay, but on a candlestick, and it giveth light to all that are in the house; Therefore let your light so shine before this people, that they may see your good works and glorify your Father who is in heaven (3 Ne. 12:13–16)

And why take ye thought for raiment? Consider the lilies of the field how they grow; they toil not, neither do they spin; And yet I say unto you, even Solomon, in all his glory, was not arrayed like one of these (3 Ne. 13:28–29)

For it is better that ye should deny yourselves of these things, wherein ye will take up your cross, than that ye should be cast into hell. (3 Ne. 12:30)

Give not that which is holy unto the dogs, neither cast ye your pearls before swine (3 Ne. 14:6)

Enter ye in at the strait gate; for wide is the gate, and broad is the way, which leadeth to destruction, and many there be who go in thereat; Because strait is the gate, and narrow is the way, which leadeth unto life, and few there be that find it (3 Ne. 14:13–14)

Beware of false prophets, who come to you in sheep's clothing, but inwardly they are ravening wolves (3 Ne. 14:15)

Ye shall know them by their fruits. Do men gather grapes of thorns, or figs of thistles? Even so every good tree bringeth forth good fruit; but a corrupt tree bringeth forth evil fruit. A good tree cannot bring forth evil fruit, neither a corrupt tree bring forth good fruit. Every tree that bringeth not forth good fruit is hewn down, and cast into the fire. Wherefore, by their fruits ye shall know them (3 Ne. 14:16–20)

Other sheep I have which are not of this fold; them also I must bring, and they shall hear my voice; and there shall be one fold, and one shepherd (3 Ne. 15:17)

If ye shall always do these things blessed are ye, for ye are built upon my rock. But whoso among you shall do more or less than these are not built upon my rock, but are built upon a sandy foundation; and when the rain descends, and the floods come, and the winds blow, and beat upon them, they shall fall, and the gates of hell are ready open to receive them (3 Ne. 18:12–13)

I know my sheep, and they are numbered (3 Ne. 18:31)

Behold, I am the light which ye shall hold up—that which ye have seen me do (3 Ne. 18:24)

Ye have sold yourselves for naught, and ye shall be redeemed without money (3 Ne. 20:38)

So shall he sprinkle many nations (3 Ne. 20:45)

for they will sell me for silver and for gold, and for that which moth doth corrupt and which thieves can break through and steal (3 Ne. 27:32)

OTHER METAPHORES FOUND IN THE LATER CHAPTERS OF THE BOOK OF MORMON ARE:

to sing ceaseless praises with the choirs above (Morm. 7:7)

for it shall be brought out of darkness unto light (Morm. 8:16)

the sword of vengeance hangeth over you (Morm. 8:41)

it will kindle a flame of unquenchable fire upon you (Morm. 9:5)

that we may rid our garments of the blood of our brethren (Morm. 9:35)

all shall stand before his bar, being redeemed and loosed from this eternal band of death, which death is a temporal death (Morm. 9:13)

Behold, when ye shall rend that veil of unbelief (Ether 4:15)

because of the mountain waves which broke upon them (Ether 6:6) who is the father of all lies (Ether 8:25)

the things which they had beheld with an eye of faith (Ether 12:19)

author and finisher of their faith (Moro. 6:4)

chosen vessels of the Lord (Moro. 7:31)

this tabernacle of clay (Moro. 9:6)

NOTES

1. Watson, *Classical Hebrew Poetry,* 263; see 251–72.
2. Watson, *Classical Hebrew Poetry,* 254–55, italics in original.
3. Caird, *Language and Imagery of the Bible,* 145, see 144–59.

CHAPTER EIGHT

SIMILES

SIMILE CURSES AND SIMILE BLESSINGS

Like metaphors, similes draw a comparison between two things. *A simile is a figure of speech in which one thing is compared to another thing, often through the use of the words* as *or* like. Some similes are classified as "simile curses" or "simile blessings," and will be discussed later in this chapter.

Similes make a comparison more obvious than do metaphors because they use the words *as* and *like*. But they also make it less likely that the comparison is real, but rather that it is symbolic and emblematic. According to Sands, some similes in the Bible are grotesque, while others are homely but forcible, picturesque, and beautiful.[1] The similes in the Book of Mormon demonstrate remarkable variation, from grotesque to beautiful, from condemnatory and damning to consoling and reassuring.

There are a great many similes in the Book of Mormon, and many of them are repeated several times, so our list cannot be considered comprehensive. The existence of so many, varied, and beautiful similes is an indicator of the inspiration of the prophetic authors of the Book of Mormon, and of the literary significance and sophistication of the text. We will list the similes used in the Book of Mormon in the order in which they are presented in the text.

> I beheld multitudes of people even as it were in number as many as the sand of the sea (1 Ne. 12:1)

> and the brightness [of the justice of God] was like unto the brightness of a flaming fire (1 Ne. 15:30)

has spoken unto you like unto the voice of thunder (1 Ne. 17:45)

even as a dried reed (1 Ne. 17:48)

it is likened unto [the remnant] being nourished by the Gentiles and being carried in their arms and upon their shoulders (1 Ne. 22:8)

must be consumed as stubble (1 Ne. 22:23)

the righteous must be led up as calves of the stall (1 Ne. 22:24)

they had hardened their hearts against him, that they had become like unto a flint (2 Ne. 5:21)

[the devil and his angels] shall go away into everlasting fire, prepared for them; and their torment is as a lake of fire and brimstone, whose flame ascendeth up forever and ever and has no end.2 (2 Ne. 9:16; Alma 12:17)

[the Gentiles] shall be like unto a father to [the Lamanites] (2 Ne. 10:18)

those who shall be destroyed shall speak unto them out of the ground, and their speech shall be low out of the dust, and their voice shall be as one that hath a familiar spirit (2 Ne. 26:16)

the nations that fight against Zion . . . shall be as a dream of a night vision . . . even as unto a hungry man which dreameth, and behold he eateth but he awaketh and his soul is empty (2 Ne. 27:3)

the words of the faithful shall speak as if it were from the dead (2 Ne. 27:13)

them that seek deep to hid their counsel from the Lord . . . your turning of things upside down shall be esteemed as the potter's clay (2 Ne. 27:27)

the fruitful field shall be esteemed as a forest (2 Ne. 27:28)

for the earth shall be full of the knowledge of the Lord as the waters cover the sea (2 Ne. 30:15)

I speak unto you as the voice of one crying from the dust (2 Ne. 33:13)

be presented as the first-fruits of Christ unto God (Jacob 4:11)

our lives passed away like as it were unto us a dream (Jacob 7:26)

[guilt] which is like an unquenchable fire (Mosiah 2:38)

except they humble themselves and become as little children (Mosiah 3:18)

and becometh as a child, submissive, meek, humble, patient, full of love (Mosiah 3:19)

their doings shall be as a stumbling block before them (Mosiah 7:29)

the children of men . . . are as a wild flock which fleeth from the shepherd, and scattereth, and are driven, and are devoured by the beasts of the forest (Mosiah 8:21)

the life of king Noah shall be valued even as a garment in a hot furnace (Mosiah 12:3; see also vv. 10–12)

shall be driven before like a dumb ass (Mosiah 12:5; 21:3)

shall be driven and scattered to and fro, even as a wild flock is driven by wild and ferocious beasts (Mosiah 17:17)

they fought like lions for their prey (Mosiah 20:11)

as numerous almost, as it were, as the sands of the sea (Alma 2:27; Morm. 1:7)

ye workers of iniquity . . . have gone astray, as sheep having no shepherd (Alma 5:37)

[the people in Ammonihah] fled from the presence of Alma and Amulek even as a goat fleeth with her young from two lions (Alma 14:29)

if ye do not remember to be charitable, ye are as dross, which the refiners do cast out, (it being of no worth) and is trodden under foot of men (Alma 34:29)

Nephi and Lehi were encircled about as if by fire (Hel. 5:23; see also vv. 44–45)

the faces of Nephi and Lehi . . . did shine exceedingly, even as the faces of angels (Hel. 5:36)

the Holy Spirit of God did come down from heaven, and did enter into their hearts, and they were filled as if with fire (Hel. 5:45)

like a dog to his vomit, or like a sow to her wallowing in the mire (3 Ne. 7:8)

whoso repenteth and cometh unto me as a little child, him will I receive (3 Ne. 9:22)

O ye people of these great cities . . . how oft have I gathered you as a hen gathered her chickens under her wings (3 Ne. 10:4)

Therefore, whoso heareth these sayings of mine and doeth them, I will liken him unto a wise man, who built his house upon a rock (3 Ne. 14:24–27)

Satan desireth to have you, that he may sift you as wheat (3 Ne. 18:18)

they shall be as salt that hath lost its savor (3 Ne. 16:15)

a remnant of the house of Jacob . . . shall be among them as a lion among the beasts of the forest, and as a young lion among the flocks of sheep, who, if he goeth through both treadeth down and teareth in pieces, and none can deliver (3 Ne. 20:16)

I will gather my people together as a man gathereth his sheaves into the floor (3 Ne. 20:18)

But unto you that fear my name, shall the Son of Righteousness arise with healing in his wings; and ye shall go forth and grow up as calves in the stall (3 Ne. 25:2–3)

the earth should be wrapt together as a scroll (3 Ne. 26:3)

and twice were they cast into a den of wild beasts; and behold they did play with the beasts as a child with a suckling lamb, and received no harm (3 Ne. 28:22) for he that doeth this shall become like unto the son of perdition (3 Ne. 30:7)

heaped up as dung upon the face of the land (Morm. 2:15)

the Nephites . . . began to be swept off by them even as a dew before the sun (Morm. 4:18)

were driven about as chaff before the wind, or as a vessel is tossed about upon the waves (Morm. 5:16)

And they were small, and they were light upon the water, even like unto the lightness of a fowl upon the water (Ether 2:16)

would hold water like unto a dish (Ether 2:17)

ye shall be as a whale in the midst of the sea (Ether 2:24)

they were drunken with anger, even as a man who is drunken with wine (Ether 15:22)

the way to judge is as plain, that ye may know with a perfect knowledge, as the daylight is from the dark night (Moro. 7:15)

SIMILE CURSES

Mark J. Morrise discussed the prevalence of simile curses in the ancient Near East, with special reference to their use in the Old Testament and the Book of Mormon.[3] As defined by Morrise, *a simile curse is "a special form of malediction or denunciation."* It consists of an event and "an application of that event to the subject of the curse."[4] A notable example occurred in the war between the Nephite forces led by Captain Moroni and Zerahemnah, commander of the Lamanite forces, when a Nephite soldier

> smote Zerahemnah that he took off his scalp and it fell to the earth. . . . And it came to pass that the soldier who stood by, who smote off the scalp of Zerahemnah, took up the scalp from off the ground by the hair, and laid it upon the point of his sword, and stretched it forth unto them, saying unto them with a loud voice: Even as this scalp has fallen to the earth, which is the scalp of your chief, so shall ye fall to the earth

> except ye will deliver up your weapons of war and depart with a covenant of peace. (Alma 44:12–14)

Morrise argues that simile curses occur in three different forms in both the Old Testament and Book of Mormon: (a) treaty curses, (b) curses in religious covenants, and (c) prophetic curses. Below are some instances of simile curses found in the Book of Mormon:

> rending their garments in token, or as a covenant, that they would not forsake the Lord their God; or, in other words, if they should transgress the commandments of God, or fall into transgression, and be ashamed to take upon them the name of Christ, the Lord should rend them even as they had rent their garments (Alma 46:21; see also v. 29)

> Yea, and I [Abinadi] will suffer even until death, and I will not recall my words, and they shall stand as a testimony against you. And if ye slay me ye will shed innocent blood, and this shall also stand as a testimony against you at the last day. (Mosiah 17:10; see also vv. 13–19. The fulfillment of Abinadi's curse is recorded in Mosiah 19:20.)

> If the Gentiles do not repent after the blessing which they shall receive, after they have scattered my people–Then shall ye, who are a remnant of the house of Jacob, go forth among them; and ye shall be in the midst of them who shall be many; and ye shall be among them as a lion among beasts of the forest, and as a young lion among the flocks of sheep, who, if he goeth through both treadeth down and teareth in pieces, and none can deliver. (3 Ne. 20:15–16; see vv. 17–20)

SIMILE BLESSINGS

Some simile occurrences have primarily a positive application, and are used as a covenant to commit the people to greater righteousness and faithfulness. The Title of Liberty is one such simile blessing:

> And it came to pass that [Captain Moroni] rent his coat; and he took a piece thereof, and wrote upon it—In memory of our God, our religion, and freedom, and our peace, our wives, and our children—and he fastened it upon the end of a pole. And he fastened on his head-plate, and his breastplate, and his shields, and girded on his armor about his loins; and he took the pole, which had on the end thereof his rent coat, (and he called it the title of liberty), and he bowed himself to the earth, and he prayed mightily unto his God for the blessings of liberty to rest upon his brethren, so long as there should a band of Christians remain to possess the land. (Alma 46:12–13)

A great example of a simile blessing is the story of the converted Lamanites, later called the Anti-Nephi-Lehis or the Ammonites, who buried their swords so that they would no longer be stained with blood.

> And now it came to pass that when . . . all the people [Anti-Nephi-Lehis] were assembled together, they took their swords, and all the weapons which were used for the shedding of man's blood, and they did bury them up deep in the earth.
>
> And this they did, it being in their view a testimony to God, and also to men, that they never would use weapons again for the shedding of man's blood (Alma 24:17–18)

COMBINED SIMILE CURSE AND SIMILE BLESSING

The Book of Mormon also contains examples of simile events that may eventuate in either curses or blessings. The following two examples are illustrative.

> Moroni said unto them; Behold, we are a remnant of the seed of Jacob; yea, we are a remnant of the seed of Joseph, whose coat was rent by his brethren into many pieces; yea, and now behold, let us remember to keep the command-

> ments of God, or our garments shall be rent by our brethren, and we be cast into prison, or be sold, or be slain. Yea, let us preserve our liberty as a remnant of Joseph; yea, let us remember the words of Jacob, before his death, for behold, he saw that a part of the remnant of the coat of Joseph was preserved and had not decayed. And he said—Even as this remnant of garment of my son hath been preserved, so shall a remnant of the seed of my son be preserved by the hand of God, and be taken unto himself, while the remainder of the seed of Joseph shall perish, even as the remnant of his garment. (Alma 46:23–24)
>
> And their leader, Zemnarihah, was taken and hanged upon a tree, yea, even upon the top thereof until he was dead. And when they had hanged him until he was dead, they did fell the tree to the earth, and did cry with a loud voice, saying: May the Lord preserve his people in righteousness and in holiness of heart, that they may cause to be felled to the earth all who shall seek to slay them because of power and secret combinations, even as this man hath been felled to the earth. (3 Ne. 4:28–29)

Likewise, the use of the Liahona was accompanied by both blessings and cursings:

> the ball or director, which led our fathers through the wilderness, which was prepared by the hand of the Lord that thereby they might be led, every one according to the heed and diligence which they gave unto him.
>
> Therefore, as they were unfaithful they did not prosper nor progress in their journey, but were driven back, and incurred the displeasure of God upon them; therefore they were smitten with famine and sore afflictions, to stir them up in remembrance of their duty. (Mosiah 1:16–17)

NOTES

1. Sands, *Literary Genius of the Old Testament,* 52.
2. This phraseology is probably hyperbole rather than exactly correct.
3. Morrise, "Simile Curses."
4. Morrise, "Simile Curses," 1.

CHAPTER NINE

CHIASMUS

Chiasmus is one of the most notable and distinctive literary forms in all scripture.[1] The name "chiasmus" comes from the Greek letter Chi (X), which is descriptive of the format of this literary form. A chiasm involves a first line of two elements (A and B), followed by a second line in which the elements are reversed or inverted (B and A). A simple example is

> He who fails to prepare,
> prepares to fail.

This can be diagramed as follows:

According to John W. Welch, who is the first LDS scholar to publish an article on the subject of chiasmus:

> The awareness of [chiasmus], except in isolated cases, remained a part of the intellectual subconsciousness of modern Western Europe until frequent chiasmal passages were discovered in the Bible. Since that time in the mid-nineteenth century, there have been several reputed scholars, mostly theological, who have published on the subject. Their works indicate that, although some chiasms appear in Greek, Latin and English, the form was originally Hebrew and dates at least to the eighth and tenth centuries B.C. in Isaiah and in the Psalms.[2]

It may be stated with great confidence that Joseph Smith was not aware of such a literary device, nor were other notable LDS scholars such as Sidney Sperry and Hugh Nibley until Welch's article. Yet the discovery of hundreds of chiasms since 1969 in the Book of Mormon leads to the inescapable conclusion that the book was not written by modern individuals such as Joseph Smith, but instead was written by prophets steeped in Hebrew literature. The Book of Mormon is what is purports to be: a work of scripture of very ancient date that chronicles the history and teachings of an group of people of Hebrew origin who traveled from Jerusalem to the New World and settled there.

Welch notes that in most literary traditions, such as Greek, Latin, and English, chiasms are almost never composed of more than two elements, whereas in Hebrew literature, chiasms are often very complex and extended. Indeed, if a chiasm is complex and extended, it is almost certain that the chiasm was composed by a person with extensive training in Hebrew literature.

Another aspect of the construction of a chiasm needs to be explained here. While many chiasms have a simple AB/BA or ABC/CBA construction, some chiasms are created with a "turning point," such as ABC/D/CBA, with D being the turning point. Typically, the turning point is crucial to the meaning of the chiasm and the author wishes to emphasize it in a special way. We shall illustrate this later in this chapter when we discuss the extended chiasm in Alma 13:1–9, in which the term "rest" is the turning point emphasized by Alma the younger.

I believe that most people learn about a subject by being presented with a number of examples of that subject. Thus it is time to turn to examples of chiasmus presented in the Book of Mormon.

SIMPLE CHIASMUS

A simple chiasm is an inverted parallelism in an AB/BA sequence. Two statements (A and B) are made, and then two parallel statements (B and then A) are made in reverse order. The key word or words in each statement may be identical, or they may be synonymous or antithetical. I have drawn some examples from Parry, and have used the format utilized by him, that is AB/BA.[3]

A Vengeance
  B is mine,
  B and I
A will repay (Morm. 3:15)[4]

A all things whatsoever ye would that men
  B should do to you,
  B do ye even so
A to them (3 Ne. 14:12)

A Whoso repenteth and cometh unto me as a little child,
  B him will I receive, for of such is the kingdom of God.
  B Behold, for such I have laid down my life, and taken it up again;
A therefore repent, and come unto me ye ends of the earth, and be saved. (3 Ne. 9:22)

A which covenant was given and administered by the devil,
  B to combine against all righteousness.
  B Therefore they did combine against the people of the Lord,
A and enter into a covenant (3 Ne. 6:28–29)

A Yea, the people of Nephi hath he loved,
  B and also hath he chastened them;
  B yea, in the days of their iniquities hath he chastened them
A because he loveth them. (Hel. 14:31)[5]

A And the Lord commanded him that
  B he should arise.
  B And he arose
A and stood before him. (3 Nephi 11:20)

A And the multitude did see and hear
  B and bear record;
  B and we know their record is true
A for they all of them did see and hear (3 Ne. 17:25)

A And it shall come to pass that I will establish
  B my people,
    C O house of Israel.
  B And behold, this people
A will I establish in this land (3 Ne. 20: 21–22)

A hewn down and cast into the fire, from whence there is no return.
  B For their works do follow them,
  B for it is because of their works
A that they are hewn down; (3 Ne. 27:11–12)

A And also we shall perish,
  B for in them we cannot breathe,
  B save it is the air which is in them;
A therefore we shall perish. (Ether 2:19)

A to prepare a place for the children of men.
  B And now I know that this love which thou hast had for the children of men is charity;
  B Wherefore, except men shall have charity
A they cannot inherit that place which thou hast prepared in the mansions of thy Father. (Ether 12:33–34)

COMPLEX CHIASMUS

A complex chiasm involves three or more statements presented in an inverted ABC/CBA pattern. Three or more elements or statements are proffered, and they are followed by identical, synonymous, or antithetical elements or statement that are given in reverse order.

A Make the heart of this people fat,
  B and make their ears heavy,
    C and shut their eyes—
    C lest they see with their eyes,
  B and hear with their ears,
A and understand with their heart, (2 Ne. 16:10)[6]

A before the coming of the great and dreadful day of the Lord;
  B and he shall turn the heart of the fathers
    C to the children,
    C and the heart of the children
  B to their fathers,
A lest I come and smite the earth with a curse (3 Ne. 25:5–6)[7]

A and ye will not nourish the tree
  B therefore ye cannot have the fruit thereof.
    C And thus, if ye will not nourish the word, looking forward with an eye of faith to the fruit thereof, ye can never pluck of the fruit of the tree of life.
      D But if ye will nourish the word,
      D yea, nourish the tree as it beginning to grow,
    C by your faith with great diligence, and with patience,
  B looking forward to the fruit there,
A it shall take root; and behold it shall be a tree springing up unto everlasting life. (Alma 32:39–41)

See also Mosiah 5:10–12; Alma 13:2–9; 32:37–43; 42:13; Helaman 6:21–26; 13:24–25; 3 Nephi 15:17–21; 18:27–35; 21:24–28; Moroni 8:8–24.

COMBINATION CHIASM AND ALTERNATE

A combination chiasm and alternate is a complex passage of scripture that includes both a chiasm and one or more alternates. (Alternates will be discussed in the next chapter.)

A1 Behold, I have written upon these plates the very things
B1 which the brother of Jared saw;
C1 and there never were greater things made manifest
C1 than those which were made manifest
B1 unto the brother of Jared.
A2 Wherefore the Lord hath commanded me
A1 **B2** to write them;
B2 and I have written them.
A2 **a** And he commanded me
b that I should seal them up;
a and he also hath commanded
b that I should seal up
c the interpretation thereof;
b wherefore I have sealed up
c the interpreters,
a according to the commandments of the Lord (Ether 4:4–5)

A **a** And because of the knowledge of this man
b he could not be kept from beholding within the veil;
B **a** and he saw the finger of Jesus, which
b when he saw, he fell with fear; for he knew
B **a** that it was the finger of the Lord;
b and he had faith no longer, for he knew, nothing doubting.
A **a** Wherefore, having this perfect knowledge of God,
b he could not be kept from within the veil (Ether 3:19–20)[8]

A **a** O Lord, wilt thou grant unto me that I may have strength,
b that I may suffer with patience these afflictions which shall come upon me,
c because of the iniquity of this people.
B O Lord, wilt thou comfort my soul, and give unto me suc-

cess,

C and also my fellow laborers who are with me—

C yea, Ammon, and Aaron, and Omner, and also Amulek and Zeezrom and also my two sons—yea, even all these wilt thou comfort, O Lord.

B Yea, wilt thou comfort their souls in Christ,

A a Wilt thou grant unto them that they may have strength,

b that they may bear their afflictions which shall come upon them

c because of the iniquities of this people. (Alma 31:31–33)[9]

A Behold, I give unto you power,

B a that whatsoever ye shall seal on earth

b shall be sealed in heaven;

B a and whatsoever ye shall loose on earth

b shall be loosed in heaven;

A and thus shall ye have power among this people. (Hel. 10:7)[10]

A a the people did harden their hearts,

b and did seek to kill them, even as the Jews at Jerusalem sought to kill Jesus, according to his word.

B a And they did cast them into furnaces of fire,

b and they came forth receiving no harm.

B a And they also cast them into dens of wild beasts, and they did play with the wild beasts even as a child with a lamb;

b and they did come forth from among them, receiving no harm.

A a Nevertheless, the people did harden their hearts, for they were led by many priests and false prophets to build up many churches,

b and to do all manner of iniquity (4 Nephi 1:31–43)[11]

See also 2 Nephi 1:13–23; Jacob 5:7–9; Mosiah 4:11–12; Alma 13:1–9; Helaman 6:7–13; 3 Nephi 19:25–30.

CHIASMS WITHIN A CHIASM

One or more shorter chiasms within a longer chiasm

One of the most notable and complex passages of scripture in the Book of Mormon is found in Alma 13:1–9. This passage is poetic at its very heart. It presents a series of remarkable revelations concerning the priesthood, the preexistence, and the "preparatory redemption" in a complex poetic form. This is the first chiasm that I personally discovered, and came as a result of several weeks of reading and rereading this passage, pondering on its meaning, and attempting to diagram the chiasm I had found.[12] The trigger for me was that in the middle of his sermon concerning the priesthood to the people in Ammonihah, Alma inserted the phrase "And thus it is. Amen." I had previously read Noel Reynolds analysis of the arrangement of First Nephi, and his specific assertion that each section was closed with this same phrase.[13] I was motivated to look for a chiasm, and after much study was able to identify the basic elements of it. These are:

A order of his son (v. 2)
  B ordained (v. 3)
    C called (v. 3)
      D foreknowledge of God (v. 3)
        E prepared (v. 3)
          F foundation of the world (v. 5)
            G Son (v. 5)
              H high priesthood (v. 6)
                I rest (v. 6) (turning point)
              H high priesthood (v. 7)
            G Son (v. 7)
          F foundation of the world (v. 7)
        E prepared (v. 7)
      D foreknowledge (v. 7)
    C called (v. 8)
  B ordained (v. 8)
A order of the Son (v. 9)

After later study, the passage became much more complex to me, so I now present the complex diagram of this passage of scripture.

ALMA 13:1–9

a And again, my brethren, I would cite your minds forward
b to the time when the Lord God
c gave these commandments unto his children;
a and I would that you should remember
b that the Lord God
c d ordained priests, after his *holy* order, [extended alternate]
A e which was after the order of his Son,
f to teach these things unto the people.
B d and those priests were ordained
A 1 e after the order of his Son
2 in a manner
3 f that thereby the people might know
2 in what manner
1 to look forward to his Son for redemption.
2 and this is the manner [repetition]
B after which they were ordained
C g being called
h and prepared
i from the foundation of the world
D according to the foreknowledge of God,
4 on account of their exceeding great faith and good works;
5 in the first place being left to choose good or evil;
5 therefore they having chosen good,
4 and exercising exceeding great faith,
6 are called with a *holy* calling
6 yea, with that *holy* calling [repetition]
7 which was prepared with
7 and according to, a preparatory redemption for such.

6 And thus they have been called to this *holy* calling

4 on account of their faith, [repetition]

8 while others would *reject the spirit of God*
on account of the *hardness of their hearts*
and the *blindness of their minds*, [synonymia]

9 while, if it had not been for this they might have had as great privilege as their brethren.

9 Or in fine, in the first place they were on the same standing with their brethren;

10 g thus this *holy* calling

11 h being prepared

E i from the foundation of the world

8 for such as would not harden their hearts,

F being in and through the atonement of the Only Begotten Son

11 who was prepared—

10 j And thus being called by this *holy* calling,

G k and ordained unto the high priesthood

l of the *holy* order of God,

f to teach his commandments unto the children of men,

H that they also might enter into his rest—

G m This high priesthood

n being after the order

F of his Son

n which order

E was from the foundation of the world,
or in other words,

o being without beginning of days or end of years,

h being prepared

i from eternity to all eternity [synonymia and repetition]

D according to his foreknowledge in all things—

B Now they were ordained with a *holy* ordinance
C j being called with a *holy* calling
B k and ordained with a *holy* ordinance
l and taking upon them the high priesthood [extended alternate] of the *holy* order
j which calling
k and ordinance
l and high priesthood [extended alternate]
o is without beginning or end—
l m Thus they become high priests forever,
A n after the order of the Son,
the Only Begotten of the Father, [prosapodosis]
o who is without beginning of days or end of years,
who is full of grace
and equity
and truth. [synonymia]
And thus it is. Amen.

See also 1 Nephi 1:15–18; 2 Nephi 24:9–18.

LITERARY STRUCTURE OF ALMA'S SERMON TO THE ZORAMITES (ALMA 32:35–42)

A Yea, because it is light;
B and whatsoever is light is good,
C because it is discernible,
B therefore ye must know that it is good;
A and now behold, after ye have tasted this light
is your faith perfect?
Behold, I say unto you, Nay;
neither must ye lay aside your faith,
for ye have only exercised your faith [repetition]
to plant the seed
that ye might try the experiment to know
if the seed was good. [repetition]

And behold, as the tree beginneth to grow, ye will say:
a Let us nourish it with great care,
b that it may get root,
c that it may grow up,
d and bring forth fruit unto us.
a And now behold, if ye nourish it with much care
A **b** it will get root,
c and grow up,
d and bring forth fruit.
B But if ye neglect the tree
B and take no thought for its nourishment,
A behold it will not get root; [chiasm and antithetical]
and when the heat of the sun cometh and scorcheth it,
because it hath no root [repetition] it withers away,
and ye pluck it up and cast it out.
Now, this is not because the seed was not good [repetition],
A neither is it because the fruit thereof
would not be desirable;
but it is because your ground was barren,
B and ye will not nourish the tree,
C therefore ye cannot have the fruit thereof.
D And thus, if ye will not nourish the word,
E looking forward with an eye of faith
C to the fruit thereof
C ye can never pluck of the fruit
B of the tree of life.
D But if ye will nourish the word,
D yea, nourish the tree as it beginneth to grow,
a by your faith
b with great diligence,
c and with patience
C looking forward to the fruit thereof,
it shall take root; [counterpoint]
B and behold it shall be a tree springing up unto everlasting life.
b And because of your diligence
a and your faith
c and your patience [extended alternate]

D with the word, nourishing it,
that it may take root in you, [counterpoint]
C behold, by and by ye shall pluck the fruit thereof,
which is most precious,
a which is sweet
b above all that is sweet,
a and which is white
b above all that is white,
a yea, and pure
b above all that is pure; [alternate]
C and ye shall feast upon this fruit
even until ye are filled,
that ye hunger not,
neither shall ye thirst. [synonymia]
Then, my brethren,
a ye shall reap the rewards of your faith,
b and your diligence,
c and your patience, [extended alternate]
and long-suffering,
B waiting for the tree
A to bring forth much fruit unto you.

HOW MANY CHIASMS CAN BE FOUND IN THE BOOK OF MORMON?

I have attempted to count all of the chiasms identified by Donald Parry in the Book of Mormon text, and to classify them according to their chiasmic structure.[14] Please see the accompanying table. By my count, Parry identified 325 chiasms. In addition, I have identified another 109 chiasms in the text. The great majority (83 percent) of the chiasms I have found are "simple" chiasms, that is AB/BA chiasms. However, the majority of Parry's chiasms (62 percent) are complex or extended, with only 38 percent being simple. Obviously, Parry is much more astute in finding complex chiasms than am I. The sheer number of such chiasms is truly remarkable, but when we add in the complexity of many of these chiasms, the enormity of the chiastic nature of the Book of Mormon text is more than remarkable, it is extraordinary.

CHIASMS IN THE BOOK OF MORMON

[not including the Isaiah passages]

Chiasms	**Parry**	**Duke**
AB A	4	0
AB BA (simple)	121	91
ABC BA	21	1
ABC CB	0	1
ABC CBA	58	10
ABCD CBA	11	1
ABCD DCBA	45	3
ABCDE DCBA	11	0
ABCDE EDCBA	21	0
ABCDEF EDCBA	4	0
ABCDEF FEDCBA	15	0
ABCDEFG FEDCBA	1	0
ABCDEFG GFEDCBA	3	0
ABCDEFGH HGFEDCBA	5	1
ABCDEFGHI HGFEDCBA	1	1
ABCDEFGHI IHGFEDCBA	2	0
ABCDEFGHIJ JIHGFEDCBA	1	0
ABCDEFGHIJK KJIHGFEDCBA	1	0
TOTAL	325	109
Percent Complex Chiasms	62%	17%

NOTES

1. Parry, *Book of Mormon Text Reformatted,* xxxii–xxxiv.
2. Welch, "Chiasmus," 69.
3. Parry, *Book of Mormon Text Reformatted, op. cit.*
4. The repetition of identical words in reverse order is called "*epanodos or inversion*" by Bullinger, *Figures of Speech,* 299–300.
5. Parry, *Book of Mormon Text Reformatted,* 374
6. Parry, *Book of Mormon Text Reformatted,* 84
7. Parry, *Book of Mormon Text Reformatted,* 424
8. Parry, *Book of Mormon Text Reformatted,* 458
9. Parry, *Book of Mormon Text Reformatted,* 269
10. Parry, *Book of Mormon Text Reformatted,* 362
11. Parry, *Book of Mormon Text Reformatted,* 435
12. James T. Duke, "The Literary Structure and Doctrinal Significance of Alma 13:1-9," *Journal of Book of Mormon Studies* 5/1 (Spring 1996): 103-118.
13. Reynolds, "Nephi's Outline," 56.
14. Parry, *Book of Mormon Text Reformatted, op. cit.*

CHAPTER TEN

ALTERNATES

Chiasms and alternates are the two major forms of parallelism. As we discussed in the last chapter, the basic form of chiasmus is four lines in an AB/BA pattern. In contrast, the typical form of the alternate type of parallelism is four lines in an ab/ab pattern, in which the first and third lines are parallel and the second and fourth lines are parallel.[1] This, of course, is the way many poems and the lyrics of songs are written in English. In English poetry and song, the typical way of forming a parallelism is end-rhyme, in which the last word of the first line rhymes with the last word of the second line. Often, the last word of the second line will rhyme with the last word of the fourth line. Because we don't have the original plates from which the Book of Mormon was translated, and because we don't know the original language (either reformed Hebrew or reformed Egyptian), we can't tell if the lines in the Book of Mormon contain rhymes. We can say that any rhymes in the translated English version of the scripture are rare, and such as do exist may be accidental.

We will begin our discussion with simple alternates and then progress to more complex ones. In a "simple identical" alternate, there are four lines, and lines one and three contain an identical word of phrase, and lines two and four contain an identical word of phrase. We call it "simple" because it has only four lines. Alternates with more than four lines are typically called "extended alternates."[2] We will present only a few examples of each type, recognizing that there are hundreds of alternates found in the Book of Mormon.

IDENTICAL SIMPLE ALTERNATES

Four words or phrases in an ab/ab pattern, in which the a's and b's are identical.

a unto thy Father
  b who is in secret;
a and thy Father,
  b who seeth in secret,
shall reward thee openly (3 Ne. 13:18)

they did cause that the multitude should kneel down upon the face of the earth, and
a should pray unto the Father
  b in the name of Jesus.
a And the disciples did pray unto the Father
  b also in the name of Jesus. (3 Ne. 19:6–7)

SIMPLE ALTERNATES

Four words or phrases in an ab/ab pattern. Both the a's and the b's have corresponding but not identical elements.

Simple alternates are composed of four lines arranged in an ab/ab pattern. Lines one and three (the "a" lines) have corresponding or contrasting (but not identical) elements, and the same is true of lines two and four (the "b" lines). However, there are also many instances in which identical words are found in the "a" lines, and contrasting words are found in the "b" lines.

a until I did cry out unto the Lord Jesus Christ for mercy,
  b did I receive a remission of my sins.
a But behold, I did cry unto him
  b and I did find peace to my soul. (Alma 38:8)

a But behold, because of the exceedingly great length of the war between the Nephites and the Lamanites
  b many had become hardened,
a because of the exceedingly great length of the war;
  b and many were softened because of their afflictions (Alma 62:41)

REPEATED ALTERNATES

Repetitions of identical words or phrases in an ab/ab/ab pattern.

Repeated alternates contain at least six lines. Lines one, three, and five (the "a" lines) contain either identical or contrasting words or phrases, and lines two, four, six (the "b" lines) contain identical or contrasting words or phrases. Typically the "a" lines are identical and the "b" lines are contrasting, but the reverse may also be true.

a but every man fared in this life
  b according to the management of the creature;
a therefore every man prospered
  b according to his genius,
a and that every man conquered
  b according to his strength (Alma 30:17)[3]

a all churches which are built up
  b to get gain
a and all those who are built up
  b to get power over the flesh
a and those who are built up
  b to become popular in the eyes of the world (1 Ne 22:23)[4]

a But if he murdered
  b he was punished unto death;
a and if he robbed
  b he was also punished;
a and if he stole
  b he was also punished;
a and if he committed adultery
  b he was also punished;
a yea, for all this wickedness
  b they were punished (Alma 30:10)[5]

a Let us nourish it
b with great care,
c that it may get root
d that it may grow up,
e and bring forth fruit unto us.
a And now behold, if ye nourish it
b with much care
c it will get root,
d and grow up
e and bring forth fruit (Alma 32:37)[9]

a Behold, are ye stripped of pride?
b I say unto you, if ye are not ye are not prepared to meet God,
c Behold ye must prepare quickly;
d for the kingdom of heaven is soon at hand
e and such an one hath not eternal life.
a Behold, I say, is there one among you who is not stripped of envy?
b I say unto you that such an one is not prepared;
c and I would that he should prepare quickly,
d for the hour is close at hand, and he knoweth not when the time shall come;
e for such an one is not found guiltless. (Alma 5:28–29)[10]

a whoso should possess this land of promise,
b from that time henceforth and forever,
should serve him, the true and only God,
c or they should be swept off
d when the fulness of his wrath should come upon them.
And now, we can behold the decrees of God concerning this land,
a that it is a land of promise;
b and whatsoever nation shall possess it shall serve God,
c or they shall be swept off
d when the fulness of his wrath shall come upon them.
And the fulness of his wrath cometh upon them when they are ripened in iniquity.

a For behold, this is a land which is choice above all other lands;

b wherefore he that doth possess it shall serve God

c or shall be swept off; for it is the everlasting decree of God.

d And it is not until the fulness of iniquity among the children of the land, that they are swept off (Ether 2:8–10)[11]

a behold, I am fair, and I will dance before him and I will please him,

b insomuch that he will desire me to wife;

c wherefore if he shall desire to thee that ye shall give unto him me to wife, then shall ye say:

d I will give her if ye will bring unto me the head of my father, the king.

And now Omer was a friend to Akish; wherefore, when Jared had sent for Akish,

a the daughter of Jared danced before him that she pleased him,

b insomuch that he desired her to wife.

c And it came to pass that he said unto Jared: Give her unto me to wife.

d And Jared said unto him: I will give her unto you, if ye will bring unto me the head of my father, the king. (Ether 8:10–12)

a And I also saw gold,

b and silver,

c and silks

d and scarlets

e and fine-twined linen,

f and all manner of precious clothing;

g and I saw many harlots.

And the angel spake unto me, saying:

a Behold the gold

b and the silver,

c and the silks,

d and the scarlets,

e and the fine-twined linen,

f and the precious clothing,
g and the harlots
are the desires of this great and abominable church. (1 Ne. 13:7–8)[12]

EXTENDED ALTERNATES

Three of more elements are repeated in an abc/abc pattern.

With extended alternates, there are at least six lines. Lines one and four (the "a" lines) contain complementary words or phrases, lines two and five (the "b" lines) contain complementary words or phrases, and lines three and six (the "c" lines) contain complementary words or phrases.

a Zenock spake concerning these things
b because they testified particularly concerning us,
c who are the remnant
d of their seed.
a Behold, our father Jacob also
b testified concerning
c a remnant
d of the seed of Joseph.
c And behold, are not we a remnant
d of the seed of Joseph?
b And these things which testify of us (3 Ne 10:16–17)

IDENTICAL DUPLICATE ALTERNATE

Four of more lines in an aa/bb pattern.

In this type of alternate, lines one and two are considered the "a" lines, and are parallel in that they contain identical words or phrases. Likewise, lines three and four (the "b" lines) contain identical words or phrases.

For I remember the word of God,
a which saith by their works ye shall know them;
a for if their works
b be good,
b then they are good also (Moro. 7:5)

HOW MANY ALTERNATES ARE THERE IN THE BOOK OF MORMON?

Any attempt to count the actual number of alternates in the Book of Mormon is exceedingly difficult, and depends on one's ability to find such alternates and one's judgment as to which passages are alternates and which are not. With this in mind, I have attempted to estimate, at least in a rough way, the number of alternates that may be present in the Book of Mormon. In the table below, I have first counted the alternates identified by Parry[13] and then added the ones that I have judged to be alternates that are not identified as such by Parry. The listing below does not include the many alternates found in the Isaiah passages in the Book of Mormon.

AN ENUMERATION OF ALTERNATES FOUND BY PARRY AND DUKE

Alternates	**Parry**	**Duke**
ab ab (simple)	208	90
ab ab ab	30	7
ab ab ab a	1	0
ab ab ab ab	5	1
ab ab ab ab ab	1	0
ab ab ab ab ab ab	1	0
ab ab ab ab ab ab ab	1	0
ab ab ba	0	1
abc abc	63	11
abc ab	0	1
abc abc abc	3	0
abc abc abc abc	1	0
abcd abcd	24	4
abcd abcd abcd	2	0
abcde abcde	11	1
abcdef abcdef	7	0
abcdef abcdef abcdef abcdef abcdef	1	0
abcdefg abcdefg	1	0
Total Number of Alternates	360	116
Percent Complex Alternates	42%	22%

NOTE: Isaiah contains alternates of the types: aabb and aabbccddee. See also 3 Nephi 29, in chapter 5.

By my count, Parry has identified 360 alternates, and I have identified an additional 116. Thus, there is a grand total of 476 alternates in the Book of Mormon. As the reader will see, the alternates identified by Parry are much more likely to be complex passages, whereas the great majority of alternates identified by me are simple alternates. One should note that the complexity of the types of alternates found in the Book of Mormon represents a high level of literary achievement and sophistication. The literary structure of the Book of Mormon is in the classical Hebrew style and therefore is a strong indication that the text was originally written by authors who came from a Hebrew heritage.

NOTES

1. Willis, "Alternating (ABA'B') Parallelism," 49–76. See also Parry, *Book of Mormon Text Reformatted,* ix–xiv.
2. Parry, *Book of Mormon Text Reformatted,* xiii–xiv.
3. Parry, *Book of Mormon Text Reformatted,* 263.
4. Parry, *Book of Mormon Text Reformatted,* 48.
5. Parry, *Book of Mormon Text Reformatted,* 262
6. Parry, 428. Compare Matthew 21:22, Enos 1:15, D&C 6:5.
7. Parry, 405. Compare Matthew 7:7, Luke 11:9.
8. Parry, *Book of Mormon Text Reformatted,* 186.
9. Parry, *Book of Mormon Text Reformatted,* 272.
10. Parry, *Book of Mormon Text Reformatted,* 206.
11. Parry, *Book of Mormon Text Reformatted,* 455.
12. Parry, *Book of Mormon Text Reformatted,* 21
13. Parry, *Book of Mormon Text Reformatted, opt. cit.*

CHAPTER ELEVEN

HALF-LINE PARALLELISM, COUPLETS, AND TRICOLON

One of the most exciting new discoveries in the study of Hebrew poetry is the "internal" or "half-line" parallel. This is perhaps the simplest form of parallelism, which adds a fascinating set of examples of Hebrew verse structure in the Book of Mormon. After discussing this form of parallelism, we will next present some examples of couplets, or two-sentence parallelisms. Then we turn to what have become known as tricolon by Hebrew scholars, which are three-sentence parallelisms. Within these categories, the parallelisms are listed in order of their presentation in the Book of Mormon, although they could be classified in other ways.

INTERNAL (HALF-LINE) PARALLELISMS

One of the newly discovered aspects of Biblical and Hebrew literature has come to be known by the title "internal" of "half-line" parallelisms.[1] Very simply put, these are sentences in which the first part of the sentence is matched by a parallel phrase in the second part of the sentence. The two matched phrases form a complete sentence of unusual beauty and significance. Wilfred Watson, one of the greatest interpreters of Hebrew poetry, did not discuss this form of poetry in his earlier work, but has written much in recent years concerning this form of Hebrew expression.[2]

Latter-day Saints are perhaps most familiar with the famous half-line parallelism in 2 Nephi 2:25, which reads:

> Adam fell that men might be, and men are that they might have joy.

Many other instances of half-line parallelism are found in the Book of Mormon, including the following:

> and if all the things which I saw are not written, the things which I have written are true (1 Ne. 14:30)

> Now, he says that the Lord has talked with him, and also that angels have ministered unto him (1 Ne. 16:38)

> And it came to pass that according to his word he did destroy them; and according to his word he did lead them (1 Ne. 17:31)

> Behold, I am full of the Spirit of God, insomuch that my frame has no strength (1 Ne. 17:47)

> he shall do none other work, save the work which I shall command him (2 Ne. 3:8)

> Behold, he hath heard my cry by day, and he hath given me knowledge by visions in the nighttime. (2 Ne. 4:23)

> And the Lord spake it, and it was done. (2 Ne. 5:23)

> But wo unto him that has the law given, yea, that has all the commandments of God (2 Ne. 9:27)

> pray unto him continually by day, and give thanks unto his holy name by night (2 Ne. 9:52)

> Jacob shall not now be ashamed, neither shall his face now wax pale (2 Ne. 27:33)

> Hearken unto us, and hear ye our precept (2 Ne. 28:5)

> And we also had many revelations, and the spirit of much prophecy (Jacob 1:6)[3]

> But before ye seek for riches, seek ye for the kingdom of God (Jacob 2:18)

Ye have broken the hearts of your tender wives, and lost the confidence of your children (Jacob 2:35)

for the end is nigh at hand, and the season speedily cometh (Jacob 5:71)[4]

for father fought against father, and brother against brother (Mosiah 9:2)[5]

Nevertheless, the Lord seeth fit to chasten his people; yea, he trieth their patience and their faith (Mosiah 23:21)

every knee shall bow, and every tongue confess (Mosiah 27:31)[6]

for thou hast not lied unto men only but thou hast lied unto God (Alma 12:3)

That they might not be hardened against the word, that they might not be unbelieving (Alma 16:17)

that their hearts had been changed; that they had no more desire to do evil (Alma 19:33)

these our dearly beloved brethren, who have so dearly beloved us (Alma 26:9)

therefore they were poor as to things of the world;[7] and also they were poor in heart (Alma 32:3)

and ye shall feast upon this fruit even until ye are filled, that ye hunger not, neither shall ye thirst (Alma 32:42)

this mortal does not put on immortality, this corruption does not put on incorruption (Alma 40:2)

For behold, justice exerciseth all his demands, and also mercy claimeth all which is her own (Alma 42:24)

O ye wicked and ye perverse generation; ye hardened and ye stiffnecked people (Hel. 13:29)

I came unto my own, and my own received me not (3 Ne. 9:16)

and it was not a harsh voice, neither was it a loud voice (3 Ne. 11:3)

The eye hath never seen, neither hath the ear heard . . . And no tongue can speak, neither can there be written by any man . . . (3 Ne. 17:16–17)

And they were married, and given in marriage (4 Ne. 1:11)

and even as she is, so are they (Morm. 5:18)

thou art a God of truth, and canst not lie (Ether 3:12)

tongue cannot tell neither can it be written (Moro. 9:19)

COUPLETS (TWO-LINE PARALLELISMS)

Couplets are familiar to all people who love poetry or drama, since much of classical literature such as Shakespeare's plays are composed of couplets. These are two parallel lines or sentences that match each other, that is, they are parallel statements.[8] It is sometimes difficult to distinguish between half-line parallels and couplets because the punctuation of sentences does not always allow this distinction. Thus, we have judged couplets to be slightly longer than half-line parallels, but the classification of phrases as either half-line parallels or couplets is, at least in some cases, somewhat arbitrary.

for when a man speaketh by the power of the Holy Ghost
the power of the Holy Ghost carrieth it unto the hearts of the children of men (2 Ne. 33:1)

That perhaps they might bring them to the knowledge of the Lord their God,
and convince them of the iniquity of their fathers (Mosiah 28:2)

and his soul began to be harrowed up under a consciousness of his own guilt;
yea, he began to be encircled about by the pains of hell (Alma 14:6)

to bring, if it were possible, their brethren, the Lamanites, to the knowledge of the truth,
to the knowledge of the baseness of the traditions of their fathers (Alma 17:9)[9]

that perhaps they might bring them unto repentance;
that perhaps they might bring them to know of the plan of redemption (Alma 17:16)

And thus the work of the Lord did commence among the Lamanites;
thus the Lord did begin to pour out his Spirit upon them (Alma 19:36)

What shall I do that I may have this eternal life of which thou hast spoken?
Yea, what shall I do that I may be born of God? (Alma 22:15)

the king did bow down before the Lord, upon his knees;
yea, even he did prostrate himself upon the earth (Alma 22:17)

seeing that the Lord had granted unto them according to their prayers,
and that he had also verified his word unto them in every particular (Alma 25:17)

and thou didst visit them in thine anger with speedy destruction.
And thou didst hear me because of mine afflictions and my sincerity (Alma 33:10-11)

For behold, this life is the time for men to prepare to meet God;
yea, behold the day of this life is the day for men to perform their labors (Alma 34:32)[10]

For I know that thou wast in bonds;
yea, and I also know that thou wast stoned for the word's sake (Alma 38:4)

ye shall be delivered out of your trials, and your troubles, and your afflictions,
and ye shall be lifted up at the last day (Alma 38:5)

Now, my son, I would not that ye should think that I know these things of myself,
but it is the Spirit of God which is in me which maketh these things known unto me (Alma 38:6)

Do not endeavor to excuse yourself in the least point because of your sins, by denying the justice of God;
but do you let the justice of God, and his mercy, and his long-suffering have full sway in your heart (Alma 42:30)

behold, the very powers of hell would have been shaken forever;
yea, the devil would never have power over the hearts of the children of men (Alma 48:17)

which would lay a foundation for serious consequences among the people of Nephi,
yea, which consequences would lead to the overthrow of their liberty (Alma 50:32)

and they are strict to remember the Lord their God from day to day;
yea, they do observe to keep his statutes, and his judgments, and his commandments[11] continually (Alma 58:40)

But behold, great has been the slaughter among our people,
yea, thousands have fallen by the sword (Alma 60:4)

For we know not but what ye yourselves are seeking for authority.
We know not but what ye are also traitors to your country (Alma 60:18)

Ye know that ye do transgress the laws of God,
and ye do know that ye do trample them under your feet (Alma 60:33)

having restored peace to the land of Zarahemla, among their own people,
having inflicted death upon all those who were not true to the cause of freedom (Alma 62:11)

behold, I declare unto you that except ye shall repent your houses shall be left unto you desolate.
Yea, except ye repent, your women shall have great cause to mourn in the day that they shall give suck (Hel. 15:1–2)

I am the light and the life of the world.
I am Alpha and Omega, the beginning and the end (3 Ne. 9:18)[12]

and then will I gather them in from the four quarters of the earth;
and then will I fulfill the covenant which the Father hath made unto all the people of the house of Israel (3 Ne. 16:5)

And it shall be a testimony unto the Father than ye do always remember me.
and if ye do always remember me ye shall have my Spirit to be with you (3 Ne. 18:7)

Therefore, what manner of men ought ye to be?
Verily I say unto you, even as I am. (3 Ne. 27:27)

but I, knowing that these things must surely be made known,
and that all things which are hid must be revealed upon the house-tops (Morm. 5:8)

lest he shall come out in justice against you—
lest a remnant of the seed of Jacob shall go forth among you as a lion (Morm. 5:24)

And the day soon cometh that your mortal must put on immortality,
and these bodies which are now moldering in corruption must soon become incorruptible bodies (Morm. 6:21)

for there are none save it be the Lamanites and robbers that do exist upon the face of the land.
And there are none that do know the true God save it be the disciples of Jesus (Morm. 8:9–10)

O the depravity of my people!
They are without order and without mercy. (Moro. 9:18)

we know that many of our brethren have deserted over unto the Lamanites,
and many more will also desert over unto them (Moro. 9:24)

And I would exhort you, my beloved brethren, that ye remember that every good gift cometh of Christ.
And I would exhort you, my beloved brethren, that ye remember that he is the same yesterday, today, and forever (Moro. 10:9–19)[13]

And behold, they shall proceed forth out of the mouth of the everlasting God;
and his word shall hiss forth from generation to generation. (Moro. 10:28)

TRICOLON (THREE-LINE PARALLELS)

Tricolon are three sentences or phrases that are composed to be parallel to one another.[14] The three lines fit together in a special way and form a complete entity or expression.

for my soul delighteth in the scriptures,
and my heart pondereth them,
and writeth them for the learning and profit of my children (2 Ne. 4:15)

O Lord, wilt thou redeem my soul?
Wilt thou deliver me out of the hands of mine enemies?
Wilt thou make me that I may shake at the appearance of sin? (2 Ne. 4:31)

for the Spirit speaketh the truth and lieth not.
Wherefore, it speaketh of things as they really are,
and of things as they really will be (Jacob 4:13)

and all things shall be revealed unto the children of men
which ever have been among the children of men,
and which ever will be even unto the end of the earth (2 Ne. 27:11)

And they that make a man an offender for a word,
and lay a snare for him that reproveth in the gate,
and turn aside the just for a thing of naught (2 Ne. 27:32)

Go amongst thy brethren, the Lamanites,
and bear with patience thine afflictions,
and I will give unto you success (Alma 26:27)

Behold, I say unto you, is not a soul at this time as precious unto God as a soul will be at the time of his coming?
Is it not as necessary that the plan of redemption should be made known into this people as well as unto their children?
Is it not as easy at this time for the Lord to send his angel to declare these glad tidings unto us as unto our children, or as after the time of his coming? (Alma 39:17–19)

It is because you have hardened your hearts;
yea, ye will not hearken unto the voice of the good shepherd;
yea, ye have provoked him to anger against you (Hel. 7:18)

Behold, he is a god,[15] for except he was a god he could not know of all things.
For behold, he has told us the thoughts of our hearts, and also has told us things;

and even he has brought unto our knowledge the true murderer
of our chief judge. (Hel. 9:41)

O Lord, do not suffer that this people shall be destroyed by the
sword;
but O Lord, rather let there be a famine in the land,
to stir them up in remembrance of the Lord their God (Hel. 11:4)

And the battle commenced in this the sixth month;
and great and terrible was the battle thereof,
yea, great and terrible was the slaughter thereof (3 Ne. 4:11)

And the highways were broken up,
and the level roads were spoiled,
and many smooth places became rough (3 Ne. 8:13)

Judge not, that ye be not judged.
For with what judgment ye judge, ye shall be judged;
and with what measure ye mete, it shall be measured to you
again. (3 Ne. 14:1–2)

have we not prophesied in thy name,
and in thy name have cast out devils,
and in thy name done many wonderful works? (3 Ne. 14:22)

And behold, ye are the children of the prophets;
and ye are of the house of Israel;
and ye are of the covenant which the Father made with your
fathers (3 Ne. 20:25)

And now we call the proud happy;
yea, they that work wickedness are set up;
yea, they that tempt God are even delivered (3 Ne. 24:15)

And the Lord did prosper them exceedingly in the land;
yea, insomuch that they did build cities again where there had
been cities burned.

Yea, even that great city Zarahemla did they cause to be built again (4 Ne. 1:7–8)

And they began to be divided into classes;
and they began to build up churches unto themselves to get gain,
and began to deny the true church of Christ. (4 Ne. 1:26)

But behold, it shall come to pass that they shall be driven and scattered by the Gentiles;
and after they have been driven and scattered by the Gentiles,
behold, then will the Lord remember the covenant which he made unto Abraham and unto all the house of Israel. (Morm. 5:20)

And may the Lord Jesus Christ grant that their prayers may be answered according to their faith;
and may God the Father remember the covenant which he hath made with the house of Israel;
and may he bless them forever, through faith on the name of Jesus Christ. Amen. (Morm. 9:37)

And now, if I have no authority for these things, judge ye;
for ye shall know that I have authority when ye shall see me,
and we shall stand before God at the last day (Ether 5:6)

being armed with weapons of war,
having shields, and breastplates, and head-plates,
and being clothed after the manner of war (Ether 15:15)

And the church did meet together oft, to fast and to pray,
and to speak one with another concerning the welfare of their souls.
And they did meet together oft to partake of bread and wine, in remembrance of the Lord Jesus. (Moro. 6:5–6)
And awake, and arise from the dust, O Jerusalem;
yea, and put on thy beautiful garments, O daughter of Zion;
and strengthen thy stakes and enlarge thy borders forever (Moro. 10:31)

CONCLUSION

I believe the conclusion is inescapable that the Book of Mormon contains numerous parallelistic passages that are similar in many respects to the most beautiful parallelistic passages in the Old Testament and in the teachings of Jesus. What is known as poetic in the Old Testament is comparable to what most people think of as prose passages in the Book of Mormon. It is thus time to recognize that much of the Book of Mormon is composed in parallelistic passages, many of two lines and some extended passages of many lines. These parallelistic passages take many forms, and the ones identified here are typically not part of chiasms, alternates, or other types of parallelisms. Instead they stand on their own as simple parallelisms—beautiful, artistic, poetic, and meaningful.

Much of the beauty of the language of the Book of Mormon is created by parallelistic statements, and the parallelism found in the Book of Mormon is characteristic of Hebrew poetic and literary expressions. Much of the text of the Book of Mormon is poetic in structure and presentation. It is a monumental but still largely unappreciated literary accomplishment.

NOTES

1. Watson, *Traditional Techniques in Classical Hebrew Verse.* In his earlier work, Watson did not discuss this type of poetic form, and notes that much of his earlier work needs to be modified in light of this new discovery (see p. 22).
2. Watson, *Traditional Techniques in Classical Hebrew Verse,* 104–91.
3. This is an instance of what is called "verb gapping," in that the words *we had* are left out of the second phrase. See chapter 24.
4. This verse is similar to Jacob 5:29.
5. Another example of verb-gapping, in that the verb *fought* is left out of the second phrase.
6. This is also an example of verb-gapping with the omission of the verb *shall.*
7. This sentence is part of a prior alternate according to Parry.
8. Watson, *Classical Hebrew Poetry,* 11–15.
9. The second line here is also an example of verb-gapping.
10. This couplet is classified as synonymous by Parry.
11. This is also an example of a triplet (see chapter 13).
12. This last sentence in the couplet is itself a half-line parallelism, which demonstrates that the type of Hebrew-derived poetry found in the Book of Mormon is often complex and sophisticated.
13. Parry classified this couplet as polysyndeton or "many ands."
14. See Watson, *Traditional Techniques in Classical Hebrew Verse,* 332.
15. This is part of a previous alternate.

CHAPTER TWELVE

LONGER PARALLELS

In this chapter, we discuss a number of longer parallel scriptural passages found in the Book of Mormon. Having identified half-line parallels, couplets, and tricolon, we need to recognize that the Book of Mormon contains many longer passages, of from four to seventeen lines, that have a form of parallelism, but are not part of chiasms or alternates or other known types of parallelism. However, they are obviously scriptural passages that possess a parallelistic nature. Typically, words or phrases are repeated to create the parallels. Most of these have a distinct poetic feeling and sensibility, and the literary value of these passages is usually apparent. The writers of the Book of Mormon took great pains to beautify and adorn the text so that it would be memorable and significant to the reader.

I have found that putting these passages into a poetic format enables us to identify the parallel structure better than if they are left in their original sentence format, as the manuscript of the Book of Mormon was originally translated. For ease of identification, I present these passages in the same order in which they are found in the Book of Mormon. I have underlined words in these passages that are used repetitively in a parallelistic fashion.

> Now I, Nephi, did not work the timbers after the manner which was learned by men,
> neither did I build the ship after the manner of men;
> but I did build it after the manner which the Lord had shown unto me;
> wherefore, it was not after the manner of men (1 Ne. 18:2)

and they shall be gathered together to the lands of their inheritance;
and they shall be brought out of obscurity and out of darkness;
and they shall know that the Lord is their Savior and their Redeemer,
the mighty One of Israel. (1 Ne. 22:11)

And again, the Lord God hath commanded
that men should not murder;
that they should not lie,
that they should not steal;
that they should not take the name of the Lord their God in vain;
that they should not envy;
that they should not commit whoredoms,
and that they should do none of these things;
for whoso doeth them shall perish (2 Ne. 26:32)

That perhaps they might bring them to the knowledge of the Lord their God,
and convince them of the iniquity of their fathers;
and that perhaps they might cure them of their hatred towards the Nephites,
that they might also be brought to rejoice in the Lord their God,
that they might become friendly to one another (Mosiah 28:2)

that the word of God might have no obstruction,
but that it might go forth throughout all the land,
that his people might be convinced concerning the wicked traditions of their fathers,
and that they might be convinced that they were all brethren (Alma 23:3)

Yea, cry unto God for all thy support;
yea, let all thy doings be unto the Lord,
and whithersoever thou goest let it be in the Lord;
yea, let all thy thoughts be directed unto the Lord;
yea, let the affections of thy heart be placed upon the Lord forever (Alma 37:36)

Counsel with the Lord in all thy doings,
and he will direct thee for good;
yea, when thou liest down at night lie down unto the Lord,
that he may watch over you in your sleep;
and when thou risest in the morning
let thy heart be full of thanks unto God (Alma 37:37)

I say unto thee, my son, that the plan of restoration is requisite with the justice of God;
for it is requisite that all things should be restored to their proper order.
Behold, it is requisite and just, according to the power and resurrection of Christ,
that the soul of man should be restored to its body,
and that every part of the body should be restored to itself.
And it is requisite with the justice of God that men should be judged according to their works (Alma 41:2–3)

O remember, remember, my sons, the words which king Benjamin spake unto his people;
yea, remember that there is no other way nor means whereby man can be saved,
only though the atoning blood of Jesus Christ, who shall come,
yea, remember that he cometh to redeem the world.
And remember also the words which Amulek spake unto Zeezrom, in the city of Ammonihah;
for he said unto him that the Lord surely should come to redeem his people,
But that he should not come to redeem them in their sins,
but to redeem them from their sins (Hel. 5:9–10)

Yea, that same being who did plot with Cain,
that if he would murder his brother Abel it should not be known unto the world.
And he did plot with Cain and his followers from that time forth.
And also it is that same being who put it into the hearts of the people to build a tower sufficiently high that they might get to heaven.

And it was that same being who led on the people who came from that tower into this land;

who spread the works of darkness and abominations over all the face of the land,

until he dragged the people down to an entire destruction, and to an everlasting hell.

Yea, it is that same being who put it into the heart of Gadianton

to still carry on the work of darkness, and of secret murder;

and he has brought it forth from the beginning of man even down to this time (Hel. 6:27–29)

O how foolish and how vain,

and how evil, and devilish,

and how quick to do iniquity,

and how slow to do good,

are the children of men;

yea, how quick to hearken unto the words of the evil one;

and to set their hearts upon the vain things of the world!

Yea, how quick to be lifted up in pride;

yea, how quick to boast, and do all manner of that which is iniquity;

and how slow are they to remember the Lord their God,

and to give ear unto his counsels,

yea, how slow to walk in wisdom's paths! (Hel. 12:3–5)[1]

But we read that in the great and last day

there are some who shall be cast out,

yea, who shall be cast off from the presence of the Lord;

Yea, who shall be consigned to a state of endless misery (Hel. 12:25–26)

For I will, saith the Lord,

that they shall hide up their treasures unto me;

and cursed be they who hide not up their treasures unto me;

for none hideth up their treasures unto me save it be the righteous;

and he that hideth not up his treasures unto me,

cursed is he, and also the treasure (Hel. 13:19)

And then shall ye lament, and say:
O that I had repented, and had not killed the prophets, and stoned them, and cast them out.
Yea, in that day ye shall say:
O that we had remembered the Lord our God in the day that he gave us our riches,
and then they would not have become slippery that we should lose them (Hel. 13:33)

Behold, verily, verily, I say unto you,
I will declare unto you my doctrine.
And this is my doctrine,
and it is the doctrine which the Father hath given unto me;
and I bear record of the Father,
and the Father beareth record of me,
and the Holy Ghost beareth record of the Father and me;
and I bear record that the Father commandeth all men, everywhere,
to repent and believe in me. (3 Ne. 11:31–32; see also 3 Ne. 11:35–36)

And my Father sent me that I might be lifted up upon the cross;
and after that I had been lifted up upon the cross,
that I might draw all men unto me,
that as I have been lifted up by men
even so should men be lifted up by the Father,
to stand before me, to be judged of their works,
whether they be good or whether they be evil—
and for this cause have I been lifted up;
therefore, according to the power of the Father
I will draw all men unto me,
that they may be judged according to their works. (3 Ne. 27:14–15)

Know ye that ye are of the house of Israel.
Know ye that ye must come unto repentance, or ye cannot be saved.
Know ye that ye must lay down your weapons of war . . .
Know ye that ye must come to the knowledge of your fathers (Morm. 7:2–5)

And he knoweth their prayers,
that they are in behalf of their brethren.
And he knoweth their faith,
for in his name could they remove mountains;
and in his name could they cause the earth to shake;
and by the power of his word did they cause prisons to tumble to the earth
yea, even the fiery furnace could not harm them,
neither wild beast nor poisonous serpents,
because of the power of his word. (Morm. 8:24)

and it shall come in a day when it shall be said that miracles are done away;
and it shall come even as if one should speak from the dead.
And it shall come in a day when the blood of saints shall cry unto the Lord,
because of secret combinations and the works of darkness.
Yea, it shall come in a day when the power of God shall be denied,
and churches become defiled and be lifted up in the pride of their hearts;
yea, even in a day when leaders of churches and teachers shall rise in the pride of their hearts,
even to the envying of them who belong to their churches.
Yea it shall come in a day when there shall be heard of fires, and tempests,
and vapors of smoke in foreign lands;
And there shall also be heard of wars, rumors of wars, and earthquakes in divers places.
Yea, it shall come in a day when there shall be great pollutions upon the face of the earth;

there shall be murders, and robbings, and lying
and deceivings, and whoredoms, and all manner of abominations[2] (Morm. 8:26–31)

O ye pollutions, ye hypocrites, ye teachers,
who sell yourselves for that which will canker,
<u>why</u> have ye polluted the holy church of God?
<u>Why</u> are ye ashamed to take upon you the name of Christ?
<u>Why</u> do ye not think that greater is the value of an endless happiness
than that misery which never dies—because of the praise of the world?
<u>Why</u> do ye adorn yourselves with that which hath no life,
and yet suffer the hungry, and the needy,
and the naked, and the sick, and the afflicted[3]
to pass you, and notice them not?
Yea, <u>why</u> do ye build up your secret abominations to get gain,
and cause that widows should mourn before the Lord,
and also orphans to mourn before the Lord (Morm. 8:38–40)

Yea, and <u>who</u> can comprehend the marvelous works of God?
<u>Who shall say</u> that it was not a miracle
that by his word the heaven and the earth should be;
and by the <u>power of his word</u> man was created of the dust of the earth;
and by the <u>power of his word</u> have miracles been wrought?
And <u>who shall say</u> that Jesus Christ did not many mighty miracles[4] (Morm. 9:16–18)

CONCLUSION

The passages we have quoted in this chapter are longer parallel passages that have not been previously connected to any of the parallelistic forms identified by such people as John Welch and Donald Parry. Many are created by the use of repetitious words or phrases, but they have a certain free-form poetic character that sets them apart from other types of parallelistic expressions. They are often very beautiful in tone and language, and many have become favorite passages of people who read the Book of Mormon frequently. We regard these passages as having special literary worth, and commend them to the reader as further evidence that the Book of Mormon was created as a great literary treasure by its prophetic authors.

Because of space considerations, we have not included many passages that could have been used to illustrate the type of parallelism that we are discussing here. They have their own distinctive feeling, and there is a free-form character to these passages. They are beautiful and distinctive, and are among the best-loved passages of scripture among Latter-day Saint people.

For further study, see also the following passages: 1 Nephi 1:9–10; 2 Nephi 26:26–28; Alma 5:6–10; 10:19–21; 22:15; 33:4–11; 50:22; Helaman 3:20; 6:37–38; 8:25–27; 12:18–19; 13:19; 13:38; 3 Nephi 5:21–24 ("surely"); 26:3; 27:10–11; 28:9–11; 28:19–22; 30:1; 4 Nephi 1:3; 1:17–18; 1:24; Mormon 3:9–10; 9:2; 9:24–25; Ether 10:26–28; 12:3–4; 12:8–16; Moroni 6:5–6; 7:46–47; 9:21–22.

NOTES

1. Parry classifies this passage as an extended synonymous.
2. The last two lines are identified as synonymia by Parry.
3. These two lines are identified as synonymia by Parry.
4. This line is also an example of antenantiosis (see chapter 20).

CHAPTER THIRTEEN

WORD PAIRS AND DISTINCTIVE WORD COMBINATIONS

INTRODUCTION

One of the most significant literary forms found in the Bible is word pairs.[1] These are variously referred to as parallel pairs, synonymous pairs, stock word pairs, standing pairs, fixed pairs, A-B pairs, and sound pairs.[2] Avishur defined word pairs as

> pairs of synonymous, antonymous, or heteronymous words, whose components are found in tandem as a result of mutual affinity . . . combined in one of the established and accepted modes of pairing that reflect coordination . . . between the components, and there must exist sufficient examples confirming its provenance. The usage of the pair must be repeated in well defined and formulated stylistic phenomena; and not be a unique, single occurrence in a manner of casual affinity.[3]

The Hebrew and other Canaanite people frequently employed significant combinations of two words. In comparing Ugaritic and Hebrew poetry, language experts found many pairs of words that occurred in both languages. In 1972, Mitchell Dahood published a list of 609 word pairs found in both languages, and later added 66 more in 1975 and 344 in 1981.[4] Adele Berlin concluded that

> There existed a stock of fixed word pairs which belonged to the literary tradition of Israel and Canaan, and poets [and prophets], specially trained in their craft, drew on this stock to aid in the . . . composition of parallel lines . . . That leaves us with the notion of a stock of fixed pairs—the poets' dictionary, as it has been called . . . This stock of pairs, once numbering a few dozen, is now over a thousand and still growing.[5]

Berlin called the discovery and analysis of word pairs "one of the major achievements of modern biblical research."[6] This study gained a great boost with the discovery of Ugaritic texts in the 1930s.[7] Yet many books on Hebrew literature and poetry still do not comment directly on the phenomenon of word pairs.[8]

Calvert Watkins noted that what philologists call *formulas* are set word pairs that "make reference to culturally significant features—'something that matters'—and it is this which accounts for their repetition and long-term preservation."[9] The word pair *goods and chattels* is a formula with at least a thousand-year history that is still used in English today.[10] "The collection of such utterances, such formulaic phrases, is part of the poetic repertory of . . . individual languages."[11]

Kevin Barney and John Tvedtnes have both studied word pairs and word groups in the Book of Mormon. Barney articulated a fundamental ambition. "For some time I have felt that an analysis as to whether word pairs exist in the Book of Mormon would provide an interesting test of the Book of Mormon's authenticity."[12] He reported on forty word pairs he had discovered that are found in both the Old Testament and the Book of Mormon, with some also found in other Canaanite languages. He concluded that his list was not exhaustive, and he expected that "other scholars will be able to add to this list."[13]

Tvedtnes responded by identifying and discussing a number of other word groupings in the Book of Mormon, including *firm/steadfast/immovable, old/young, bond/free, flocks/herds,* and *gold/silver/precious things,* among others.[14] Our wish is also to respond to Barney's expectation by adding to the list of word pairs and other word combinations in the Book of Mormon, with the explicit hope that the discovery of these word groupings will add further proof to the authenticity of this great book of scripture.

FORMATS FOR WORD PAIRS

We find that word pairs typically are found in two different formats: parallel pairs and conjoined pairs.

Parallel Pairs. Word pairs in the Bible usually occur in parallel constructions, with the first word (the so-called A word) in the first parallel line, and the second word (the B word) in the second parallel line. Watson and most other biblical scholars argued that one of the important criteria for identifying a word pair is that the two words occur in parallel lines, such as

> like *snow* in summer,
> and like *rain* at harvest (Proverbs 26:1).[15]

Barney and Tvedtnes also use examples that follow this type of parallelism.

Conjoined Pairs. A second format, which is more common in the Book of Mormon, is two words that are connected with a conjunction such as the word *and,* as in *gold and silver.* We call these conjoined pairs, which display a different type of parallelism—both words are on the same line and adjacent. As we examine biblical usage more closely, we note that conjoined pairs also occur frequently in the Bible. This type of parallelism is more obvious but also less noticed by Biblical scholars. The pair *good/evil,* for example, is utilized twenty-five times in parallel constructions in the Book of Mormon, and twenty-four times in conjoined constructions.

EXTENDED WORD COMBINATIONS

In addition to word pairs, Biblical scholars observed the occurrence of three parallel words, which Berlin called "triplets."[16] Avishur also recognized the existence of "quadruplets," or four parallel words.[17] Five or more words or phrases may be referred to as "literary lists," which Koskenniemi called "word-groups."[18] Donald Parry's discussion of synonymia[19] recognized the existence of extended lists of synonymous words or expressions. Thus, a significant literary form found in the Bible and, as we will show here, in the Book of Mormon, is the presence of combinations of two, three, four, or more words and phrases, used in parallel or conjoined format.

While kneeling beside my father in family prayer, I often heard him pray for "the poor and the needy, the sick and the afflicted." Only later did I realize my father was using a saying from the Book of Mormon (Alma 1:27). There are many scriptural expressions such as this one that utilize a combination of words that have a poetic ring to them and are familiar to those of us who read the book frequently. Examples include *great/abominable, carnal/sensual/devilish,* and *nations/kindreds/tongues/peoples.*

It is to the analysis and explanation of these word combinations that this chapter is addressed. We identify many word pairs and discuss the ways in which the prophetic authors of the Book of Mormon employed word combinations to make the text more familiar and intriguing, to provoke interest and recognition, and to improve the remembrance and retention of the passage. We hope that this chapter will further the identification of such an important literary format employed by the prophets who wrote this ancient scripture.

WORD PAIRS

Every culture creates its own stock of traditional word combinations that are familiar to its people, and both the

Israelites and the Nephites had their own stock of expressions.[20] The Lehi colony brought with them their language with its many institutionalized expressions that formed their cultural foundation. Other expressions later were developed by the Nephite people, led by their prophets who, because they spoke for God, exercised a great influence on the language of the people. These latter word combinations are found only in the Book of Mormon and not in the Bible.

The great majority of these scriptural word combinations are not typically employed by modern English-speaking people in common parlance. So people today may communicate their familiarity with the scriptures to other knowledgeable individuals simply through the use of word combinations. For example, just saying the expression "great and abominable" carries a wealth of meanings to hearers who are familiar with the Book of Mormon, while leaving other people wondering concerning the meaning of what is being said.

Many words in both the Bible and Book of Mormon occur in pairs, such as *gold/silver* and *eat/drink*. Such word pairs are typical of Hebrew literary usage,[21] but many occur in other languages and cultures as well.[22] It would be difficult to imagine a society without words for *up/down, in/out, male/female, hot/cold, father/mother,* and many other combinations. However, some combinations are more unusual and less obvious, such as *honey/oil* or *David/son of Jesse.* Watson also noted that the A word (the word in the first parallel phrase) is more common and important, whereas the B word (the word in the second phrase) may be more varied and perhaps archaic.

Koskenniemi found the following word pairs that were developed in Old English but have become standard in modern English, and will be familiar to our readers: *far/wide, part/parcel, honest/true, really/truly, lo/behold, words/deeds, body/soul,* and *fame/fortune.*[23] Such words might have been expected to be employed by Joseph Smith if he were the author of the Book of Mormon, but they are not, which attests to the claim that the book is of ancient origin. The American people employ such word combinations so frequently that they are commonplace and even trite in our language.

Many secular authors utilize two or more words or expressions with synonymous or complementary meanings. Usually such combinations appear only once, and these simply reflect ordinary usage that occurs when an author seeks to expand the meaning of a word by adding a synonym. At other times, however, the intent of the writer is more symbolic and poetic, using two words to create a special effect on the minds and hearts of the readers, to heighten emotion, and to create sayings that are more easily remembered. This is true of the alliterative expression "*marvelous work and a wonder.*" Many word pairs are components of the stock of pairs that are part of the language of the people. But many may also be the creation of a prophet who seeks to use a poetic pair of words to catch the attention of the hearer or reader. The more frequently a pair of words is used in a text such as the Book of Mormon, the greater our assurance that it is included in the stock of words that are standardized in the language being studied.

Most but not all of the word pairs in the Book of Mormon are nouns, but they may be almost any part of speech. Sometimes the two words are linked theologically or legally, as are *justice/mercy.* Some are simply word pairs people tie together in a stereotypical way, such as *husband/wife.* Other pairs like *good/evil* exhibit antithetical meanings. Some are adjectives, such as *great/abominable,* which in this case in the Book of Mormon always modify the noun *church.* Some words or expressions appear many times in the Book of Mormon so that they carry a special sound or recognition to people who read the book frequently. For example, the word pair "wickedness and abominations" occurs forty-two times in the Book of Mormon.

Watson argued that in the Hebrew language and culture there were many word pairs that were "ready made and already existing in tradition."[24] Word pairs were "handed down through tradition and known to both poet and audience."[25] He compared the Hebrew language to the classical language of Greece, and noted that word pairs appear frequently in Homer.[26] Word pairs were especially important in oral communications, including sermons.

TYPES OF WORD PAIRS

Watson classified the types of word pairs preserved in the Old Testament, which included the following:[27]

Synonymous (the "components are synonyms or near-synonyms and therefore almost interchangeable"[28]). Examples include *flocks/herds, sins/iniquities, prophecy/revelation* and *wicked/perverse.*

Antithetical[29] (words with opposite meaning): *heaven/earth, night/day, quick/slow, temporally/spiritually,* and *first/last.*

Correlative (both words indicate examples of the same category)[30]: *blind/lame, gold/silver, eat/drink, fear/tremble,* and *broken heart/contrite spirit.*

Figurative (poetic words or phrases): *great/abominable, plain/precious, great/last, true/living,* and *lost/fallen.*

WORD PAIRS THAT OCCUR IN BOTH THE BOOK OF MORMON AND THE OLD TESTAMENT

I present a few of the more prominent examples of these word pairs in chart 1. It must be noted that sometimes the words appear in a different order or sentence format than the one that is quoted here. For example, some word pairs may be reversed, so "vain and foolish" becomes "foolish and vain." However, other word pairs always stand in the same word order. The pair "great and abominable" is never reversed—it is never stated as "abominable and great." The expression "wives and concubines" is also never reversed.

The first number in a parenthesis is the number of times this word pair is utilized in the Book of Mormon. The second number represents the times the word pair is found in the Bible, usually the Old Testament. For all the pairs that are used many times, it is obvious that they were stock pairs familiar to any Hebrew person.

CHART 1
WORD PAIRS IN BOTH THE BOOK OF MORMON AND THE BIBLE

gold and silver (43/153)[31]
heaven and earth (28/104)
power and authority (25/5)
justice and mercy (17/1)
great and terrible (15/12)
signs and wonders (14/15)[32]
life and death (13/14)
body and soul (11/2)
death and hell (10/9)
fast and pray/fasting and prayer (10/5)
famine and pestilence (9/26)
eat and drink (9/81)
sins and iniquities (9/15)
statutes and judgments (9/57)
flesh and blood (8/2)
true and living God (8/2)
the last shall be first (8/13)
a king and a ruler (8/5)
strait and narrow path (8/1)
his will and pleasure(8/2)
iniquities and abominations (7/1)

the life and the light (7/2)
smitten and afflicted (7/1)[33]
wives and concubines (7/7)
male and female (7/16)
just and true (7/2)
vain and foolish (7/1)
hunger and thirst (7/7)[34]
poor and needy (6/36)
broken heart and a contrite spirit (6/1)
power and glory (6/4)
faith and diligence (6/3)
a mourning and a lamentation (5/5)
quake and tremble (5/1)
my rock and my salvation (5/11)
the beginning and the end (5/14)
fear and tremble (5/5)
light and knowledge (5/1)
good and bad (4/13)
joy and gladness (4/12)
weeping and wailing (2/2)
a marvelous work and a wonder (2/1)

WORD PAIRS FOUND ONLY IN THE BOOK OF MORMON

The word pairs presented in chart 2 are found only in the Book of Mormon and do not appear in paired fashion in the Old Testament. It is quite possible that these word pairs were once employed by Biblical authors but have since been lost. In addition, the peoples of the Book of Mormon developed their own culture and traditions, and their own linguistic formulas and legacy. While there were important links to Hebrew culture, there were also many ways in which the descendants of Lehi avoided Hebrew practices and sought to develop their own independent values and norms. Nephi said that he had not taught his children much about the Jews because their works were the works of darkness (2 Ne. 25:2).[35]

CHART 2
WORD PAIRS FOUND ONLY IN THE BOOK OF MORMON

wickedness and abominations (42)
wars and contentions (27)
great and marvelous (27)
priests and teachers (21)
prophecy and revelation (13)
great and abominable church (12)
plain and precious things (10)
gift and power of God (10)
great and last day (10)
kept and preserved (10)
forever and ever (9)
saw and bear record (8)
mortal or immortal/immortality (8)
riches and vain things of world (8)
henceforth and forever (8)
lost and fallen (8)
rights and privileges (7)
driven and slain (7)
wars and rumors of wars (7)
oaths and covenants (7)
in and through (7)
great and eternal (6)
wicked and perverse (6)

heard and bear record (5)

heed and diligence (5)

liberty and freedom (5)

both temporally and spiritually (5)

gall of bitterness/ bonds of iniquity (4)

TRIPLETS

Triplets are three words or phrases that exhibit complementary meanings and are presented in a distinctive and poetic way.[36] They suggest analogous or complementary meanings that are similar but not identical.[37] The three words usually would not appear in a thesaurus as synonyms, so "complementary" is a more accurate characterization than "synonymous."[38] When a writer presents three words or clauses together, they are even more conspicuous and remarkable than word pairs, at least for many of us. These triplets are presented in chart 3. Again, the numbers in parentheses identify the instances in the Book of Mormon and the Bible.[39]

CHART 3
TRIPLETS IN BOTH THE BOOK OF MORMON AND THE BIBLE

their gold, and their silver, and all their precious things (16/6)[40]

Abraham, Isaac, and Jacob/God of Abraham, and God of Isaac, and God of Jacob (13/23)

men, women, and children (9/7)

the judgments, and the statutes, and the commandments of the Lord (7/14)

in the name of the Father, and of the Son, and of the Holy Ghost (7, with an additional four in other formats/1)

faith, hope, and charity (7/1)

famine, and pestilence, and the sword (4/24)

eat, drink, and be merry (4/4)
signs, and wonders and miracles (3/2)
for thine is the kingdom, and the power, and the glory (1/1)[41]

TRIPLETS FOUND ONLY IN THE BOOK OF MORMON

yesterday, today, and forever (6)
hunger, thirst, and fatigue (5)
carnal, sensual, and devilish (4)
death, hell, and an endless torment (4)
might, mind, and strength (4)
the power, and the mercy, and the justice of God (3)
your diligence and your faith and your patience (3)
envyings and strifes and malice (3)
weeping, and wailing, and gnashing of teeth (2)

QUADRUPLETS

Quadruplets is a somewhat inelegant term utilized by Avishur[42] to label four words or phrases with complementary meaning presented in a poetic fashion. Quadruplets typically possess a recognizable and noteworthy lilt or meter that makes them especially poetic and beautiful. Watkins gave the example in English of the quadruplet *oats, peas, beans and barley grow,* which he called "a masterpiece of the Indo-European poet's formulaic verbal art."[43]

Such combinations of words or phrases are obviously not simple, run-of-the-mill attempts by ordinary authors to convey everyday meaning. They are wisely and poetically constructed to be striking and to capture the mind and the heart. A few of these quadruplets are utilized several times by Book of Mormon authors, but most appear only once in the text. (See chart 4.) Again, the number of usages is found in parentheses after the quotation. Following are some of the notable examples of complementary quadruplets in the Book of Mormon. The first example is the only one also found in the Old Testament.[44]

CHART 4
QUADRUPLETS IN THE BOOK OF MORMON

neither on the north, nor on the south, nor on the east, nor on the west (7/10)

nations, kindreds, tongues and people (employed 4 times in the Book of Mormon, but also in the Testimony of the Three Witnesses and the Testimony of the Eight Witnesses)[45]

faith and diligence and patience and long-suffering (2)

the hardness of their hearts, and the deafness of their ears, and the blindness of their minds, and the stiffness of their necks (2)

the poor and the needy, and the sick and the afflicted (2)

in his power, and in his might, majesty, and dominion (2)

signs and wonders, and types, and shadows (1)

LITERARY LISTS

Finally, there are numerous passages in the Book of Mormon with more than four complementary words or clauses (see chart 5). Literary lists are words or phrases presented in a kind of enumeration that has a poetic or literary style.[46] Such literary lists are usually classified as "synonymia" by Parry.[47] The classic example is found in Isaiah 3:18–23, and repeated in 2 Nephi 13:18–23, in which Isaiah noted the ways in which the "daughters of Zion" act in provocative manners especially in their dress.[48] These are not merely lists of words but take on special meaning because they form an ensemble that exhibits a unity and purpose. Watson noted that a selective listing is another form of merismus (see our discussion below).[49]

CHART 5
SELECTED LITERARY LISTS IN THE BOOK OF MORMON

Five: *glory/ might/ majesty/ power/ dominion* (Alma 5:50)[50]

Six: *bows/ arrows/ swords/ cimeters/ stones/ slings* (Mosiah 10:8)[51]

Seven: *thou/ son/ daughter/ man-servant/ maid-servant/ cattle/ stranger* (Mosiah 13:18)[52]

Eight: *thunderings/ lightnings/ tempest/ fire/ smoke/ vapor of darkness/ opening of the earth/ mountains which shall be carried up* (1 Ne. 19:11)[53]

Ten: *flocks/ herds/ fatlings/ grain/ gold/ silver/ precious things/ silk/ fine-twined linen/ homely cloth* (Alma 1:29).[54]

Thirteen: *evil doings/ lyings/ deceivings/ whoredoms/ secret abominations/ idolatries/ murders/ priestcrafts/ envyings/ strifes/ wickedness/ abominations* (3 Ne. 30:2)[55]

Fourteen: *sorceries/ idolatry/ idleness/ babblings/ envyings/ strife/ wearing costly apparel/ pride/ lying/ thieving/ robbing/ committing whoredoms/ murdering/ all manner of wickedness* (Alma 1:32)

Nineteen: *Lamanites/ Nephites/ wars/ contentions/ dissensions/ preaching/ prophecies/ shipping/ building of ships/ building of temples/ synagogues/ sanctuaries/ righteousness/ wickedness/ murders/ robbings/ plunderings/ abominations/whoredoms* (Hel. 3:14; See also Ether 9:17–19)

Twenty-six: *haughty/ stretched-forth necks/ wanton eyes/ mincing/ tinkling with their feet/ tinkling ornaments/ cauls/ round tires like the moon/ chains/ bracelets/ mufflers/ bonnets/ ornaments of the legs/ headbands/ tablets/ ear-rings/ rings/ nose jewels/ changeable suits of apparel/ mantles/ wimples/ crisping-pins/ glasses/ fine linen/ hoods/ veils* (2 Ne. 13:16–23 and Isa. 3:16–23)

Counting these instances is often arbitrary and complicated, either because the author presents a subject and then gives instances of the subject, or because the beginning and the ending of a list are not always completely clear. Also, two things are sometimes combined into a single entity, such as *flocks/herds.*

THE SIGNIFICANCE OF WORD COMBINATIONS

As noted previously, many authors utilize two or three sequential synonyms in ordinary writing, so the Book of Mormon is not unique in this sense. However, the repeated usage of the same word pairs, usually in the same order, does seem to be common in both the Book of Mormon and the Bible. They may be very common in other languages as well, such as Old German or Middle English.[56] Some expressions, such as *great/abominable*, are utilized only by a single author, in this case Nephi, and not by other writers. Other combinations, such as *great/marvelous* and *power/authority* are extensively employed by virtually all Book of Mormon authors.

Similarly, Book of Mormon writers appealed to such patterns in order to enliven their expressions and to sway the minds and hearts of their readers. To be sure, these prophetic authors, like the prophets who wrote the Bible, did not indicate that they were writing poetry, creating parallelistic patterns, or using other literary forms and figures of speech. We are left to study these questions out in our minds and attempt to arrive at some conclusions about the usage of word combinations and other literary forms. The following possibilities occurred to me.

Literary Functions. What literary functions do such word combinations perform? Biblical and Book of Mormon authors obviously took great care in constructing poems and sermons that contained many figures of speech as well as theological teachings. One reason that the prophets employed so many literary devices is

> to facilitate smooth, imaginative verse composition and so maintain the attention of a potentially critical audience. By using the technique of adding style, a set of traditional patterns and a measure of economy, the trained [prophet] is able to keep up the flow . . . The listening [or reading] audience needs aids to attention, and assistance in following the movement of the [sermon or scripture] . . . It must also be charmed by the familiar, yet aroused and captivated by the unexpected.[57]

Several word combinations are especially notable because they use alliteration, at least when they are translated into English. It is almost certain that in the original language of the people of the Book of Mormon many more expressions were alliterative, because there are many alliterative expressions in the Old Testament. Examples in the Book of Mormon include *work/wonder, weep/wail, plain/precious,* and *life/light.*

Many other word combinations have become notable literary expressions, such as *a broken heart/a contrite spirit, strait/narrow, wars/rumors of war, great/eternal, steadfast/immovable, gall of bitterness/bonds of iniquity, carnal/sensual/devilish, weeping/wailing/gnashing of teeth,* and *the hardness of their hearts/the deafness of their ears/the blindness of their minds/the stiffness of their necks*. Perhaps they have special meaning to us because we have read and spoken them many times.

Standard Hebrew Word Pairs. As before noted, several stock word pairs are utilized many times, both in the Book of Mormon and the Bible. These include *gold/silver, heaven/earth, flocks/herds, eat/drink, famine/pestilence,* and *sins/iniquities.* These were almost certainly part of Hebrew culture and literary style and had become stock expressions in the Hebrew language. The saying *sackcloth/ashes* obviously expresses a Hebrew cultural practice. I hesitate to say these are trite expressions, but they are sayings that every Hebrew person would easily recognize and understand.

Echoes of the Law of Moses. The word-pair *statutes/judgments* and the triplet *judgments/statutes/commandments* are employed frequently in both the Book of Mormon and the Old Testament, and repeat the language of the law of Moses, especially in Deuteronomy. Ellis Rasmussen noted that Deuteronomy

> teaches that those who inherit a promised land do so on condition that they remain faithful to the Lord, pure in heart, generous to the poor, and devoted to God's Law. In a formula that appears several times, the people are promised that they will receive blessings for obedience to God and punishment for disobedience (Deuteronomy 27–30). Book of Mormon prophets taught similar doctrines, and they also indicated that such principles were divinely given long before Moses.[58]

The Book of Mormon also employed the pairs *oaths/covenants* and *performances/ordinances* that apply specifically to the law of Moses.

Theological Terms. Some word combinations command special theological significance. This is especially true of *justice/mercy,* a combination that is found only in the Book of Mormon. Other examples are *life/light, flesh/blood,* and *rock/salvation.* They are the subject of considerable theological discussion and elucidation by LDS scholars, especially justice and mercy. Other expressions with theological significance include *true/living God, life/light of the world, God of Abraham/God of Isaac/God of Jacob, in the name of the Father/and of the Son/and of the Holy Ghost,* and *for thine is the kingdom/and the power/and the glory.*

Universals/Merisms. Some word pairs or phrases are intended to encompass everything, that is, to be universalistic statements. A *merism* is a linguistic term that signifies a combination of two or more words that are used to stand for a whole entity. For example, *head and foot* do not just identify these two body parts, but signify the whole body. Likewise, *body and soul* is an expression that means the whole person.[59] Examples in the Book of Mormon include *nations/kindreds/tongues/peoples, yesterday/today/forever, power/might/majesty/dominion,* and *henceforth/forever.* Some word combinations, such as *heaven/earth* and *good/evil,* express opposites (antitheticals), but are also intended to project universal application. (see Chapter 17).

Repetition. Some word combinations are renowned because of the frequency with which they are repeated, especially the sayings *wickedness/abominations* (employed 42 times), *great/marvelous* (27 times), *wars/contentions* (27 times), and *power/authority* (26 times). When I counted these word combinations, I was surprised how frequently they were employed.

Mnemonic or Remembrance Function. Word combinations serve as a device to help listeners and readers remember the ideas and doctrines presented. To the extent to which the Book of Mormon prophets delivered sermons to teach the people, they undertook to express key phrases that were easily recognizable to the listeners. The expression *great/abominable* comes to mind as a good example here, but all of the sayings used many times also served this function.

Because some Biblical and Book of Mormon expressions are repeated many times, they may be considered trite (as are some Shakespearean expressions today). Others, employed only once or twice, are famous because of their wonderful literary value. The prophets expressed the language of God in the language of their people, but they did so with great flair and literary significance.

OTHER LITERARY COMBINATIONS

As we noted earlier, most commentators on biblical literature argue that word pairs must belong to the same grammatical class, that is, the same parts of speech.[60] We believe we have followed this rule consistently. It is obvious, however, that the Book of Mormon prophets employed other combinations of words that involve different parts of speech. These are yet to be studied and discussed fully, and we hope they will be the subject of further research in coming years. These involve the following types of stock word combinations (the number in parentheses is the number of usages found in the Book of Mormon/Old Testament):

(1) Combinations of an adjective and a noun, such as *eternal life* (30/30), *everlasting destruction* (9/1), *deep sleep* (6/10), *holy order(6/0), mighty power* (4/7), *mighty change* (4/0), and *eternal round* (3/0).

(2) Combinations of a verb and a noun, such as *harden your hearts* (37/8), *stir up* (33/15), *get gain* (18/1), *take up arms* (17/0), *set your hearts upon* (12/4), *lift up your heads* (10/9), *harrow up his mind* (10/0), *laid before [the judges]* (8/10), *pour out his spirit* (6/3), *labor with their hands* (6/0), and *publish peace* (3/2).

(3) Prepositional phrases, that is, two nouns linked by a preposition, such as: *face of the land* (77/0), *face of the earth* (60/4), *Son of God* (57/1 in O.T. and 51 N.T.), *kingdom of god* (37/ 69), *remission of your sins* (28/8 in N.T.), *voice of the people* (25/1), *ends of the earth* (23/27), *shedding of blood* (23/38), *foundation of the world* (22/3 with the word *earth* replacing the word *world), spirit of prophecy* (19/1 in N.T.), *traditions of your [their] fathers* (19/0), *spirit of god* (18/19), *sins of the world* (17/1 in N.T.), *bands of death* (13/0), *holy order of god* (10/0), *inquired of the Lord* (9/12), *lake of fire and brimstone* (9/2 in N.T.), *instrument in the hands of god* (8/0), and *chains of hell* (6/0).

We have not counted any of these expressions as word pairs because they do not fit the criteria for word pairs identified by Watson and others. However, they claim a significance in their own right. All are used frequently enough to qualify as traditional stock expressions in the language of the Nephites.

CONCLUSION

> The Book of Mormon is what it claims to be—an ancient text with roots in seventh-century B.C. Jerusalem. Word pairs [of Semitic origin] exist in the Book of Mormon because Lehi and his family were direct participants in the oral and literary traditions of that time and place, traditions which, to some extent at least, they passed on to their descendants.[61]

In this chapter we identified over a hundred word pairs utilized in the Book of Mormon, as well as numerous triplets, quadruplets, and literary lists, for a total of more than two hundred word combinations. Because many are repeated frequently, there are well over a thousand usages of word combinations we have discovered. We are assured that there are many more word combinations yet to be enumerated in this sacred scripture. We also recognized other types of word combinations, such as an adjective and a noun, a verb and a noun, and prepositional phrases, which we believe are perhaps as traditional, formulaic, and significant as word pairs.

The use of word pairs and other combinations of words is one of the most notable and as yet unappreciated aspects of the literary style of the Book of Mormon. It is my hope that we will ponder the deeper meanings of these expressions and that they will give us further light and knowledge (to conclude with a familiar word pair found in Alma 9:23).

NOTES

1. For an extensive discussion of the history of the study of word pairs, see Avishur, *Stylistic Studies,* 1–52. See also James T. Duke, "Word Pairs and Distinctive Word Combinations in the Book of Mormon," *Journal of Book of Mormon Studies (forthcoming).*
2. Watson, *Classical Hebrew Poetry,* 128–44. See scattered references to word pairs in Watson's later work, *Traditional Techniques in Classical Hebrew Verse.*
3. Avishur, *Stylistic Studies,* 1.

4. Dahood, "Ugaritic-Hebrew Parallel Pairs," 1:71–382. See also articles by the same title and author in 2:1–33, and 3:1–178. In response to critics, Dahood acknowledged that some of the so-called pairs are not strictly pairs because they are identical words, such as *father/father* (3:4).
5. Berlin, *Dynamics of Biblical Parallelism,* 65–66. Berlin also noted that "a word may elicit a number of different associations. Linguists usually rank them statistically, from the most common to the least. For example, *man* will usually elicit *woman,* but it will elicit *boy* in a smaller number of cases" (71).
6. Berlin, *Dynamics of Biblical Parallelism,* 65.
7. Avishur, *Stylistic Studies,* 6–43.
8. Fokkelman, *Reading Biblical Poetry.*
9. Watkins, *How to Kill a Dragon,* 9.
10. Watkins, *How to Kill a Dragon,* 9.
11. Watkins, *How to Kill a Dragon,* 10.
12. Barney, "Poetic Diction," 23. See also Barney, "Understanding Old Testament Poetry," 51–54.
13. Barney, "Poetic Diction," 23.
14. Tvedtnes, "Word Groups," 262.
15. Watson, *Classical Hebrew Poetry,* 128.
16. Berlin, *Dynamics of Biblical Parallelism,* 626-633.
17. Avishur, *Stylistic Studies,* 629.
18. Koskenniemi, *Repetitive Word Pairs,* 12. See also Watkins's discussion of "indexical lists," *How to Kill a Dragon,* 46.
19. Parry, *Book of Mormon Text Reformatted,* iii–ix.
20. See Bullinger, *Figures of Speech,* 657–72, for a discussion of a figure of speech called "hendiadys," which involves two words expressing a single thought. These two words are always the same parts of speech, and are always joined with the conjunction *and.*
21. Watson, *Classical Hebrew Poetry,* 128–44.
22. Jeep, *Alliterating Word-Pairs;* Avishur, *Stylistic Studies.*
23. Koskenniemi, *Repetitive Word Pairs,* 11. In the index, Koskenniemi has listed several hundred word pairs encompassing forty-two pages (120–162).
24. Watson, *Classical Hebrew Poetry,* 137.
25. Watson, *Classical Hebrew Poetry,* 138.
26. Watson, *Classical Hebrew Poetry,* 136–37.
27. Watson, *Classical Hebrew Poetry,* 131–35. Watson also discussed augmented word-pairs, epithetic word-pairs, identical or repetitive pairs, fixed and variant pairs, distant word-pairs, reversed word-pairs, and numerical word-pairs.
28. Watson, *Classical Hebrew Poetry,* 31. While the usage of the word *synonym* has become standard in both Biblical and Book of Mormon literary analysis, I prefer the term *complementary,* because many of the pairs labeled as

synonyms would not appear in lists of synonyms in a thesaurus.

29. Watson used the word *autonymic* here.

30. I admit that I find the categories "synonymous" and "correlative" difficult to distinguish in practice.

31. See also a triplet with the addition of *precious things.*

32. See also the triplet *signs/wonders/miracles* and the quadruplet *signs/wonders/types/shadows.*

33. The triplet *stricken/smitten of God/afflicted* is found in Isaiah 53:4.

34. See also the triplet *hunger/thirst/fatigue.* The seven usages in the Bible extend from Deuteronomy to Revelations, so this was a very common expression of the Hebrew people. Christ used this pair twice, once in a conjoined pair (Matt. 5:6) and once in a parallel pair (John 6:35).

35. Other word pairs are found in the following scriptures (number of usages in parentheses): 1 Nephi 3:7 (2); 1 Nephi 19:23 (3); 2 Nephi 3:24 (2); Enos 1:4 (2); Omni 1:28 (4); Mosiah 5:15 (4); Mosiah 13:30 (4); Mosiah 18:29 (1); Mosiah 21:35 (2); Mosiah 25:11 (2 and 4); Mosiah 18:2 (2); Alma 1:21 (1); Alma 9:10 (3); Alma 10:4 (4); Alma 13:17 (2); Alma 13:26 (4); Alma 17:5 (2); Alma 17:14 (2); Alma 26:15 (2); Alma 40:23 (3); Alma 42:23 (3); Helaman 1:15 (3); Helaman 3:37 (4); Helaman 4:25 (1 and 3); Helaman 6:14 (2); Helaman 6:17 (2); Helaman 7:16 (4); Mormon 4:11 (3); and Ether 11:15 (3).

36. Avishur, *Stylistic Studies,* 626–33.

37. Bullinger, *Figures of Speech,* 673, utilized the term *hendiatris* to describe a figure of speech which involves "three words used, but one thing meant."

38. The triplet *grain/wine/oil* appears in both the Bible and in Ugaritic. Dahood, "Ugaritic-Hebrew Parallel Pairs," 1:250.

39. Other triplets (used only once or twice) are found in the following scriptures: 1 Nephi 12:23 (2); Mosiah 20:1 (1); Alma 9:11 (2); Alma 9:20 (1); Alma 13:9 (2); Helaman 5:12 (2); Helaman 6:8 (1); 3 Nephi 6:14 (2); and Mormon 5:15 (2).

40. Originally discussed by Tvedtnes, "Word Groups," 266–67.

41. This expression is employed only once, but it has become very famous and recognizable because it is used in the Lord's Prayer.

42. Avishur, *Stylistic Studies,* 629.

43. Watkins, *How to Kill a Dragon,* 47.

44. The following quadruplets each appear only once in the Book of Mormon: 1 Nephi 14:23; 16:35; 22:24, 2 Nephi 6:18; 10:6; 25:29; 28:14; 32:7; Jacob 5:76; Mosiah 2:13; 4:4; 5:15; 15:5; 16:2; Alma 14:18; 40:12; 43:9; 43:26; 45:11; 48:13; Helaman 3:17; 4:20; 6:30; 7:5; 9:21; 10:5; 15:12, 3 Nephi 4:4; 6:15; 8:17; Mormon 2:23; 9:6; Moroni 8:8. As noted earlier, the notable quadruplet *heart/might/mind/strength* appears only in the Doctrine and Covenants (D&C 4:2 and 59:5).

45. Also utilized in a different format in 3 Nephi 26:4. The word pair *kindreds/nations* is found in Psalms 27:22.
46. See Watson's discussion of lists, and what he calls "tours" and "expansion" in *Classical Hebrew Poetry,* 349–56.
47. Parry, *Book of Mormon Text Reformatted,* iii–ix.
48. According to Bullinger, this is a classic example of "synthroesmos," or enumeration. This is a method of amplification in which a number of examples are given when one larger statement would have sufficed. E. W. Bullinger, *Figures of Speech,* 436–37. Many other lists in the Book of Mormon could also be classified under this figure of speech.
49. Watson, *Classical Hebrew Poetry,* 321.
50. See also Alma 4:9; Mosiah 3:19; 3 Nephi 8:12; 8:19; and Moroni 6:9
51. See also Omni 1:25; Mosiah 3:5; 11:8; 29:14; Alma 43:47; 46:12; 3 Nephi 16:9; 17:9, and 4 Nephi 1:5.
52. See also Mosiah 9:16; Alma 2:12; 43:20; 50:21, Helaman 1:14; and 1 Nephi 18:25. Tvedtnes, "Word Groups," 268, also noted the list *cow/ox/ass/horse/goat/wild goat/wild animals.*
53. See also 2 Nephi 5:15; Mosiah 11:8; Alma 4:6; 9:26; 44:5; 62:39–40; Helaman 12:4; 3 Nephi 16:10; 17:7.
54. See also Jarom 1:8.
55. See also 2 Nephi 13:1–3 with a list of fifteen.
56. Koskenniemi, *Repetitive Word Pairs.*
57. Koskenniemi, *Repetitive Word Pairs,* 33.
58. Rasmussen, "Deuteronomy," 1:378.
59. Watson, *Classical Hebrew Poetry,* 321.
60. Watson, *Classical Hebrew Poetry,* 128.
61. Barney, "Poetic Diction," 28–29.

CHAPTER FOURTEEN

IDIOMATIC EXPRESSIONS

Idioms are colloquial sayings that are symbolic rather than being literally true, and are specific to a given language or culture.[1] It is difficult for foreigners to understand idioms without explanation. They are a great barrier to learning the meanings of another language and culture, and are often misunderstood and mistranslated. Examples from English are "he is in a pickle," "to give a bride a shower," "bite the bullet," and "being in hot water."

There are relatively few such idioms in the Book of Mormon, indicating that Mormon and other writers knew that their words would be translated and made available to people who would not understand Hebrew idiomatic expressions. However, it is also possible that there are many idioms in the text of the Book of Mormon that may not be recognized by people such as ourselves who are far removed from the language and culture of the Nephite people. As people who have lived in a foreign country know, you can believe you understand an expression because you know the meaning of every word used, while being oblivious to the idiomatic nature of the expression and while missing the wealth of meanings conveyed by it.

Some words or phrases in the Book of Mormon we shall call "idiomatic expressions." These are statements that are common expressions in the language of the people of Lehi, but which are unusual and somewhat odd and curious in the English into which the book was originally translated. English-speaking people either never or rarely use these idiomatic expressions found in the Book of Mormon.

Most readers of the book have come to understand and accept these expressions, so their idiomatic nature may not be fully appreciated. For example, the word "exceedingly" is easily understood by people whose native language is English, although it is rarely used in either verbal or written form today. But it is a common expression in the Book of Mormon, appearing 245 times. It also is used 28 times by the writers of the Old Testament. The adjectival form "exceeding," as in "exceeding faith" or "exceeding joy," is used another 42 times in the Book of Mormon.

Some idiomatic expressions are peculiar to the Book of Mormon, but many others are also found in the Old Testament, which indicates that the latter are typical Hebrew expressions.[2] For example, the word "behold" appears 1,401 times in the Book of Mormon and 1,057 times in the Old Testament, which demonstrates that this is an expression common to both the Lehi colony and the Hebrews. English-speaking people almost never use this expression in either spoken or written form. On the other hand, the phrase "it came to pass" is used a total of 1,325 times in the Book of Mormon but is found only three times in the Old Testament, indicating perhaps that it is an idiomatic expression that is unique to the Nephite culture.

In the list of idiomatic expressions that follows, I have divided the list into those unique to the Book of Mormon and those that are also found in the Old Testament. I have indicated only one scriptural reference for each expression, although many of them appear frequently in the scriptures.

As with any literary form, variations in style or presentation are found with some of these idiomatic expressions. Many idiomatic expressions are found in the book of Isaiah and are quoted in the Book of Mormon. Here I have only listed those expressions found in Isaiah that are found in other contexts in the Book of Mormon rather than in the quoted Isaiah passages. These are listed in rough alphabetical order of the most important word in the idiomatic expression.

IDIOMS UNIQUE TO THE BOOK OF MORMON

bear record (1 Ne. 14:29)
became for themselves (3 Ne. 1:29)
call the name of the place (1 Ne. 16:13)
called under that head (Alma 3:10)
cease to strive with them (1 Ne. 7:14)
cross his words (Mosiah 10:16)
cross him (Hel. 9:19)
days of probation (1 Ne. 15:33)
dissenting away (3 Ne. 3:11)
due time of the Lord (1 Ne. 14:26)
dwindle in unbelief (2 Ne. 1:10)
engraven the heads of them upon the plates (Jacob 1:4)
one eternal round (1 Ne. 10:19)
expedient (Mosiah 29:16)
in fine (Omni 1:3)
foolish imaginations of his heart (1 Ne. 17:20)
gotten great hold upon (Alma 8:9)
hardness of their hearts (1 Ne. 2:18)
high birth (Alma 51:8)
hinderment (Mosiah 27:9)
imagined up unto themselves (Morm. 9:10)
in and through (Mosiah 3:17, 18)
maketh manifest (Jarom 1:4)
matchless power (Alma 49:28)
mysteries of God (1 Ne. 2:16)
nine moons (Omni 1:21)
the mother of [abominations] (1 Ne. 14:9)[3]
the office of their ministry (Moro. 7:31)
press forward (1 Ne. 8:24)
rising generation (3 Ne. 1:30)

save it be (Morm. 8:15)
set my back towards (Alma 8:24)
shadow of changing (Morm. 9:10)
his soul mourned and refused to be comforted (Ether 15:3)
for the space of a time (1 Ne. 16:17)
for the space of many generations (2 Ne. 1:18)
sow filthiness (Mosiah 7:30-31)
stay their hand (3 Ne. 3:8)
a thing of naught (1 Ne. 19:9)
unfolded unto them (Mosiah 29:35)
visited by sword, and by famine (2 Ne. 1:18)
visitations (2 Ne. 1:12)
warm contention (Alma 50:26)[4]
a wine-bibber (Mosiah 11:15)
wise purpose (W of M 1:7)
wo (Mosiah 11:20)[5]
wonderfully great army (Alma 51:11)[6]
work of death (Hel. 4:5) and work of destruction (Hel. 11:2)

IDIOMS FOUND IN BOTH THE BOOK OF MORMON AND THE OLD TESTAMENT

at hand (3 Ne. 1:16; Gen. 27:41)
the arm of the Lord (2 Ne. 28:32; Isa. 53:1)
make bare his arm (1 Ne. 22:10; 3 Ne. 20:35; Isa. 52:10)
behold (1 Ne. 1:17; Gen. 1:29)
before our eyes (Mosiah 1:5; Deut. 6:22)
branch (1 Ne. 15:12; Isa. 14:19)
breathe out [much threatenings] (1 Ne. 18:17; Ps. 27:12)
build up [churches unto themselves] (4 Ne. 1:41; Deut. 25:9)
captivity (1 Ne. 14;4; Num. 21:29)
out of captivity (1 Ne. 13:16; Ezra 2:1)

cast off (1 Ne. 15:33; 2 Kgs. 23:27)
children of men (Mosiah 3:5; Gen. 11:5)
crooked paths (Alma 7:20; Isa. 40:4)
cut off (2 Ne. 1:17; Gen. 17:14)
confederate (Hel. 9:20; Gen. 14:13)
in my days (Omni 1:2; 2 Kgs. 20:19)
depths of the sea (1 Ne. 17:48; Ps. 68:23)
dig a pit (2 Ne. 28:8; Eccl. 10:8)
durst not (Alma 1:17; Job 32:6)
ends of the earth (Morm. 9:21; Deut. 33:17)
exceedingly (1 Ne. 18:15; Gen. 7:19)
the face of the earth (1 Ne. 14:14; Gen. 4:14)
let fall [the sword] (3 Ne. 3:8; Ruth 2:16)
he fled from before them (Mosiah 17:4; Ex. 4:3)
maketh flesh his arm (2 Ne. 4:34; Jer. 17:5)
from the foundation of the earth (Mosiah 4:6; Ps. 102:25)
fountain of living waters (1 Ne. 11:25; Jer. 2:13)
four quarters [of the earth] (1 Ne. 19:17; Jer. 49:36)
go the way of all the earth (Mosiah 1:9; Josh. 23:14)
and it had an end (Hel. 1:13; Ezek. 35:5)
had made an end (1 Ne. 7:1; Gen. 27:30)
by the hand of [my industry] (Alma 10:4; Gen. 38:20)
the hand of the Lord (1 Ne. 5:14; 2 Ne. 1:6; Job 12:9)
hardened [in iniquity] (Hel. 16:12; Dan. 5:20)
one heart (2 Ne. 1:21; Jer. 32:39)
the Lord shall hiss (2 Ne. 29:2; Isa. 7:18)
hither and thither (1 Ne. 17:26; 2 Kgs. 2:8)
a hundredth part (W of M 1:5; Neh. 5:11)
insomuch (Alma 51:32; Ps. 106:40)
isles of the sea (1 Ne. 22:4; Esth. 10:1; Isa. 24:15)
jot or tittle (Alma 34:13; 3 Ne. 1:25; 12:18; Matt. 5:18

know of a surety (1 Ne. 5:8; Gen. 15:13)
the land of (Omni 1:13; Gen. 4:16)
lifted up (1 Ne. 16:2; Deut. 8:14)
living water (1 Ne. 11:25; Zech. 14:8)
make an end (Omni 1:3; Deut. 20:9)
all manner of (Ether 13:26; Gen. 18:11)
after the manner of (1 Ne. 11:18; Gen. 18:10)
which are meet for [repentance] (Alma 9:30; Deut. 3:18)
multitudes (1 Ne. 12:21; Joel 3:14)
murmur (1 Ne. 16:3; Ex 16:7; Num. 16:11)
publish peace (Mosiah 15:17; Isa. 52:7 uses "publisheth" peace)
rehearse unto them (Mosiah 8:2; Ex. 17:14)
return upon your own heads (2 Ne. 29:5; Obad. 1:15)
my rock (1 Ne. 13:37; 2 Sam. 22:3)
rod of his mouth (2 Ne. 30:9; Isa. 11:4)
my seed and the seed of my brethren (1 Ne. 12:19; Gen. 17:7)
set his hand (2 Ne. 6:2; Isa. 11:11)
deep sleep (2 Ne. 1:13; Isa. 19:10)
sore battle (Morm. 4:19; 2 Sam. 2:17)
spoken by the mouth (1 Ne. 5:13; 2 Chr. 36:22)
stiffneckedness (1 Ne. 2:11; Ex. 33:3)
stir them up (Alma 4:19; Ps. 78:38)[7]
a tender plant (Mosiah 14:2; Isa. 53:2)
good tidings (Mosiah 15:14; Isa. 52:7)
thought it [expedient] (Mosiah 1:9; Dan. 4:2)
by times or at seasons (Mosiah 18:4; Dan. 2:21)
[his heart] took courage (Hel. 1:22; 2 Chr. 15:8)
tree of life (1 Ne. 11:25; Gen. 2:9; Prov. 11:30)
utter destruction (3 Ne. 3:4; 1 Kgs. 20:42)
utterly refuse (Morm. 3:11; Ex. 22:17)
vineyard of God (all of Jacob 5; Alma 13:23; Isa. 1:8)

visit you [with utter destruction] (3 Ne. 3:4; Gen. 50:24)
walk humbly [before the Lord] (Ether 6:30; Micah 6:8)
watchmen (Mosiah 12:22; Isa. 56:10; Jer. 6:17)
water my pillow by night (2 Ne. 33:3; Ps. 6:6)
waxed [strong] (Jarom 1:5; Gen. 26:13)
went forth (3 Ne. 1:23; Gen. 8:7)
the wilderness (1 Ne. 2:2; Gen. 21:14)[8]
written on the heart (2 Ne. 8:7; Jer. 31:33)

CONCLUSION

Idiomatic expressions are an essential part of the common language and literature of any people. The great majority of the idiomatic expressions in the Book of Mormon are not typically used by people who speak or write the English language. Therefore, Joseph Smith did not simply borrow the common language of his time. Instead, many of these idiomatic expressions are found in the language and literature of the Hebrew people. Other expressions seem to be exclusive to the Book of Mormon people. It is common for every nation to develop its own idioms and unique expressions, and this is what seems to have occurred among the Book of Mormon people.

The study of the idiomatic expressions found in the Book of Mormon should convince honest readers that Joseph Smith did not create the book from his own American experience and culture. Instead, these idiomatic expressions give further proof not only of the Hebrew roots of the people of the Book of Mormon, but also of the ancient foundations of the literary style of its authors.

NOTES

1. Bullinger, *Figures of Speech,* 819–60.This is a very useful discussion of idioms used in the Bible, which derive from both Greek and Hebrew.
2. A wonderful source for idioms found in the Bible is Lamsa, *Idioms in the Bible Explained.*
3. The Old Testament never uses the word *mother* in an idiomatic way, but always in reference to a specific mother. However, the phrase "the mother of," as in "the mother of abominations" or "the mother of all wars" is a common idiomatic phrase among people in the Middle East today.
4. The Old Testament never uses the word *warm* as an adjective.
5. The Old Testament uses the word *woe* frequently, but never the word *wo.* This difference between the Old Testament and the Book of Mormon may be due to the styles of the translators rather than to expressions found in the original languages.
6. The Old Testament uses the word *wonderfully* as an adverb but never as an adjective.
7. The Old Testament uses the expression *stir up.*
8. This word is used 257 times in the Old Testament and 214 times in the Book of Mormon

CHAPTER FIFTEEN

ANTITHETICALS

Antithetical statements are among the most prominent and distinctive literary forms in all scriptures, and occur frequently in the Book of Mormon. *An antithetical, also called an antithesis,*[1] *is a word or phrase that is stated opposite to another word or phrase.* The first word is usually referred to as the "thesis." Thus, a thesis and an antithesis are opposites that are inseparably linked together, and the reader cannot fully appreciate an antithetical without also knowing the thesis to which it is attached. Such antitheticals are common in any language, and children often learn the meaning of words by being taught their opposites, such as up and down, in and out, or boy and girl.

The ultimate antithesis is the conflict between God and Satan, which leads to many other antitheticals such as good and evil. Prophets use antithetical expressions to communicate many important ideas, such as conflict between two or more groups, principles, or ideas. An antithetical is also frequently used as a means of expressing a universal (see chapter 17), which is a statement that includes everyone or everything. Parry has identified a very large number of antitheticals in the Book of Mormon text.[2] He typically identified these by using numbers (e.g., 1 and 2) to mark the opposite words or phrases. It is highly recommended that the serious student of the Book of Mormon obtain a copy of Parry's book for earnest and thoughtful study.

SIMPLE ANTITHETICAL

A simple antithetical is two words or phrases with opposite meanings. The list below is not a comprehensive list of the antitheticals used by the prophetic writers of the Book of Mormon. As is our common practice, we give only one reference for such expressions, even though many appear more than once in the text. These examples are the result of my own observations.

to dwell in the kingdom of God, or to be cast out (1 Ne. 15:35)

good or bad (2 Ne. 2:11)

enticed by the one or the other (2 Ne. 2:16)

to act for themselves and not to be acted upon (2 Ne. 2:26)

out of darkness unto light (2 Ne. 3:5)

they who are not for me are against me, saith our God (2 Ne. 10:16)

both Jew and Gentile (2 Ne. 26:33)

from the beginning of the world to the ending thereof (2 Ne. 27:7)

my mortal shall put on immortality (Enos 1:27)

heaven and earth (Mosiah 13:19)

the first and the last (Alma 11:39)

stand or fall (Alma 41:7)

we will perish or conquer (Alma 44:8)

choose life or death (Hel.14:31)

in the body or out of the body (3 Ne. 28:15)

mortal or immortal (3 Ne. 28:18)

both temporally and spiritually (Morm. 2:15; 1 Ne. 14:7)

Doubt not, but be believing (Morm. 9:27)

by day and by night (Ether 14:23)

as the daylight is from the dark night (Moro. 7:15)

the quick and the dead (Moro. 10:34)

EXTENDED ANTITHETICALS

either to the convincing of them unto peace and life eternal,
or unto the deliverance of them to the hardness of their hearts and
the blindness of their minds (1 Ne. 14:7)

For the things which some men esteem to be of great worth, both
to the body and soul,
others set an naught and trample unto their feet (1 Ne. 19:7)

remember that ye are free to act for yourselves--
to choose the way of everlasting death
or the way of eternal life (2 Ne. 10:23)[3]

I trust that you do not worship idols,
but that ye do worship the true and living God (Alma 7:6)

mortality raised to immortality,
corruption to incorruption (Alma 41:4)

And they did not come unto Jesus with broken hearts and contrite
spirits,
but they did curse God, and wish to die (Morm. 2:14)

DIALECTIC

A dialectic is a series of opposites or antitheticals. A dialectic may include as few as two contrasts or an extended list of opposites. In most cases, each contrast involves two direct opposites, such as old and young. However, in at least one case, three categories are identified: the aged, the middle aged, and the rising generation (Alma 5:49). We quote below some of the most notable antitheticals in the Book of Mormon. These are in addition to the numerous ones identified by Parry.[4]

both Jew and Gentile,
both bond and free,
both male and female (2 Ne. 10:16)[5]

to preach unto all, both old and young,
both bond and free;
yea, I say unto you the aged, and also the middle aged, and the rising generation (Alma 5:49)[6]

whether he desireth good or evil,
life or death,
joy or remorse of conscience (Alma 29:5)[7]

black and white,
bond and free,
male and female;
and he remembereth the heathen, and all are alike unto God,
both Jew and Gentile (2 Ne. 26:33)

both the old and young,
both bond and free,
both male and female,
both the wicked and the righteous (Alma 11:44; see also Alma 1:30 and Mosiah 25:8–11)[8]

A CLASSIC DIALECTIC

The best example of a dialectic[9] in all scripture is found in 2 Nephi 2:11, in which Nephi discusses the significance of opposition and illustrates such opposition by using seven antithetical contrasts in one verse.

For it must needs be, that there is an opposition in all things.
If not so, my firstborn in the wilderness,
righteous could not be brought to pass, neither wickedness,
neither holiness nor misery,
neither good nor bad.
Wherefore, all things must needs be a compound in one;
wherefore, if it should be one body it must needs remain as dead,
having no life neither death,
nor corruption nor incorruption,
happiness nor misery,
neither sense nor insensibility. (2 Ne. 2:11)

ANTITHETICAL CHIASMS

Antithetical chiasms are antithetical statements arranged in a chiastic ABBA pattern as discussed in chapter 9.

A and he hath spoken unto you in a still, small voice,
  B but ye were past feeling,
  B that ye could not feel his words;
A wherefore, he has spoken unto you like unto the voice of thunder (1 Ne. 17:45)

ANTITHETICAL ALTERNATES

Antithetical alternates are antithetical statements arranged in an ab/ab pattern. For a more extensive discussion of alternates, see chapter 10.

a for if iniquity shall abound
  b cursed shall be the land for their sakes,
a but unto the righteous
  b it shall be blessed forever (2 Ne. 1:7)

Behold there are save two churches only;
a the one
  b is the church of the Lamb of God,
a and the other
  b is the church of the devil (1 Ne. 14:10)[10]

a for unto him that receiveth
  b I will give more;
a and from them that shall say, We have enough,
  b from them shall be taken away even that which they have (2 Ne. 28:30)
a I was in the darkest abyss,
  b but now I behold the marvelous light of God.
a My soul was racked with eternal torment;
  b but I am snatched, and my soul is pained no more (Mosiah 27:29)

a And if their works were good in this life, and the desires of their hearts were good
    b that they should also, at the last day, be restored unto that which is good.
a And if their works are evil
    b they shall be restored unto them for evil (Alma 41:3)

a except there were a punishment
    b which also was eternal as the life of the soul should be,
a affixed opposite to the plan of happiness,
    b which was as eternal also as the life of the soul (Alma 42:16)

a many had become hardened,
    b because of the exceedingly great length of the war;
a and many were softened
    b because of their afflictions (Alma 62:41)

a I am Alpha
    b and Omega,
a the beginning
    b and the end (3 Ne. 9:18; see also Alma 11:39)

a Some
    b were lifted up in pride,
a and others
    b were exceedingly humble
a some
    b did return railing for railing
a while others
    b would receive railing and persecution (3 Ne. 6:13)[11]

a Behold, this is not my doctrine,
    b to stir up the hearts of men with anger, one against another;
a but this is my doctrine,
    b that such things should be done away (3 Ne. 11:30–31)

a Verily, verily, I say unto you, that this is my doctrine,
    b and whoso buildeth upon this buildeth upon my rock,
        c and the gates of hell shall not prevail against them.

a And whoso shall declare more or less than this, and establish it for my doctrine,
  b the same cometh of evil, and is not built upon my rock, but he buildeth upon a sandy foundation,
    c and the gates of hell stand open to receive such when the floods come and the winds beat upon them. (3 Ne. 11:39–40)

a Even so every good tree
  b bringeth forth good fruit;
a but a corrupt tree
  b bringeth forth evil fruit (3 Ne. 14:17)

a ask not,
  b that ye may consume it on your lusts,
a but ask with a firmness unshaken,
  b that ye will yield to no temptation,
  but that ye will serve the true and living God. (Morm. 9:28)

a all things which are good
  b cometh of God;
a and that which is evil
  b cometh of the devil (Moro. 7:12)

Other antithetical alternates we have found include Alma 42:27; 3 Nephi 15:2; Mormon 2:13; Alma 26:26; Helaman 3:22; and Moroni 9:4.

CONCLUSION

The Book of Mormon authors used antitheticals extensively in their presentation of gospel principles. Antitheticals are usually more easily identified than many other literary forms, and some of the most significant gospel teachings are presented in this format.

Most of us use a form of an antithetical in order to learn the meaning of a concept. Once we have identified the opposite of a concept, such as when we are presented with a contrast, then we understand the concept better. Thus antitheticals are used as a teaching device to help us understand a principle by also seeing its opposite, and to learn the consequences of a choice we make by also learning what will happen to us if we choose an opposite pattern of behavior.

When we come to recognize antitheticals in our reading of scriptures, we gain a fuller appreciation of the gospel of Jesus Christ, as opposed to the teachings of the Evil One. We begin to see the gospel in a different way, and we begin to read the scriptures with new eyes.

NOTES

1. Donald Parry used the terms "antime" and "antimetabole," but I prefer the term "antithetical." See Parry, *Book of Mormon Text Reformatted,* xxvii–xxx; see also Bullinger, *Figures of Speech,* 301–3, 715–18.
2. Parry, *Book of Mormon Text Reformatted.*
3. This is an example of exergasia according to Parry, as well as an antithetical
4. Parry, *Book of Mormon Text Reformatted.*
5. This is an example of anaphora according to Parry.
6. This is an example of synonymia according to Parry.
7. This is part of an extended alternate according to Parry.
8. This is an example of both anaphora and synonymia.
9. Karl Marx is famous for his use of the dialectic, and for the many anthithetical contrasts he used. It should be noted that this scriptural dialectic was published long before Marx began to use the dialectic in his writings.
10. This is labeled prosapodosis by Parry.
11. Parry diagramed this as a chiasm.

CHAPTER SIXTEEN

APHORISMS AND MEMORABLE AND POETIC PHRASES

Many aphorisms and other memorable and poetic phrases are found in the Book of Mormon. These are some of the most significant literary aspects of the Book of Mormon. While the book is full of history and sermons, it is also replete with wonderful poetic phrases that capture the imagination and the heart and mind.[1] Those of us who often read the Book of Mormon come to love certain ways of phrasing the important principles found in the book, and these expressions rest upon our minds as sweet memories and distillations of eternal truths and gospel principles.

APHORISMS

An aphorism is a brief statement of a truth or principle. Aphorisms are short sayings, maxims, epigrams, expressions and truisms. In a brief phrase or sentence, an eternal principle is captured and expressed simply yet beautifully. Many eloquent and moving aphorisms are contained within a larger statement, such as "wickedness never was happiness," so we have edited them to a shorter length. We have done this because we recognize that many people remember and take to heart only a short part of the fuller scripture. The choice of aphorisms is a very personal matter, so I have selected the ones that are most significant to me. Dozens and perhaps hundreds more could be noted. These are presented in the order in which they appear in the Book of Mormon.

It is better that one man should perish than that a nation should dwindle and perish in unbelief (1 Ne. 4:13)

the Lord is able to do all things according to his will, for the children of men, if it so be that they exercise faith in him (1 Ne. 7:12)

he that diligently seeketh shall find (1 Ne. 10:19)

the kingdom of God is not filthy, and there cannot any unclean thing enter into the kingdom of God (1 Ne. 15:34)

the guilty taketh the truth to be hard, for it cutteth them to the very center (1 Ne. 16:2)

the Lord esteemeth all flesh in one; he that is righteous is favored of God (1 Ne. 17:35)

For the things which some men esteem to be of great worth, both to the body and soul, others set at naught and trample under their feet (1 Ne. 19:7)

there is no peace, saith the Lord, unto the wicked (1 Ne. 20:22; Isaiah 48:22)

Wherefore, the righteous need not fear; for thus saith the prophet, they shall be saved, even if it so be as by fire (1 Ne. 22:17)

for the time surely must come that all they who fight against Zion shall be cut off (1 Ne. 22:19)

Wherefore, if ye shall be obedient to the commandments, and endure to the end, ye shall be saved at the last day (1 Ne. 22:31)

[God] shall consecrate thine afflictions for thy gain (2 Ne. 2:2)

the way is prepared from the fall of man, and salvation is free (2 Ne. 2:4)

For it must needs be, that there is an opposition in all things (2 Ne. 2:11)

Adam fell that men might be; and men are, that they might have joy (2 Ne. 2:25)

I know that if ye are brought up in the way ye should go ye will not depart from it (2 Ne. 4:5)

He knoweth all things, and there is not anything save he knows it (2 Ne. 9:20)

where there is no law given, there is no punishment (2 Ne. 9:25)

When they are learned, they think they are wise, and they hearken not unto the counsel of God, for they set it aside, supposing they know of themselves (2 Ne. 9:28)

Remember, to be carnally-minded is death, and to be spiritually-minded is life eternal. (2 Ne. 9:39)

ye are free to act for yourselves—to choose the way of everlasting death or the way of eternal life (2 Ne. 10:23)

the right way is to believe in Christ and deny him not (2 Ne. 25:28)

the Spirit of the Lord will not always strive with man (2 Ne. 26:11)

He doeth not anything save it be for the benefit of the world (2 Ne. 26:24)

the laborer in Zion shall labor for Zion; for if they labor for money they shall perish (2 Ne. 26:31)

wo be unto him that is at ease in Zion! (2 Ne. 28:24)

except ye shall keep the commandments of God ye shall all likewise perish (2 Ne. 30:1)

He that endureth to the end, the same shall be saved (2 Ne. 31:15)

before ye seek for riches, seek ye for the kingdom of God (Jacob 2:18)

seek not to counsel the Lord, but to take counsel from his hand (Jacob 4:10)

how blessed are they who have labored diligently in his vineyard (Jacob 6:3)

Whatsoever thing ye shall ask in faith, believing that ye shall receive in the name of Christ, ye shall receive it (Enos 1:15)

the natural man is an enemy to God (Mosiah 3:19)

are we not all beggars (Mosiah 4:19)

for it is not requisite that a man should run faster than he has strength (Mosiah 4:27)

I would that ye should be steadfast and immovable, always abounding in good works (Mosiah 5:15)

I trust there remaineth an effectual struggle to be made (Mosiah 7:18)

Lift up your heads, and rejoice, and put your trust in God (Mosiah 7:19)

Ye shall not esteem one flesh above another, or one man shall not think himself above another (Mosiah 23:7)

stand fast in this liberty wherewith ye have been made free (Mosiah 23:13)

the Lord seeth fit to chasten his people; yea, he trieth their patience and their faith (Mosiah 23:21)

how much iniquity doth one wicked king cause to be committed (Mosiah 29:17, 31) this shall ye observe and make it your law—to do your business by the voice of the people (Mosiah 39:26)

if ye have experienced a change of heart, and if ye have felt to sing the song of redeeming love, I would ask, can ye feel so now? (Alma 5:26)

Behold, are ye stripped of pride? I say unto you, if ye are not ye are not prepared to meet God (Alma 5:28)

come ye out from the wicked, and be ye separate, and touch not their unclean things (Alma 5:57)

God is mindful of every people, whatsoever land they may be in; yea, he numbered his people, and his bowels of mercy are over all the earth (Alma 26:37)

this is joy which none receive save it be the truly penitent and humble seeker of happiness (Alma 27:18)

the Lord doth grant unto all nations, of their own nation and tongue, to teach his word, yea, in wisdom, all that he seeth fit that they should have (Alma 29:8)

this is my glory, that perhaps I may be an instrument in the hands of God to bring some soul to repentance; and this is my joy (Alma 29:9)

for he beheld that their afflictions had truly humbled them and that they were in a preparation to hear the word (Alma 32:6)

blessed are they who humble themselves without being compelled to be humble (Alma 32:16)

the great question which is in your minds is whether the word be in the Son of God, or whether there shall be no Christ (Alma 34:5)

For behold, this life is the time for men to prepare to meet God; yea, behold, the day of this life is the day for men to perform their labors (Alma 34:32) that same spirit which doeth possess your bodies at the time that ye go out of this life, that same spirit will have power to possess your body in that eternal world (Alma 34:34)

O, remember, my son, and learn wisdom in thy youth; yea, learn in thy youth to keep the commandments of God. (Alma 37:35)

Counsel with the Lord in all thy doings, and he will direct thee for good (Alma 37:37)

there is no other way or means whereby man can be saved, only in and through Christ (Alma 38:9)

no unclean things can inherit the kingdom of God (Alma 40:26)

wickedness never was happiness (Alma 41:10)

only let your sins trouble you, with that trouble which shall bring you down unto repentance (Alma 42:29)

the Lord cannot look upon sin with the least degree of allowance (Alma 45:16)

Thus we see how quick the children of men do forget the Lord their God, yea, how quick to do iniquity, and to be led away by the evil one (Alma 46:8)

And thus we see how merciful and just are all the dealings of the Lord, to the fulfilling of all his words unto the children of men (Alma 50:19)

the Spirit of the Lord doth not dwell in unholy temples (Hel. 4:24)

he that hath the spirit of contention is not of me, but is of the devil (3 Ne. 11:29)

blessed are ye if ye shall keep my commandments (3 Ne. 18:14) ye must watch and pray always, lest ye be tempted by the devil, and ye be led away captive by him (3 Ne. 18:15)

I am the light which ye shall hold up—that which ye have seen me do (3 Ne. 18:24)

my wisdom is greater than the cunning of the devil (3 Ne. 21:10)

what manner of men ought ye to be? Verily I say unto you, even as I am (3 Ne. 27:27)

it is by the wicked that the wicked are punished (Morm. 4:5)

For the eternal purposes of the Lord shall roll on, until all his promises shall be fulfilled (Morm. 8:22)

Why are ye ashamed to take upon you the name of Christ? Why do ye not think that greater is the value of an endless happiness than that misery which never dies (Morm. 8:38)

whoso believeth in Christ, doubting nothing, whatsoever he shall ask the Father in the name of Christ it shall be granted him (Morm. 9:21)

For the Lord worketh not in secret combinations, neither doth he will that man should shed blood, but in all things hath forbidden it, from the beginning of man (Ether 8:19)

ye receive no witness until after the trial of your faith (Ether 12:6)

I give unto men weakness that they may be humble (Ether 12:27)

all things which are good cometh of God; and that which is evil cometh of the devil (Moro. 7:12)

> Whatsoever thing ye shall ask the Father in my name, which is good, in faith believing that ye shall receive, behold, it shall be done unto you (Moro. 7:26)

> perfect love casteth out all fear (Moro. 8:16)

> If ye have faith ye can do all things which are expedient unto me (Moro. 10:23)

LONGER APHORISMS

Some aphorisms are considerably longer than the ones we have presented above. Indeed, they may be longer than is normally acceptable as an aphorism. However, they present such a wise and inspired statement of truth that I have included them in this section.

> I will go and do the things which the Lord hath commanded, for I know that the Lord giveth no commandments unto the children of men, save he shall prepare a way for them that they may accomplish the things which he commandeth them. (1 Ne. 3:7)

> Cursed is he that putteth his trust in man, or maketh flesh his arm, or shall hearken unto the precepts of men, save their precepts shall be given by the power of the Holy Ghost (2 Ne. 28:31)

> Wherefore, ye must press forward with a steadfastness in Christ, having a perfect brightness of hope, and a love of God and of all men. Wherefore, if ye shall press forward, feasting upon the word of Christ, and endure to the end, behold, thus saith the Father: Ye shall have eternal life. (2 Ne. 31:20)

> if ye would hearken unto the Spirit which teacheth a man to pray ye would know that ye must pray; for the evil spirit teacheth not a man to pray, but teacheth him that he must not pray (2 Ne. 32:8)

It is given unto many to know the mysteries of God; nevertheless they are laid under a strict command that they shall not impart only according to the portion of his word which he doth grant unto the children of men, according to the heed and diligence which they give unto him. (Alma 12:9)

after a people have been once enlightened by the Spirit of God, and have had great knowledge of things pertaining to righteousness and then have fallen away into sin and transgression, they become more hardened, and thus their state becomes worse than though they had never known these things (Alma 24:30)

good and evil have come before all men; he that knoweth not good from evil is blameless; but he that knoweth good and evil, to him it is given according to his desire, whether he desireth good or evil, life or death, joy or remorse of conscience (Alma 29:5)

there were many who died, firmly believing that their souls were redeemed by the Lord Jesus Christ; thus they went out of the world rejoicing . . . and those who died in the faith of Christ are happy in him, as we must needs suppose (Alma 46:39, 41)

For the Lord suffereth the righteous to be slain that his justice and judgment may come upon the wicked; therefore ye need not suppose that the righteous are lost because they are slain; but behold, they do enter into the rest of the Lord their God (Alma 60:13)

Now this is the commandment: Repent, all ye ends of the earth, and come unto me and be baptized in my name, that ye may be sanctified by the reception of the Holy Ghost, that ye may stand spotless before me at the last day (3 Ne. 27:20)

> Be wise in the days of your probation; strip yourselves of uncleanness; ask not, that ye may consume it on your lusts, but ask with a firmness unshaken, that ye will yield to no temptation, but that ye will serve the true and living God (Morm. 9:28)

> let us labor diligently; for if we should cease to labor, we should be brought under condemnation; for we have a labor to perform whilst in this tabernacle of clay, that we may conquer the enemy of all righteousness, and rest our souls in the kingdom of God (Moro. 9:6)

POETIC PHRASES

The Book of Mormon contains many beautiful poetic and symbolic expressions and phrases. Such phrases are often figurative, or are stated in a notable and memorable way. Some draw a comparison that is symbolic and not factually real, such as being "armed" with righteousness. Many poetic phrases are metaphors or similes and are listed in chapters 7 and 8.

In this section, I have not included any passages from Isaiah, although the book of Isaiah is full of poetic passages. In addition, I have not included here any passages from the dream of Lehi, which is discussed in chapter 6 as an allegory. The Book of Mormon contains numerous poetic passages that are remarkable for their variety as well as beauty. It is unthinkable that an unschooled young man such as Joseph Smith could have written a book in so short a time that contains so many notable poetic phrases and images.

In the following listing, I have presented the quotations with the key word in roughly alphabetical order, recognizing that my own choice of the key word may be different from the choices made by others.

> altered the management of affairs among the Nephites (Alma 49:11)

> in the anguish of his soul (Mosiah 19:7)

awakened to a remembrance of the deliverance of our fathers (Mosiah 9:17)

bearing down in pure testimony (Alma 4:19)

beneath the glance of an all-searching eye (Mosiah 27:31)

Use boldness but not overbearance (Alma 38:12)

breathe out much threatenings (1 Ne. 18:17; Mosiah 19:3)

changed in the twinkling of an eye from mortality to immortality (3 Ne. 28:8)

cold and silent grave, from whence no traveler can return (2 Ne. 1:14)

consign us to an awful destruction (Alma 26:19)

the course of the Lord is one eternal round (1 Ne. 10:19)

But behold, he was dead, and had gone the way of all the earth (Alma 62:37)

having great desires to know of the mysteries of God (1 Ne. 2:16)

drunk damnation to their own souls (Mosiah 3:25)

effectual struggle (Mosiah 7:18)

endurance of faith (Moro. 3:3; 8;3)

the energy of my soul (1 Ne. 16:24; Alma 5:43)

eternal gulf of misery and woe (2 Ne. 1:13)

exceedingly tender and chaste and delicate (Jacob 2:7)

he did exhort them with all the feeling of a tender parent (1 Ne. 9:37)

expert in the devices of the devil (Alma 11:21)

they were expressly repugnant to the commandments of God (Mosiah 29:36)

expressly promised and firmly decreed (Alma 9:24)

with that awful fear of death which fills the breasts of all the wicked (Morm. 6:7)

they fell away into forbidden paths and were lost (1 Ne. 9:28)

fiery flying serpents (1 Ne. 17:41)

foolish imaginations of his heart (1 Ne. 17:20)

glad tidings of great joy (Hel. 16:14)

having first obtained mine errand from the Lord (Jacob 1:17)

many hearts died, pierced with deep wounds (Jacob 2:35)

let your hearts be full, drawn out in prayer (Alma 34:27)

hearts knit together in unity and love (Mosiah 18:21)

an ignominious death (Alma 1:15)

I wish from the inmost part of my heart, yea, with great anxiety even unto pain (Alma 13:27)

that joy which is unspeakable and full of glory (Hel. 5:44)

lifted up his hand upon the Gentiles and set them up for a standard (1 Ne. 22:6)

looking beyond the mark (Jacob 4:14)

for that lucre which doth corrupt the soul (Mosiah 29:40)

view this mortal body raised in immortality, and this corruption raised in incorruption (Alma 5:15)

the nurture and admonition of the Lord (Enos 1:1)

the office of his ministry (Moro. 7:31)

one eternal round (1 Ne. 10:19)

peaceable followers of Christ (Moro. 7:3)

perfect brightness of hope (2 Ne. 31:30)

they did point the finger of scorn at me (1 Ne. 9:33)

for they did prick their hearts with the word (Jarom 1:12)

pure and delightsome (2 Ne. 30:6)

scorched with a burning heat (Alma 15:3)

his sharpness was the sharpness of the power of the word of God (2 Ne. 1:26)

and did shed tears of joy before the Lord, because of the multitude of his tender mercies (Ether 6:12)

sing the song of redeeming love (Alma 5:26; 26:13)

snatched us from our awful, sinful, and polluted state (Alma 26:17)

for I speak in the energy of my soul (Alma 5:43)

And while I was thus struggling in the spirit (Enos 1:10)

stand fast in this liberty wherewith ye have been made free (Mosiah 23:13)

still small voice (1 Ne. 17:45)

stir them up in the ways of remembrance (1 Ne. 2:24)

tremble under a consciousness of his guilt (Alma 12:1)

try the virtue of the word of God (Alma 31:5)

how unsearchable are the depths of the mysteries of him (Jacob 4:8) she being a virgin, a precious and chosen vessel (Alma 7:10)

walking with a clear conscience before God (Mosiah 2:27)

watchful unto prayer (Alma 34:39; Morm. 6:4)

the word of the justice of the Eternal God (1 Ne. 12:18)

the work of death (Alma 44:20)

workings in the Spirit (1 Ne. 19:20)

MEMORABLE VERSES AND PHRASES

Every person who reads the Book of Mormon in any serious way comes to appreciate the great number of memorable phrases and verses in the book. These are longer and somewhat different from the aphorisms discussed earlier, although the distinction is often an arbitrary one. Most Latter-day Saints have many favorite verses that have special meaning to them. Each person can choose for themselves what verses they consider to be most memorable. Many of these memorable verses could also be included in our list of aphorisms above, so the classification of verses is quite arbitrary. These are a few of my personal favorites verses.

For my soul delighteth in the scriptures, and my heart pondereth them, and writeth them for the learning and the profit of my children (2 Ne. 4:15)

O how great the goodness of our God, who prepareth a way for our escape from the grasp of this awful monster; yea, that monster, death and hell, which I call the death of the body, and also the death of the spirit (2 Ne. 9:10)

we being a lonesome and a solemn people, wanderers, cast out from Jerusalem, born in tribulations, in a wilderness, and hated of our brethren (Jacob 7:26)

And now, my beloved brethren, I would that ye should come unto Christ, who is the Holy One of Israel, and partake of his salvation, and the power of his redemption. (Omni 1:26)

Behold, I tell you these things that ye may learn wisdom; that ye may learn that when ye are in the service of your fellow beings ye are only in the service of your God (Mosiah 2:17)

I would desire that ye should consider on the blessed and happy state of those that keep the commandments of God. For behold, they are blessed in all things, both temporal and spiritual; and if they hold out faithful to the end they are received into heaven, that thereby they may dwell with God in a state of never-ending happiness (Mosiah 2:41)

And now I would that ye should be humble, and be submissive and gentle; easy to be entreated; full of patience and long-suffering; being temperate in all things; being diligent in keeping the commandments of God at all times; asking for whatsoever things ye stand in need, both spiritual and temporal; always returning thanks unto God for whatsoever things ye do receive (Alma 7:23)

O that I were an angel, and could have the wish of mine heart, that I might go forth and speak with the trump of God, with a voice to shake the earth, and cry repentance unto every people! (Alma 29:1)

but behold I say unto you, that by small and simple things are great things brought to pass; and small means in many instances doth confound the wise (Alma 37:6)

Behold, it has been made known unto me by an angel, that the spirits of all men, as soon as they are departed from this mortal body, yea, the spirits of all men, whether they be good or evil, are taken home to that God who gave them life (Alma 40:11)

Now I would that ye should remember that God has said that the inward vessel shall be cleansed first, and then shall the outer vessel be cleansed also (Alma 60:23)

Behold, I come unto my own, to fulfill all things which I have made known unto the children of men from the foundation of the world, and to do the will, both of the Father and of the Son (3 Ne. 1:14)

their hearts were swollen with joy, unto the gushing out of many tears, because of the goodness of God in delivering them out of the hands of their enemies (3 Ne. 4:33)

therefore, I was visited of the Lord, and tasted and knew of the goodness of Jesus (Morm. 1:15)

[Ether] began to prophesy unto the people, for he could not be restrained because of the Spirit of the Lord which was in him (Ether 12:2)

And if men come unto me I will show unto them their weakness. I give unto men weakness that they may be humble; and my grace is sufficient for all men that humble themselves before me; for if they humble themselves before me, and have faith in me, then will I make weak things become strong unto them (Ether 12:27)

And then shall ye know that I have seen Jesus, and that he hath talked with me face to face, and that he told me in plain humility, even as a man telleth another in mine own language, concerning these things (Ether 12:39)

teach parents that they must repent and be baptized, and humble themselves as their little children, and they shall all be saved with their little children (Moro. 8:10)

Pray for them, my son, that repentance may come unto them (Moro. 8:28)

> And when ye shall receive these things, I would exhort you that ye would ask God, the Eternal Father, in the name of Christ, if these things are not true; and if ye shall ask with a sincere heart, with real intent, having faith in Christ, he will manifest the truth of it unto you, by the power of the Holy Ghost. And by the power of the Holy Ghost ye may know the truth of all things (Moro. 10:4–5)

NOTE

1. Sands refers to these as "epigrams," and notes the frequency of such sayings in the Gospels and the epistles of Paul. Sands, *Literary Genius of the New Testament*. 148–51.

CHAPTER SEVENTEEN

CLIMAX, UNIVERSALS, PARADOX, AND RHETORICAL QUESTIONS

In the next few chapters, we will discuss a number of different aspects of the literary structure of the Book of Mormon. Because of the great diversity of such literary forms, they do not fit easily together, so these next chapters will be quite diverse in their makeup. And because there are a multitude of different subjects to be discussed, we will only be able to address each one briefly.

Four interesting features of the Book of Mormon literary structure will be considered in this chapter. The first is called "climax" by some scholars, including Donald Parry,[1] and involves an unusual type of literary form in the repetition of selected words. The second feature is called universals, which are statements that attempt to include all aspects or people in a single phrase. The third to be discussed here are paradoxes, or things that seem to be contrary to what is normally expected. The last are interrogatives, or rhetorical questions.

CLIMAX

Climax is a distinctive form of parallelistic expression. *In successive clauses or sentences, the same words are found at the end of an expression and at the beginning of the next.* In the Book of Mormon, there are many instances of climax, as is true of Hebrew literature in general and the Bible in particular.

Conversely, climax is extremely unusual in English literature, and is not a literary feature to which Joseph Smith would ever have been introduced or ever have been aware. I will begin with two examples I have found, and then give several examples found by Parry.

> And he that
> believeth not my words
> believeth not my disciples; and if it be that I do not
> speak, judge ye; for ye shall know that it is I that
> speaketh at the last day.
> But he that believeth these things which I have spoken,
> him will I visit with the manifestations of my
> Spirit, and he shall know and bear record. For because of my
> Spirit he shall know (alternate) that these things are true; for it
> persuadeth to do good. And whatsoever thing
> persuadeth men to do good is of me. For
> good cometh of none save it be of
> me.
> I am the same that leadeth men to all
> good (chiasm); he that will
> not believe my words will
> not believe me—that I am; and he that will not
> believe me will not
> believe the
> Father who sent me. For behold, I am the
> Father (Ether 4:10–12)

> And they did pray for that which they most
> desired; and they
> desired that the Holy Ghost should be given unto them. And when they had thus prayed they went down unto the
> water's edge, and the multitude followed them. And it came to pass that Nephi went down into the
> water and was
> baptized. And he came up out of the water and began to

baptize. And he
baptized all those whom Jesus had chosen. And it came to pass when they were all
baptized and had come up out of the water,
the Holy Ghost did fall upon them, and they were filled with
the Holy Ghost and with
fire. And behold, they were encircled about as if it were by
fire; and it
came down from heaven, and the multitude did witness it, and did bear record; and angels did
come down out of heaven and did
minister unto them. And it came to pass that while the angels were
ministering unto the disciples (3 Ne. 19:9–15)

Scholars who desire a full exposition of climax should study the many examples found in Parry's book. The following are some notable examples.

Wherefore, he has given a
law; and where there is no
law given there is no
punishment; and where there is no
punishment there is no
condemnation; and where there is no
condemnation the mercies of the Holy One of Israel have claim upon them, because of the
atonement; for they are delivered by the power of him. For the
atonement satisfied the demands of his justice (2 Ne. 9:25–26)[2]

but the meaning of the word restoration is to bring back again
evil for
evil, or
carnal for
carnal, or

devilish for
devilish—
good for that which is
good;
righteous for that which is
righteous;
just for that which is
just;
merciful for that which is
merciful (Alma 41:13)[3]

Wherefore, there must be
faith; and if there must be
faith there must also be
hope; and if there must be
hope there must also be
charity. And except ye have
charity ye can in nowise be
saved in the kingdom of God; neither can ye be
saved in the kingdom of God if ye have not faith, neither can
ye if ye have no
hope. And if ye have no
hope ye must needs be in
despair; and
despair cometh because of iniquity (Moro. 10:20–22)[4]

And the first fruits of repentance is
baptism; and
baptism cometh by faith unto the
fulfilling the commandments; and the
fulfilling the commandments bringeth
remission of sins; And the
remission of sins bringeth
meekness, and lowliness of heart; and because of
meekness and lowliness of heart cometh the visitation of the
Holy Ghost, which
Comforter filleth with hope and perfect
love, which
love endureth by diligence unto prayer (Moro. 8:25–26)[5]

Some examples of climax are too extensive to be reproduced in this chapter. Several notable examples are found in 1 Nephi 15:13–20, Alma 42:17–20, Mormon 9:11–13, and Ether 1:7–32.

UNIVERSALS

A universal is a statement that encompasses all people or all things. It asserts the general application of an condition or principle to all of God's children. While good scientific writing tends to be qualified, with the scientist recognizing and attesting to the many conditions, restrictions or limitations to the statements being made, scriptural writing tends to be universal in its applicability. The Book of Mormon contains many notable phrases and sentence constructions that are universal in their intent and application.

both seen and heard (1 Ne. 1:18)

all nations, both unto the Jews and also unto the Gentiles (1 Ne. 13:42)

both temporally and spiritually (1 Ne. 14:7)

both to the body and soul (1 Ne. 19:7)

both in word and in deed (2 Ne. 3:24)

every living creature, both men, women, and children who belong to the family of Adam (2 Ne. 9:21)

both Jew and Gentile, both bond and free, both male and female (2 Ne. 10:16)

both in the east and in the west, and in the north, and in the south, and in the islands of the sea (2 Ne. 29:11)

both old and young (Jacob 5:63)

both roots and branch (Jacob 6:4)

neither has been, nor ever will be (Jacob 7:9)

both in heaven and in earth (Jacob 7:14, Mosiah 5:15, Alma 1:15)

forever and ever (Mosiah 2:24)

from all eternity to all eternity (Mosiah 3:5)

was, and is, and is to come (Mosiah 3:18)

those that have been, and who are, and who shall be (Mosiah 15:21)

at all times and in all things, and in all places that ye may be in (Mosiah 18:9)

all nations, kindreds, tongues and people (Mosiah 27:25)

both old and young, both bond and free, both male and female, whether out of the church or in the church (Alma 1:30; 1 Ne. 8:27)

this restoration shall come to all, both old and young, both bond and free, both male and female, both the wicked and the righteous (Alma 11:44)

both limb and joint (Alma 11:43)

both the just and the unjust (Alma 12:8)

without beginning or end (Alma 13:8)

every living soul (Alma 16:9)

if all men had been, and were, and ever would be (Alma 48:17)

the whole earth, from the sea south to the sea north, from the sea west to the sea east (Hel. 3:8, Hel. 11:20, 3 Ne. 6:2) both the Nephites and the Lamanites (Hel. 11:21)

both above the earth and beneath (Hel.n 14:11)

both great and small (3 Ne. 26:1)

both in towns and villages (Morm. 4:22)

God is the same yesterday, today, and forever (Morm. 9:9)

this promise is unto all, even unto the ends of the earth (Morm. 9:21)

flesh and blood (Ether 3:9)

all lands, nations, and countries (Ether 8:25)

both quick and dead (Moro. 10:34)

today and tomorrow, and forever (Moro. 10:8)

PARADOX

A paradox is a statement that is an apparent contradiction, but which upon greater reflection can be seen to express a truth. An example from the Bible is that leaders should be the servants of their followers (Matt. 23:11, D&C 50:26).[6] Servants seem to be the opposite of leaders, and the two have very different status, so to assert as Jesus did that leaders must be the servants of those they lead is paradoxical. It is what some would call "nonintuitive," or something that goes against intuition or common sense.

Most of the principles of the gospel are straightforward, plain, and easy to understand. However, other principles involve a paradox that is more difficult to understand and appreciate, and which requires more thought, discussion, reflection, and prayer before we can understand the principle completely.

Perhaps the greatest paradox in the scriptures, a paradox that has led to much confusion in the minds of many souls, is that Jehovah, the God of the Old Testament, should be born as Jesus Christ, a helpless baby in this mortal world, much like the rest of us. This great truth, so essential to our understanding of the plan of salvation, is best understood if we read the many sermons in the Book of Mormon concerning the purpose of Christ's mortal ministry and of his atonement (see chapter 3).

What may seem like a paradox to one person may, on the other hand, seem very straight-forward to another person. My own list of paradoxes in the Book of Mormon includes the following.

Jehovah, the God of the Old Testament, comes to earth as a mortal, is born as a child, and lives as a common man (Mosiah 3:5–9). The religious leaders of the Israelites, who have made a career of studying and teaching about God, reject Him and crucify Him.

Nephi is commanded by God to kill Laban, contrary to the Ten Commandments which forbid killing. He is told that "it is better that one man should perish than that a nation should dwindle and perish in unbelief." He kills Laban and is blessed by God (1 Ne. 4:13).

Ammon, who is a prince of the Nephites, went to preach to King Lamoni. He was offered the hand of Lamoni's daughter in marriage, which would make him a prince of the Lamanites. Instead, he became a servant of Lamoni and tended his flocks and horses. He knew more about being an effective servant than the other servants (Alma 17–18).

When people obey the commandments of God and are blessed by God with peace and prosperity, they then forget their God, harden their hearts and trample under their feet the Holy One because of their ease and prosperity. When God chastens them with many afflictions, they turn their hearts back to God, which illustrates the evil, foolishness, and vanity of God's children (Hel. 12:1–4).

Laman and Lemuel smite Nephi and Sam with a rod. They are visited by an angel who rebukes them. After the angel departs, Laman and Lemuel continue to murmur and continue to reject God and the prophetic teachings of Lehi and Nephi (1 Ne. 3:28–31).

Likewise, many people who see "signs and wonders" reject them, "turn their hearts aside," and "crucify the God of Israel" (1 Ne. 19:13–14).

People who are obedient to the commandments of God become free and gain a great measure of autonomy, whereas those who are disobedient because they don't like the supposed restrictions of the commandments of God, lose their autonomy and become slaves to Satan. (2 Ne. 2:26–27; Hel. 14:30–31)

Christ commands people to love their enemies, do good to them that hate them, and pray for them who despitefully use them and persecute them (3 Ne. 12:44)

It is by the wicked (and not the righteous) that the wicked are punished (Morm. 4:5).

Nephites who were without hope would still struggle for their lives (Morm. 5:2).

The mortal bodies of men and women were created after the body of Christ's spirit (who had not yet been born with a physical body) (Ether 3:16).

The women in Lehi's colony "did live upon raw meat in the wilderness." They did not have a variety of good foods, but they became strong like the men and "did give plenty of suck for their children" (1 Ne. 17:2).

The children of Israel, who were led by Moses in the wilderness, hardened their hearts against God. God sent "fiery flying serpents" among them to bite them. God prepared a way for them to be healed by commanding Moses to construct a rod with the image of a serpent on it. "Because of the simpleness of the way," many refused to look upon the image and died from the bites of the serpents (1 Ne. 17:41–42; Hel. 8:14–15).

It is through opposition, rather than peace, that people learn to choose good over evil (2 Ne. 2:11).

Nephi, a great prophet of God, exclaims "O wretched man that I am" because of the "temptations and the sins which do so easily beset" him (2 Ne. 4:17–18). (We usually don't think of prophets as wretched sinners.)

Unless people become as little children, they are not acceptable to God (Moro. 8:10).

Alma the Younger was struck dumb by an angel. When he was carried, weak and dumb, to his father, his father rejoiced (rather than sorrowing), "for he knew that it was the power of God" (Mosiah 27:19–20).

After the Anti-Nephi-Lehis refused to fight the Lamanites and 1,005 of them were slain, more than that number of Lamanites were converted and joined the people of God (Alma 24:21–26).

Alma desired to preach the gospel as an angel, but realized that he sinned in this wish because God works in a different way to bring his children to the truth (Alma 29:1–3).

During the time of Captain Moroni, in the midst of some of the worst wars in Nephite history, was a time when "there never was a happier time among the people of Nephi, since the days of Nephi, than in the days of Moroni" (Alma 50:23).

When people have known the truth and then have fallen away, they become more hardened and rebellious than those who have never known the truth (Alma 24:30).

After many years in which the Nephites were more righteous than the Lamanites, and had attempted to preach the gospel to them, the situation was reversed and the Lamanites became more righteous and sent missionaries to the Nephites (Hel. 6:1–4).

"because of their faith in the Lamb of God their garments are made white in his blood" [which is usually red] (1 Ne. 12:11; Alma 34:36).

RHETORICAL QUESTIONS[7]

The Book of Mormon is replete with instances in which a speaker (or writer) asks a rhetorical question, which is a question used for rhetorical effect to induce the listener or reader to ponder or think of an answer.[8] In most cases in the Book of Mormon, the speaker quickly answers his own question.

Here we can only give a sampling of instances in which rhetorical questions are posed to the reader (or listener). We urge our readers to become aware of the use of rhetorical questions and of their frequent usage by Book of Mormon authors.

> Know ye not that there are more nations than one? Know ye not that I, the Lord your God, have created all men . . . ? Know ye not that the testimony of two nations is a witness unto you that I am God, that I remember one nation like unto another? (2 Ne. 29:7–8)

> And now, I would ask of you, my beloved brethren, wherein the Lamb of God did fulfil all righteousness in being baptized by water? (2 Ne. 31:6)

> How could ye speak with the tongue of angels save it were by the Holy Ghost? (2 Ne. 32:2)

> But what could I have done more in my vineyard? Have I slackened mine hand, that I have not nourished it? (Jacob 5:47)

> I say unto you, my brethren, you that belong to this church, have you sufficiently retained in remembrance the captivity of your father? Yea, and have you sufficiently retained in remembrance his mercy and long-suffering towards them? And moreover, have ye sufficiently retained in remembrance that he has delivered their souls from hell? (Alma 5:6; this whole chapter, Alma's discourse to the people of Zarahemla, which is the beginning of what is sometimes

> called Alma's "reform movement," is built around rhetorical questions: see also vv. 8, 9, 10, 11, 14, 18, 19, 29, 30, 31, 34, 35)
>
> Now, behold, my brethren, I would ask if ye have read the scriptures? If ye have, how can ye disbelieve on the Son of God? (Alma 33:14)
>
> Have ye not read the scriptures, which say ye must take upon you the name of Christ, which is my name? . . . And how be it my church save it be called in my name? (3 Ne. 27:5–8)
>
> Therefore, what manner of men ought ye to be? Verily I say unto you, even as I am. (3 Ne. 27:27)
>
> why have ye polluted the holy church of God? Why are ye ashamed to take upon you the name of Christ? Why do ye not think that greater is the value of an endless happiness than that misery which never dies—because of the praise of the world? (Morm. 8:38; see also vv. 39–40).
>
> In Moroni's address to unbelievers, he poses a series of questions found in Mormon 9:2–3, 9, 15, 16–19, 26.

Other rhetorical questions are found in the following passages: Jacob 2:21; 3:7; 4:17; 5:1; Alma 30:17–19; 40:7; 41:12; 42:17, 19, 21, 25, and throughout the Book of Mormon.

BEHOLD, I SAY UNTO YOU, YEA

There are at least eight instances in the Book of Mormon in which the author poses a rhetorical question and then immediately answers in the affirmative. Without exception, this takes the form of "I say unto you, yea." These instances are found in 1 Nephi 15:16; Jarom 1:2; Alma 5:9; 7:17; 32:29, 35; 49:3; and 3 Nephi 10:15.

BEHOLD, I SAY UNTO YOU, NAY

There are many more instances (thirty-one by my count) in the Book of Mormon in which the speaker poses a rhetorical question and then answers in the negative, usually with the statement "I say unto you, nay." These can be found in: 1 Nephi 17:33, 34; 2 Nephi 26:25, 26–28 (three separate questions); 31:19; Jacob 2:14; Mosiah 2:25; 5:14; 12:37; 13:26, 32; Alma 5:8, 25 (and all of Alma 5); 9:19; 11:24; 24:13; 26:31, 33; 32:18, 36; 34:11; 40:18; 42:25; 60:23; Helaman 9:28; 3 Nephi 12:26; Mormon 9:15; Moroni 7:29, 37.

NOTES

1. Parry, *Book of Mormon Text Reformatted,* xviii–xxi; Bullinger, *Figures of Speech,* 256–59.
2. Parry, *Book of Mormon Text Reformatted,* 71.
3. Ibid. 291
4. Ibid. 489
5. Ibid. 486
6. A paradox is similar in some respects to the concept of irony, or "eironeia" as it is discussed by Elder Hugh W. Pinnock, *Finding Biblical Hebrew and Other Ancient Literary Forms,* 150–53.
7. Tanner, "Responding to the Lord's Questions," 26–29, discusses questions posed by Christ to his people, including "Adam, where art thou?" "But whom say ye that I am?" "Will ye also go away?" and "Lovest thou me?"
8. Watson, *Classical Hebrew Poetry,* 338–42.

CHAPTER EIGHTEEN

DOCTRINAL TERMS, NAMES OF CHRIST, NEW WORDS, DUPLICATION, COLOPHONS

In this chapter we consider another series of literary forms as they apply to the Book of Mormon, including doctrinal terms or concepts, names of Christ, the creation of new words not found in the English language, duplication or repetition of words, and what are called colophons. Each of these topics are significant in their own right, and together they provide further evidence of the divine origin of the Book of Mormon and of the prophetic calling of Joseph Smith.

DOCTRINAL TERMS

A number of doctrinal concepts or terms are used in the Book of Mormon. Some of these are standard gospel terms discussed frequently by religious commentators representing many denominations. Others are exclusive or unique to the Book of Mormon. This is not the proper forum for an extended discussion of the doctrinal significance of these terms, so we will only identify the terms and quote a passage or two from the Book of Mormon to illustrate them. Some of these terms are defined in the scriptures cited, and others require much more study and meditation before a fuller comprehension is reached. Those who seek further enlightenment are encouraged to search the Book of Mormon and other scriptures, as well as the teachings of the prophets, for the meanings and uses of the terms.

CONDESCENSION

> Knowest thou the condescension of God? . . . And the angel said unto me again: Look and behold the condescension of God! And I looked and beheld the Redeemer of the world. . . . And the Lamb of God went forth and was baptized of [the prophet who should prepare the way] (1 Ne. 11:16; 26)

The principal meaning of this passage of scripture is that Jehovah, the God of the Old Testament, condescended to leave His eternal world and be born as a child in a relatively obscure village within a conquered nation. He did this that He might teach His people the truths of the gospel, that He might take upon Him the sins of every creature, and that He eventually would be crucified and killed by those who alleged to worship Him.

DOCTRINE OF CHRIST/MY GOSPEL

> Wherefore, my beloved brethren, I know that if ye shall follow the Son, with full purpose of heart, acting no hypocrisy and no deception before God, but with real intent, repenting of your sins, witnessing unto the Father that ye are willing to take upon you the name of Christ, by baptism–yea, by following your Lord and your Savior down into the water, according to his word, behold, then shall ye receive the Holy Ghost; yea, then cometh the baptism of fire and of the Holy Ghost; and then can ye speak with the tongue of angels, and shout praises unto the Holy One of Israel (2 Ne. 31:13; see 2 Ne. 31:2–32:6, which is too long to quote here.)

> Behold, I have given unto you my gospel, and this is the gospel which I have given unto you—that I came into the world to do the will of my Father, because my Father sent me.

And my Father sent me that I might be lifted up upon the cross; and after that I had been lifted up upon the cross, that I might draw all men unto me, that as I have been lifted up by men even so should men be lifted up by the Father, to stand before me, to be judged of their works, whether they be good or whether they be evil . . .

And it shall come to pass that whoso repenteth and is baptized in my name shall be filled; and if he endureth to the end, behold, him will I hold guiltless before my Father at that day when I shall stand to judge the world. (3 Ne. 27:13–14, 16; see also 3 Ne. 11:32–40)

REST[1]

that they might enter into his rest (Alma 13:6)

which rest is the fulness of his glory (D&C 84:24)

SEER

And the things (Urim and Thummin) are called interpreters, and no man can look in them except he be commanded, lest he should look for that he ought not and he should perish. And whosoever is commanded to look in them, the same is called seer (Mosiah 8:13)

But a seer can know of things which are past, and also of things which are to come, and by them shall all things be revealed, or rather, shall secret things be made manifest, and hidden things shall come to light (Mosiah 8:17)

PUBLISH PEACE

How beautiful upon the mountains are the feet of those who shall hereafter publish peace. . . . For O how beautiful upon the mountains are the feet of him that bringeth good tidings, that is the founder of peace, yea, even the Lord (Mosiah 14:17–18)

RESTORATION[2]

> The spirit and the body shall be reunited again in its perfect form; both limb and joint shall be restored to its proper frame, even as we now are at this time; and we shall be brought to stand before God, knowing even as we know now, and have a bright recollection of all our guilt. Now, this restoration shall come to all, both old and young, both bond and free, both male and female, both the wicked and the righteous; and even there shall not so much as a hair of their heads be lost; but every thing shall be restored to its perfect frame, as it is now, or in the body (Alma 11:42:44)

ETERNAL LIFE

> Wherefore, ye must press forward with a steadfastness in Christ, having a perfect brightness of hope, and a love of God and of all men. Wherefore, if ye shall press forward, feasting upon the word of Christ, and endure to the end, behold, thus saith the Father: Ye shall have eternal life. (2 Ne. 31:20)

> Therefore, I would that ye should be steadfast and immovable, always abounding in good works, that Christ, the Lord God Omnipotent, may seal you his, that you may be brought to heaven, that ye may have everlasting salvation and eternal life, through the wisdom, and power, and justice, and mercy of him who created all things, in heaven and in earth, who is God above all. (Mosiah 5:15)

> and they have a part in the first resurrection, or have eternal life, being redeemed by the Lord (Mosiah 15:24)

The term "eternal life" is used thirty-three times in the Book of Mormon, and is probably the equivalent of "celestial life" or being in the celestial kingdom.

FIRST RESURRECTION

> and they have a part in the first resurrection, or have eternal life, being redeemed by the Lord (Mosiah 15:24—see above under "eternal life")

> Yea, and are willing to mourn with those that mourn; yea, and comfort those that stand in need of comfort, and to stand as witnesses of God at all time and in all things, and in all places that ye may be in, even until death, that ye may be redeemed of God, and be numbered with those of the first resurrection, that ye may have eternal life (Alma 18:9; Rev. 20:6)

INNOCENT BLOOD

> Yea, and I [Abinadi] will suffer even until death, and I will not recall my words, and they shall stand as a testimony against you. And if ye slay me ye will shed innocent blood, and this shall also stand as a testimony against you at the last day (Mosiah 17:10)

> But Ammon stood forth and said unto him [the king of the Lamanites]: Behold, thou shalt not slay thy son; nevertheless, it were better that he should fall that thee, for behold, he has repented of his sins; but if thou should fall at this time, in thine anger, they soul could not be saved.

> And again, it is expedient that thou shouldst forbear; for if thou shouldst slay thy son, he being an innocent man, his blood would cry from the ground to the Lord his God, for vengeance to come upon thee, and perhaps thou wouldst lose thy soul.

> Now when Ammon has said these words unto him, he answered him, saying: I know that if I should slay my son, that I should shed innocent blood (Alma 20:17–19)

MIGHTY NATION

> the Lord God will raise up a mighty nation among the Gentiles, yea, even upon the face of this land (1 Ne. 22:7)

This mighty nation is almost certainly the United States of America.

PRIESTCRAFT

> He commandeth that there shall be no priestcrafts; for, behold, priestcrafts are that men preach and set themselves up for a light unto the world, that they may get gain and praise of the world; but they seek not the welfare of Zion (2 Ne. 26:29)

GRAFTED IN

> the natural branches of the olive tree, or the remnants of the house of Israel, should be grafted in, or come to the knowledge of the true Messiah (1 Ne. 10:14)

HOLY ORDER OF GOD

> Now, as I said concerning the holy order, or this high priesthood, there were many who were ordained and became high priests of God; and it was on account of their exceeding faith and repentance, and their righteousness before God, they choosing to repent and work righteousness rather than to perish (Alma 13:10)

> But Melchizedek having exercised mighty faith, and received the office of the high priesthood according to the holy order of God, did preach repentance unto his people (Alma 13:18; see also Alma 13:6)

KINGDOM OF HEAVEN

> Repent ye, and prepare the way of the Lord, and walk in his paths, which are straight; for behold, the kingdom of heaven is at hand, and the Son of God cometh upon the face of the earth. (Alma 7:9)

And may the Lord bless you, and keep your garments spotless, that ye may at last be brought to sit down with Abraham, Isaac, and Jacob, and the holy prophets who have been ever since the world began, having your garments spotless even as their garments are spotless, in the kingdom of heaven to go no more out. (Alma 7:25; see also Alma 7:14)

TEMPORAL DEATH

Now, there is a death which is called a temporal death; and the death of Christ shall loose the bands of this temporal death, that all shall be raised from this temporal death. The spirit and the body shall be reunited again in its perfect form; both limb and joint shall be restored to its proper frame, even as we now are at this time; and we shall be brought to stand before God, knowing even as we know now, and have a bright recollection of all our guilt. Now, this restoration shall come to all, both old and young, both bond and free, both male and female, both the wicked and the righteous; and even there shall not so much as a hair of their heads be lost; but every thing shall be restored to its perfect frame, as it is now, or in the body (Alma 11:42:44) (See also "resurrection" below.)

SPIRITUAL DEATH

And this death of which I have spoken which is the spiritual death, shall deliver up its dead; which spiritual death is hell (2 Ne. 9:12)

And now behold, I say unto you then cometh a death, even a second death, which is a spiritual death; then is a time that whosoever dieth in his sins, as to a temporal death, shall also die a spiritual death; yea, he shall die as to things pertaining unto righteousness. (Alma 12:16)

Therefore, as the soul could never die, and the fall had brought upon all mankind a spiritual death as well as a temporal, that is, they were cut off from the presence of the Lord, it was expedient that mankind should be reclaimed from this spiritual death.

Therefore, as they had become carnal, sensual, and devilish, by nature, this probationary state became a state for them to prepare; it became of preparatory state (Alma 42:9–10)

Yea, behold, this death bringeth to pass the resurrection, and redeemeth all mankind from the first death—that spiritual death; for all mankind, by the fall of Adam being cut off from the presence of the Lord, are considered as dead, both as to things temporal and to things spiritual.

But behold, the resurrection of Christ redeemeth mankind, yea, even all mankind, and bringeth them back into the presence of the Lord.

Yea, and it bringeth to pass the condition of repentance, that whosoever repenteth the same is not hewn down and cast into the fire; but whosoever repenteth not is hewn down and cast into the fire; and there cometh upon them again a spiritual death, yea a second death, for they are cut off again as to things pertaining to righteousness (Hel. 14:16–18)

PLAN OF REDEMPTION/PLAN OF HAPPINESS/ PLAN OF SALVATION

now there was a plan of redemption laid, which shall bring to pass the resurrection of the dead (Alma 12:25)

For behold, if Adam had put forth his hand immediately, and partaken of the tree of life, he would have lived forever, according to the word of God, having no space for repentance; yea, and also the word of God would have been void, and the great plan of salvation would have been frustrated (Alma 42:5)

Behold it was not expedient that man should be reclaimed

from this temporal death, for that would destroy the great plan of happiness. (Alma 42:8)

The plan is also referred to as:

the merciful plan of the great Creator (2 Ne. 9:6)

the plan of our God (2 Ne. 9:13);

the plan of the Eternal God (Alma 34:9)

the eternal plan of deliverance from death (2 Ne. 11:5)

the plan of restoration (Alma 41:2)

the plan of mercy (Alma 42:15, 31)

RESURRECTION

Now, there is a death which is called a temporal death; and the death of Christ shall loose the bands of this temporal death, that all shall be raised from this temporal death. The spirit and the body shall be reunited again in its perfect form; both limb and joint shall be restored to its proper frame, even as we now are at this time; and we shall be brought to stand before God, knowing even as we know now, and have a bright recollection of all our guilt. Now, this restoration shall come to all, both old and young, both bond and free, both male and female, both the wicked and the righteous; and even there shall not so much as a hair of their heads be lost; but every thing shall be restored to its perfect frame, as it is now, or in the body (Alma 11:42:44)

SPIRIT OF PROPHECY

And we also had many revelations, and the spirit of much prophecy; wherefore, we knew of Christ and his kingdom, which should come. (Jacob 1:6)

Wherefore, we search the prophets, and we have many revelations and the spirit of prophecy (Jacob 4:6)

And behold, I have been called to preach the word of God among all this people, according to the spirit of revelation and prophecy (Alma 8:24)

ADMINISTERED

when Ammon arose he also administered unto them, and also did all the servants of Lamoni; and they did all declare unto the people the selfsame thing (Alma 19:33)

REMNANT

Wherefore, I spake unto them, saying: Hear ye the words of the prophet, ye who are a remnant of the house of Israel, a branch who have been broken off; hear ye the words of the prophet, which were written unto all the house of Israel, and liken them unto yourselves (1 Ne. 19:24)

And the things which shall be written out of the book shall be of great worth unto the children of men, and especially unto our seed, which is a remnant of the house of Israel (2 Ne. 28:2)

Behold, now I finish the commandments which the Father hath command me concerning this people, who are a remnant of the house of Israel (3 Ne. 20:10)

HOLY CALLING

God hath called me by a holy calling, to preach the word unto this people (Alma 29:13)

And this is the manner after which they were ordained–being called and prepared from the foundation of the world according to the foreknowledge of God, on account of their exceeding faith and good works; in the first place being left to choose good or evil; therefore they having chosen good, and exercising exceedingly great faith, are called with a holy calling, yea, with that hold calling which was prepared with, and according to, a preparatory redemption for such (Alma 13:3; see also vv. 4–5)

NEW JERUSALEM

> And behold, this people will I establish in this land, unto the fulfilling of the covenant which I made with your father Jacob; and it shall be a New Jerusalem. And the powers of heaven shall be in the midst of this people; yea, even I will be in the midst of you (3 Ne. 20:22; see also 3 Ne. 21:23–25)

NAMES OF JESUS CHRIST

The Book of Mormon uses many names and titles for Jesus Christ, as do all other scriptures.[3] This is done, we assume, to emphasize a certain quality or characteristic of Christ, to allow the reader to ponder on the Savior, and perhaps also to avoid the monotony of repetition of His holy name. Susan Easton Black noted that the Book of Mormon "mentioned some form of Christ's name on an average of once every 1.7 verses."[4] She counts 101 different names or titles by which Jesus is referred to in the Book of Mormon. More mentions occur in periods of obedience, and fewer mentions occur in times of disobedience and apostacy.[5]

> His name . . . does not appear as a monotonous or chanting repetition. Each appearance of his name reveals something unique, something essential, and something deeply inspirations about him.[6]

I will list below a few of these mentions of Christ's name that have been most notable to me.

Almighty (2 Ne. 23:6)

all-powerful Creator of heaven and earth (Jacob 2:5)

Eternal God (2 Ne. 26:12)

Father of heaven (1 Ne. 22:9)

Father of heaven and of earth (2 Ne. 25:12)

very Eternal Father of heaven and of earth (Mosiah 14:4)

very Eternal Father (Mosiah 16:15)

Eternal Judge of both quick and dead (Moro 10:34)

fountain of all righteousness (1 Ne. 2:9; Ether 12:28)

great God (Alma 24:13)

great and Eternal Head (Hel. 13:38)

great and true shepherd (Hel. 15:13)

Great Mediator (2 Ne. 2:27)

Creator (2 Ne. 9:5)

God of nature (1 Ne. 19:13)

God of Abraham, and of Isaac, and of Jacob (1 Ne. 19:10)

God of Israel (1 Ne. 19:13)

God of miracles (Alma 30:44)

God of our fathers (1 Ne. 19:10)

him that is just (2 Ne. 1:10)

him who is mighty to save (2 Ne. 31:19)

Holy One (1 Ne. 21:7)

Holy One of Israel (1 Ne. 19:14)

Immanuel (2 Ne. 16:14)

Jesus Christ (Mosiah 3:8)

King (2 Ne. 16:5)

king of heaven (2 Ne. 10:14)

Lamb of God (2 Ne. 31:5–6)

Lord (1 Ne. 19:17)

Lord God (1 Ne. 22:8)

Lord God Almighty (2 Ne. 9:46)

Lord God of Hosts (2 Ne. 20:23)

Lord of Hosts (2 Ne. 15:7)

Lord Jehovah (2 Ne. 22:2)

the Lord their Redeemer (1 Ne. 19:18)

the Lord the Almighty God (Mosiah 11:21)

Lord of the vineyard (Jacob 5:15)

Lord Omnipotent (Mosiah 3:5)

Lord God Omnipotent (Mosiah 3:21)

my Maker (Enos 1:4)

our merciful God (2 Ne. 10:20)

Messiah (1 Ne. 10:5)

true Messiah (2 Ne. 1:10)

Holy Messiah (2 Ne. 2:6)

Mighty One of Israel (1 Ne. 22:12)

Mighty One of Jacob (1 Ne. 21:26)

Only Begotten of the Father (2 Ne. 25:12)

Only Begotten Son (Jacob 4:5)

The Prince of Peace (2 Ne. 19:6)

prophet (1 Ne. 22:21)

Redeemer (1 Ne. 19:23; Enos 1:27)

Redeemer of Israel (1 Ne. 21:7)

Savior (1 Ne. 21:26)

the Son of God (2 Ne. 25:16)

Son of Righteousness (3 Ne. 25:2)

Supreme Creator (Alma 30:44)

true and living God (Alma 11:27)

my well-beloved (2 Ne. 15:1)

Wonderful, Counselor, The Mighty God, The Everlasting Father, The Prince of Peace (2 Ne. 19:6)

According to Black, the most frequent mentions are the following: God (1,351 times), Lord (1,350), Christ (312), Jesus (113), Lord God (104), Lord of Hosts (52), Jesus Christ (51), Son of God (51), Son (44), Holy One of Israel (40), and Redeemer (37).[7]

NEW OR FOREIGN WORDS

The text of the Book of Mormon contains many words that are not in the English lexicon. That is to say, these are either Hebrew, Egyptian, or Nephite words. Most of the time it is not possible, at least for the average reader, to determine from which language a word is derived, although it is to be assumed that most Nephite words are either derived from Hebrew or Egyptian. Most personal names, place names, and names of coins are also strange to the English reader, but are not included here.

Irreantum— "which, being interpreted, is many waters" (1 Ne. 17:5)

Cureloms and cumoms—animals present in the lands of the Book of Mormon (Ether 9:19)

Deseret—"which, by interpretation, is a honey bee" (Ether 2:3)

Urim and Thummin—sacred seer stones referred to as "interpreters" in the Book of Mormon (Mosiah 8:13), and which were given to the brother of Jared (D&C 17:1)

Adieu [French]—Goodbye (Jacob 7:27)

Rameumptom—"Now the place was called by them Rameumptom, which, being interpreted, is the holy stand" (Alma 31:21)

Gazelem— "And the Lord said: I will prepare unto my servant Gazelem, a stone, which shall shine forth in darkness unto light" (Alma 37:23)

Liahona—"I have somewhat to say concerning the things which our fathers call a ball, or director—or our fathers called it Liahona, which is, being interpreted, a compass" (Alma 37:38)

DUPLICATION

What is called *duplication involves a word, name, or phrase that is introduced and then repeated.*[8] The classic example of a duplication is the name of Jesus Christ. Both words have the meaning of *savior,* so the name Jesus and the title of Christ both denote a savior and foreshadow the Atonement. Jesus himself, in his visit to the Book of Mormon people, often used expressions as duplications, as when he said "verily, verily." Other duplications, many drawn from Parry, are the following:

Awake, awake (2 Ne. 8:9; 3 Ne. 20:36)

Holy, holy are thy judgments, O Lord God (2 Ne. 9:46)

and others shall say, I, I am the Lord's (2 Ne. 28:3)

> Wo, wo, wo to this people (2 Ne. 28:15; 3 Ne. 9:2)
>
> For, for this intent have I written these things (Jacob 4:4)
>
> O remember, remember, my sons (Mosiah 3:1; Helaman 5:9)
>
> repent, repent (Alma 5:32)
>
> peace, peace be unto you (Helaman 5:47)
>
> Not every one that saith unto me, Lord, Lord (3 Ne. 14:21–22)
>
> Behold, verily, verily, I say unto you (3 Ne. 18:18, 3 Ne. 11:39)

Some duplications involve two usages of a word or phrase that are linked either by a conjunction or some other grammatical construction. Many examples are found in the Book of Mormon, including the ones below:

> dreamed a dream (1 Ne. 3:2; 1 Ne. 8:2)
>
> his sharpness was the sharpness of the word of God (2 Ne. 1:26)
>
> he waketh morning by morning (2 Ne. 7:4)
>
> Wo unto them that decree unrighteous decrees (2 Ne. 20:1)
>
> because of the things which are sealed up, the things which are sealed shall not be delivered (2 Ne. 27:8)
>
> For behold, I am God; and I am a God of miracles (2 Ne. 27:23)
>
> line upon line, precept upon precept, here a little and there a little (2 Ne. 28:30)
>
> A Bible! A Bible! (2 Ne. 29:3)

they shall carry them forth unto the remnant of our seed. And then shall the remnant of our seed know concerning us (2 Ne. 30:3–4)

repent ye, repent ye (2 Ne. 31:11)

that ye might know the gate by which ye should enter. For the gate by which ye should enter is repentance and baptism by water (2 Ne. 31:17)

there will be no more doctrine given until after he shall manifest himself unto you in the flesh. And when he shall manifest himself unto you in the flesh (2 Ne. 32:6)

face to face (2 Ne. 33:11)

from generation to generation (Jacob 1:3; Moro. 10:28)

cursed with a sore cursing (Jacob 3:3)

they believed in Christ and worshiped the Father in his name, and also we worship the Father in his name (Jacob 4:5)

forever and ever (Mosiah 2:24)

from all eternity to all eternity (Mosiah 3:5; Moro. 8:18)

only according to the words which I have spoken unto thee. And now I have spoken the words which the Lord God hath commanded me (Mosiah 3:22–23)

taxed with a tax (Mosiah 6:15)

peopled with a people (Mosiah 7:8)

brother against brother (Mosiah 9:2)

and I, even I, in my old age (Mosiah 10:10)

see eye to eye (Mosiah 16:1)

his glory shall be the glory of the Only Begotten of the Father (Alma 9:26) only let your sins trouble you, with that trouble which shall bring you down unto repentance (Alma 42:29)

it shall be blood for blood, yea, life for life (Alma 54:12)

I remained, with the remainder of my army (Alma 58:17)

the object of his desire, desiring that he would (Hel. 2:7)

man for man (Hel. 4:26)

Turn ye, turn unto the Lord your God (Hel. 7:17)

from multitude to multitude (Hel. 10:17)

thine anger, yea, thy fierce anger (Hel. 11:12)

restored unto grace for grace (Hel. 12:24)

led from city to city, and from land to land, and from place to place (3 Ne. 6:8)

did return railing for railing (3 Ne. 6:13)

But let your communication be Yea, yea; Nay, nay (3 Ne. 12:37)

an eye for an eye, and a tooth for a tooth (3 Ne. 12:38)

for my sake shall the Father work a work (3 Ne. 21:9)

the one on the one hand and the other on the other hand (3 Ne. 26:5)

did traffic in all manner of traffic (4 Ne. 1:46)

they did march forth from the shedding of blood to the shedding of blood (Ether 14:22)

being from everlasting to everlasting (Moro. 6:22)

no, not one (Moro. 7:17)

COLOPHONS

A colophon is one of the most recognizable and distinctive literary forms in the scriptures. A colophon is a statement by a person identifying himself, such as "I, Nephi." It represents both an introduction of oneself and an assumption of responsibility for what is spoken or written. According to John Tvedtnes, a colophon is "a statement by [an] author certifying that he is the author of his work."[9] The term in later usage also refers to a mark made by a printer that identifies the printer's name and/or other information concerning a publication, such as the type face used.

The most important instances of the use of colophons are found in the statements of Jesus Christ about himself, who introduces himself both with his own name and with his titles. Direct introductions in the Book of Mormon take the form of "I am Jesus Christ," which He uses to introduce himself to the Brother of Jared (Ether 3:14) and to the Nephites during his visit to the temple in Bountiful after his resurrection (3 Ne 9:15—in which he says: I am Jesus Christ, the Son of God"—3 Ne. 10:57, 3 Ne. 11:10, and 3 Ne. 20:31). In his revelations to the prophet Joseph Smith, Christ introduced himself as "I, Jesus Christ" three times, and "I am Jesus Christ" ten times.

Christ also introduced himself by his own titles, such as "I the Lord" (used seven times in the Book of Mormon), "I am the Lord," (used eight times), and "I, the Lord God" (used once). The latter two statements of introduction or authorship are used much more frequently in the revelations in the Doctrine and Covenants (a total of 160 times by my count). Christ also uses other titles, such as "I am Alpha and Omega," which is used once in the Book of Mormon (3 Ne. 9:18), four times in the book of Revelations, and five times in the Doctrine and Covenants.

Following the example of the Savior, the authors of the Book of Mormon frequently used a colophon to introduce themselves, especially at the beginning or ending of books or letters. Ten of the books in the Book of Mormon begin with a colophon.

> I, Nephi, having been born of goodly parents (1 Ne 1:1)
>
> And now it came to pass that after I, Nephi, had made an end (2 Ne. 1:1)
>
> For behold, it came to pass that fifty and five years had passed away from the time that Lehi left Jerusalem; wherefore, Nephi gave me, Jacob a commandment (Jacob 1:1)
>
> Behold, it came to pass that I, Enos, knowing my father (Enos 1:1)
>
> Now behold, I, Jarom, write a few words (Jarom 1:1)
>
> Behold, it came to pass that I, Omni, being commanded (Omni 1:1)
>
> And now I, Mormon, being about to deliver up the record (W of M 1:1)
>
> And now I, Mormon, make a record (Morm. 1:1)
>
> And now I, Moroni, proceed to give an account (Ether 1:1)
>
> Now I, Moroni, after having made an end of abridging the account of the people of Jared (Moro. 1:1)

In addition, Zeniff introduced the record of the Zeniff colony with a colophon (Mosiah 9:1), and Moroni introduced himself in Mormon 8:1 as he finished the record of his father Mormon.

The prophet who used the literary form of colophon most frequently was Nephi. By my count, he used the phrase "I, Nephi" 62 times in First Nephi and 23 times in Second Nephi, or a total of 85 times. Mormon used a colophon 17 times, Jacob 16 times, and Moroni 16 times.

The books of Mosiah, Alma, Helaman, Third Nephi, and Fourth Nephi do not begin with a colophon. These books are part of the abridged work of Mormon. Neither

King Benjamin nor King Mosiah used a colophon. And Alma the Younger, whose writings and teachings occupy a large portion of the Book of Mormon, used this form only four times. Others who introduced themselves with a colophon are identified below.

Christ: "I the Lord": 1 Nephi 17:14; 20:15; 2 Nephi 6:18; Jacob 2:30, 31; Mosiah 13:13; 24:14.

"I am the Lord": 2 Nephi 6:7; 8:15; 29:5; Mosiah 11:22; 12:3, 34; 26:26; 3 Nephi 24:6.

"I, the Lord God": Mosiah 24:14

Nephi: In First Nephi: Preface, 1:1, 16, 20; 3:1, 7, 9; 4:5, 14, 31; 6:1; 7:2, 3, 8, 16; 8:29; 10:1, 17 (twice); 11:33; 12:12; 13:16, 19, 20, 23; 14:14, 27; 15:1, 4, 19, 25; 16:1, 4, 7, 8, 18, 21, 22, 23, 28, 30; 17:7, 11, 15, 19, 23, 49, 52; 18:2, 3, 10 (twice), 22; 19:3, 4, 18, 22; 22:1, 2, 21, 27, 29.

In Second Nephi: 2 Nephi 1:1; 4:1, 14; 5:1, 5, 6, 12, 14, 16, 17, 18, 29, 31; 11:2; 25:1, 2, 6; 26:7; 30:1; 31:1; 32:7; 33:1, 3.

Jacob: 2 Nephi 6:2, 8; 10:1; Jacob 1:8, 14, 17, 18; 2:2; 3:1, 12; 4:1, 15; 7:3, 15, 26, 27.

Alma: Alma 5:3, 61; 9:1, 31.

Mormon: Words of Mormon 1:1, 9, 11; 3 Nephi 5:12, 20; 26:12 (twice); 28:24; 4 Nephi 1:23; Mormon 1:1, 5; 2:12; 3:11; 4:23; 5:8; 6:2, 6.

Moroni: Mormon 8:1, 12; Ether 1:1; 3:17; 5:1; 6:1; 7:1; 8:26; 9:1; 12:6, 38; 13:1; Moroni 1:1, 3; 7:1; 10:1.

Helaman: Alma 56:9; 57:36; 58:41.

Captain Moroni: Alma 54:14; 60:34, 36.

Enos: Enos 1:1, 6, 11, 17, 19.

Samuel: Helaman 13:5.

Nephi, son of Helaman: Helaman 9:26.

Pahoran: Alma 61:2, 9.

Ammoron: Alma 54:16, 23.

Chemish: Omni 1:9.

Abinadom: Omni 1:10.

Amaleki: Omni 1:12.

Zenos: "hear the words of me, a prophet of the Lord" (Jacob 5:2).

Sherem: Jacob 7:7.

Zeniff: Mosiah 9:1.

Amulek: Alma 10:2.

Giddianhi: 3 Nephi 3:9.

NOTES

1. Duke, "Literary Structure and Doctrinal Significance of Alma 13:1–9," 103–88.
2. The meaning of the term *restoration* as used here in the Book of Mormon is different from the meaning usually implied, which is that the gospel of Christ was taken from the earth and then restored again through the Prophet Joseph Smith in the latter days.
3. Sabourin, *Names and Titles of Jesus.*
4. Black, *Finding Christ,* 15.
5. Black, *Finding Christ,* 15.
6. Black, *Finding Christ,* 16.
7. Black, *Finding Christ,* 19–27.
8. Parry, *Book of Mormon Text Reformatted,* xlviii–xlix; Bullinger, *Figures of Speech,* 189–98.
9. Welch, "Colophons," 13; see also Tvedtnes, "Colophons," 32–37.

CHAPTER NINETEEN

ALLUSION, APOSTROPHE, PERSONIFICATION, REVERSE REASONING, INDUCTIVE INFERENCES, AND DIALOGUE

Several more types of literary forms or devices used by the authors of the Book of Mormon will be considered in this chapter. They represent the diversity, variety, and subtlety of the writings of the prophets, and endow the Book of Mormon with some of its unique flair, style, and elegance.

ALLUSION AND REMEMBRANCE

An allusion is a reference to past history or literature.[1] In the scriptures, the prophets use this form of speech frequently to counsel their people to remember important prophetic teachings. According to Robert Alter, "nothing confirms the literary character of biblical narrative and biblical poetry more strikingly than their constant, resourceful, and necessary recourse to allusion."[2]

The most important prophetic teachings concern the coming of Jesus Christ and the accomplishment of the Atonement. Prophets also counsel their listeners to remember God's hand in the history of his people and in the events of people's lives, such as references to God's protection while the Lehi colony was crossing the sea. This remembrance function of the scriptures is an extremely important aspect of the purpose of scriptures, because the scriptures allow us to record, recognize, and retain the memory of God's blessings to his people and the commandments he has given.

> [Christ is] to be lifted up, according to the words of Zenock, and to be crucified, according to the words of Neum, and to be buried in a sepulchre, according to the words of Zenos (1 Ne. 19:10)
>
> My brother has called upon the words of Zenos, that redemption cometh through the Son of God, and also upon the words of Zenock; and also he has appealed unto Moses (Alma 34:7; Alma 33:15; see also Hel. 15:11)
>
> the prophet Zenos did testify boldly, for the which he was slain. And behold, also Zenock, and also Ezias, and also Isaiah, and Jeremiah (Hel. 8:20; 3 Ne. 10:16)
>
> Do ye remember to have read what Zenos, the prophet of old, has said concerning prayer or worship (Alma 33:3; Hel. 15:11)
>
> all the prophets from Samuel and those that follow after, as many as have spoken, have testified of me (3 Ne. 20:24)
>
> Orihah did walk humbly before the Lord, and did remember how great things the Lord had done for his father (Ether 6:30)
>
> he remembered what the Lord had done in bringing Jared and his brother across the deep (Ether 10:2; see also Ether 15:1, 3)
>
> Ye remember that I spake unto you, and said that when the words of Isaiah should be fulfilled (3 Ne. 20:11)
>
> Remember ye the law of Moses, my servant (3 Ne. 25:4)
>
> remember also the words which Amulek spake unto Zeezrom (Hel. 5:10)

> and they began to remember the words of Nephi (Hel. 11:7; see also Alma 9:13)

> they began to remember the prophecies of Alma, and also the words of Mosiah (Hel. 4:21)

> remember, my sons, the words which king Benjamin spake unto his people (Hel. 5:9)

> remember the iniquity of king Noah and his priests (Mosiah 23:9)

> and he did exhort the people of Limhi and his brethren, all those that had been delivered out of bondage, that they should remember that it was the Lord that did deliver them (Mosiah 25:16; 27:16)

> I have spoken unto you concerning that prophet which the Lord showed unto me, that should baptize the Lamb of God, which should take away the sins of the world (2 Ne. 31:4)

> put your trust in God . . . who brought the children of Israel out of the land of Egypt, and caused that they should walk through the Red Sea on dry ground, and fed them with manna (Mosiah 7:19)

> Do they remember the travails, and the labors, and the pains of the Jews, and their diligence unto me, in bringing forth salvation unto the Gentiles? (2 Ne. 29:4)

APOSTROPHE

Apostrophe is a direct address to a person, group, or thing as if they are present and capable of listening. Examples include a sermon to all future descendants of the House of Israel, or to all unbelievers.[3]

The scriptures are meant to be read by millions of people at many different time periods, and they teach principles that are applicable to all. The Doctrine and Covenants is notable in that revelations are given to specific individuals, such as the revelations given to Oliver Cowdery in sections 8 and 9. However, they contain principles that are applicable to all of us. Many passages of scripture are addressed to specific groups of people. Others involve people who are being spoken to during sermons recorded in the scriptures.

As Mormon wrote and abridged the record that was to become the Book of Mormon, he was inspired to direct passages of the book to specific groups or types of people. While those of us who are Gentiles may gain much information and inspiration from passages addressed to the Jews or the Remnant of the House of Israel, we should take particular note of those passages that are addressed to or refer to us. Below are some examples of apostrophe included in the Book of Mormon.

> And now I speak also concerning those who do not believe in Christ (Morm. 9:1–31)
>
> O ye Gentiles, have ye remembered the Jews (2 Ne. 29:5)
>
> Hearken, O ye Gentiles (3 Ne. 30:1; Morm. 5:22; Ether 4:13; 8:23)
>
> O ye workers of iniquity (Alma 5:37)
>
> Hear ye the words of the prophet, ye who are a remnant of the house of Israel (1 Ne. 19:24; Morm. 7:1; 3 Ne. 10:5; 16:12)
>
> Hearken, O ye house of Israel (2 Ne. 21:1; 7:4; 3 Ne. 10:5)
>
> Listen, O isles, unto me (1 Ne. 21:1)
>
> Therefore I write unto you, Gentiles, and also unto you, house of Israel (Morm. 3:17)

Behold, I speak unto you as if ye were present, and yet ye are not. But behold, Jesus Christ hath shown you unto me, and I know your doing (Morm. 8:35)

PERSONIFICATION

Personification is an address to an inanimate thing as if it were a person. It involves treating something that is not human as if it were capable of acting.[4] The use of personification in the Book of Mormon generally involves an accompanying use of a metaphor.

mother Gentiles (1 Ne. 13:17)

mother of harlots (1 Ne. 13:34)

that great church, which is the mother of abominations; and she is the whore of all the earth (1 Ne. 14:9)

they are written in the book which thou beheld proceeding out of the mouth of the Jew (1 Ne. 14:23)

the words of the faithful should speak as if it were from the dead (2 Ne. 27:13)

Howl, O gate; cry, O city; thou, whole Palestina, art dissolved (2 Ne. 24:31; Isa. 14:31)

For shall the work say of him that made it, he made me not? Or shall the thing framed say of him that framed it, he had no understanding? (2 Ne. 27:27)

Break forth into joy; sing together ye waste places of Jerusalem; for the Lord hath comforted his people, he hath redeemed Jerusalem (Mosiah 12:23)

that the grave should have no victory, and that death should have no sting (Mosiah 16:7)

the blood of the innocent shall stand as a witness against them (Alma 14:11; 2 Ne. 28:10; Alma 1:13; 20:18; 37:30; 60:10; 3 Ne. 9:7)

> for the Lord will not suffer that the blood of his saints, which shall be shed by them, shall always cry unto him from the ground for vengeance upon them and yet he avenge them not (Ether 8:22)

REVERSE REASONING

Reverse reasoning involves a mode of thought or reasoning that uses negatives, and that is a reversal of the usual linear mode of reasoning or presentation. The Book of Mormon contains several notable passages that uses this type of negative or reverse reasoning.

> And if ye shall say there is no law,
> ye shall also say there is no sin.
> If ye shall say there is no sin,
> ye shall also say there is no righteousness.
> And if there be no righteousness there be no happiness.
> And if there be no righteousness nor happiness
> there be no punishment nor misery.
> And if these things are not there is no God.
> And if there is no God we are not, neither the earth;
> for there could have been no creation of things,
> neither to act nor to be acted upon;
> wherefore, all things must have vanished away. (2 Ne. 2:13)

> For as death hath passed upon all men, to fulfill the merciful plan of the great Creator,
> there must needs be a power of resurrection,
> and the resurrection must needs come unto man by reason of the fall;
> and the fall came by reason of transgression,;
> and because man became fallen they were cut off from the presence of the Lord (2 Ne. 9:6)

> Now, how could a man repent except he should sin?
> How could he sin if there was no law?
> How could there be a law save there was a punishment? (Alma 42:27)

AND THUS WE SEE—INDUCTIVE INFERENCES

Inductive inferences involve gospel principles that are inferred by the writer from the events that have been described. Induction is the major method of science. The scientist observes certain facts or sets of data and then makes inferences or conclusions concerning the application of these facts to a scientific theory or principle being studied. In a very real sense, the facts or data enable the scientist to test or "prove" a certain hypothesis derived from a theory.

In the realm of religion, inductive inferences are conclusions made by prophets, and indeed by ordinary people, about the application of gospel principles to the real world. Prophets show the people through their teachings the results of their behavior and help the people understand how gospel principles operate in the mortal world. Such inductive inferences help people to realize the workings of God in the world, and how God deals with His children in mortality.

In the Book of Mormon, the prophetic authors quite frequently use the phrase "and thus we see" to point out to the reader a conclusion that should be obvious to them, but which many may not have been able to observe or understand after reading the accounts of the people of the Book of Mormon. Some of the most important teachings of the prophets are found in these often short and pithy conclusions preceded by the phrase "and thus we see."

> And thus we see that by small means the Lord can bring about great things (1 Ne. 16:19)

> And thus we see that the commandments of God must be fulfilled. And if it so be that the children of men keep the commandments of God he doth nourish them, and strengthen them, and provide means whereby they can accomplish the thing which he has commanded them (1 Ne. 17:3)

> and thus we see that the Lord worketh in many ways to the salvation of his people (Alma 24:27)
>
> And thus we see how great the inequality of man is because of sin and transgression (Alma 28:13)
>
> And thus we see the great call of diligence of men to labor in the vineyards of the Lord (Alma 28:14)
>
> and thus we see that the devil will not support his children at the last day, but doth speedily drag them down to hell (Alma 30:60)
>
> And thus we see, that there was a time granted unto man to repent, yea, a probationary time, a time to repent and serve God (Alma 42:4)
>
> And thus we see that except the Lord doth chasten his people with many afflictions, yea, except he doth visit them with death and with terror, and with famine and with all manner of pestilence, they will not remember him (Hel. 12:3—and all of Hel. 12:1–3)
>
> and we see that his arm is extended to all people who will repent and believe on his name (Alma 19:36)
>
> And thus we see that the Lord did visit them in the fulness of his wrath, and their wickedness and abominations had prepared a way for their everlasting destruction. (Ether 14:25)

AND THUS IT IS, AMEN.

Two chapters in First Nephi end with the statement, "and thus it is. Amen." The first is chapter 9. Noel Reynolds interprets this chapter as the end of the record of Lehi, which had been abridged by Nephi (1 Ne. 1–9).[5] Chapter 22 also ends with this phrase, which brings to a conclusion the record of Nephi himself of the book of First Nephi.

However, Reynolds builds a strong case that this phrase is a signal that a major chiasmus has been completed by Nephi. The first nine books of First Nephi represent one set of stories that are arranged in chiastic order, and the rest of First Nephi represents another set of stories that are also arranged in chiastic order and complete or finish the chiasmus in the first nine chapters.

The completion of the major chiasm that the present author found in Alma 13:1–9 is signaled by the same statement "And thus it is. Amen."[6] Having read Noel Reynolds analysis of how this phrase was used by Nephi, I was sensitized to the phrase when it appeared in Alma 13:9, especially because it came in the middle of a sermon on the priesthood, and not at the end of the sermon, as would be expected by the word "Amen." So I searched for a chiasmus and found a marvelous and complex literary structure in Alma 13:1–9. This was discussed previously in chapter 5.

DIALOGUE

Finally, we note that there are several passages of scripture in the Book of Mormon that quote verbatim a dialogue between two individuals, usually between a prophet and a listener who is challenging the prophet.[7] The dialogue between Alma and Amulek, on the one hand, and Zeezrom, who was a leader of the apostates in the city of Ammonihah, is an excellent example of such dialogue. Two other examples will be quoted briefly below.

> But behold, it shall come to pass that the Lord God shall say unto him to whom he shall deliver the book:
>
> Take these words which are not sealed and deliver them to another, that he may show them unto the learned, saying: Read this, I pray thee.

> And the learned shall say: Bring hither the book and I will read them. And now, because of the glory of the world and to get gain will they say this, and not for the glory of God.
>
> And the man shall say: I cannot bring the book, for it is sealed.
>
> Then shall the learned say: I cannot read it. (2 Ne. 27:15–18)
>
> Alma said unto him, taking him by the hand: Believest thou in the power of Christ unto salvation?
>
> And he answered and said: Yea, I believe all the words that thou hast taught.
>
> And Alma said: If thou believest in the redemption of Christ thou canst be healed.
>
> And he said: Yea, I believe according to thy words (Alma 15:6–7)

Many other dialogues are quoted, at least in part, in the Book of Mormon. These include Lehi's instructions to Nephi concerning returning to Jerusalem to get the brass plates (1 Ne. 3:2–7), Nephi's talk with Zoram, the servant of Laban (1 Ne. 4:22–27), Nephi's dialogue with Laman and Lemuel concerning the building of a ship (1 Ne. 17:17–52), Ammon's dialogue with King Lamoni and Lamoni's subsequent conversion (Alma 18:14–35), King Lamoni's and Ammon's dialogue with Lamoni's father, the King of the Lamanites (Alma 20:9–27), Aaron's subsequent dialogue with King Lamoni's father that led to his conversion (Alma 22:2–18), the daughter of Jared's discussion with her father concerning his conspiracy with Akish to kill King Omer (Ether 8:9–10), and Akish's dialogue with Jared (Ether 8:11–12).

Often, only one side of the dialogue is quoted, as when Lehi responds to his wife Sariah's complaint (1 Ne. 5:2–6). In short, the Book of Mormon is filled with dialogue, and this enriches and expands the language of the book and makes it much more realistic and interesting. Dialogue is frequently an essential component of narrative, and gives it a personal character.

NOTES

1. Watson, *Classical Hebrew Poetry,* 299, defines allusion as "the reference within one body of literature to the culture and letters of another body."
2. Alter, *World of Biblical Literature,* 107.
3. Bullinger, *Figures of Speech,* 901–5.
4. Bullinger, *Figures of Speech,* 861–69; Caird, *Language and Imagery of the Bible,* 172–82. Caird uses the term *anthropomorphism* to express such personification.
5. Reynolds, "Nephi's Outline," 53–74.
6. Duke, "Literary Structure and Doctrinal Significance of Alma 13:1–9," 103–88.
7. Bullinger, *Figures of Speech,* 898–99.

CHAPTER TWENTY

EXERGASIA, EXEGESIS, HYPERBOLE, UNDERSTATEMENT, AND ANTENANTIOSIS

In this chapter, we discuss another series of literary forms found in the Book of Mormon. Some of these literary forms are easily identified by most readers. Others are misunderstood and often unappreciated. All are used by the prophets who wrote the Bible as well as those who wrote the Book of Mormon, which solidifies the ties between these two scriptures. All of them exhibit a great deal of literary sophistication, which admittedly Joseph Smith did not possess as he translated the Book of Mormon. This is added witness that he was a translator of divine records and did not create the book from his own mind or experience. For each of these literary forms, space will permit us to give only a few examples.

EXERGASIA

In the literary form known as *exergasia,*[1] *the second and subsequent lines "work out" or explain what was said in the first line.* The first line is not complete in itself, but needs further explanation and expansion.[2] The first line might be thought of as a thesis statement, with subsequent sentences filling out the meaning and adding to our understanding of the prophet's meaning and conclusion. All of our examples are drawn from Perry.[3]

We had gathered together all manner of seeds of every kind,
both of grain of every kind, and also of the seeds of fruit of every kind (1 Ne. 8:1)

Hosanna to the Lord, the most high God,
for he is God over all the earth, yea, even above all (1 Ne. 11:6)

And the mists of darkness are the temptations of the devil,
which blindeth the eyes, and hardeneth the hearts of the children of men,
and leadeth them away into broad roads, that they perish and are lost (1 Ne. 12:17)

And they came to a land,
yea, even a very beautiful and pleasant land, a land of pure water (Mosiah 23:4)

I will give unto them again the land of their fathers for their inheritance,
which is the land of Jerusalem, which is the promised land unto them forever (3 Ne. 20:29)

all things which should come upon the face of the earth,
even until the elements should melt with fervent heat,
and the earth should be wrapt together as a scroll,
and the heavens and the earth should pass away. (3 Ne. 26:3)

and they had all things common among them,
every man dealing justly, one with another (3 Ne. 26:19)

lifted up in pride,
such as the wearing of costly apparel, and all manner of fine pearls,
and of the fine things of the world. (4 Ne. 1:17)

remember that ye are free to act for yourselves—
to choose the way of everlasting death or the way of eternal life. (2 Ne. 10:23)

and blessed are they who shall seek to bring forth my Zion at
that day,
for they shall have the gift and power of the Holy Ghost;
and if they endure unto the end they shall be lifted up at the last
day,
and shall be saved in the everlasting kingdom of the Lamb;
and whoso shall publish peace, yea, tidings of great joy,
how beautiful upon the mountains shall they be. (1 Ne. 13:37)

otherwise men were fallen
and there could no good thing come unto them (Moro. 7:24)

EXEGESIS

Exegesis involves an explanation or interpretation of the meaning of a scriptural text. The prophet who is writing or giving the sermon explains the doctrine that is the subject of record. Exegesis occurs constantly in the scriptures, especially in sermons in which the speaker is explaining gospel principles. Most if not all of the sermons found in the Book of Mormon, discussed in chapter 3, can be classified as exegesis. We can identify only a few notable examples here.

3 Nephi 23:6	Jesus . . . expounded all the scriptures unto them which they had received (See also 3 Ne. 27:5)
1 Nephi 10:17–22	Nephi preached concerning the power of the Holy Ghost
1 Nephi 22	Nephi discussed and explained 1 Nephi 20–21 (Isa. 48–49)
2 Nephi 1:3–12	Nephi explained the doctrine of the promised land and of the chosen people
2 Nephi 2	Lehi explained the doctrine of the fall and of the atonement
2 Nephi 3	Lehi explained the history of the House of Israel

2 Nephi 9	Jacob explained the doctrine of the atonement
2 Nephi 25–33	Nephi discussed the meaning of the Isaiah chapters quoted in 2 Nephi 12–24.
2 Nephi 26:29	Nephi explained the meaning of priestcrafts
2 Nephi 31	Nephi discussed the doctrine of Christ
Jacob 7:10–14	Jacob explained the scriptures concerning Christ to Sherem
Mosiah 2:37–38	King Benjamin explained the effects of apostasy
Mosiah 4:4–10	King Benjamin explained the plan of salvation
Mosiah 12:20–37	Abinadi explained the meaning of "how beautiful upon the mountains"
Mosiah 16:1–6	Abinadi discussed the effects of wickedness
Alma 12:21–24	Alma discussed the events in the Garden of Eden
Alma 18:36	Alma "rehearsed and laid before [King Lamoni] the records and the holy scriptures"
Alma 21–22	Aaron to King Lamoni's father [the Lamanite king] discussed the plan of salvation
Alma 39–42	Alma to his son Corianton discussed the plan of salvation and life after death
Alma 45:19	Alma discussed being taken up by the Spirit
Helaman 5	Helaman to his sons Nephi and Lehi discussed "the man of Christ"

3 Nephi 30:23–46	Behold, I am he of whom Moses spake, saying: A prophet shall the Lord your God raise up unto you of your brethren, like unto me; him shall ye hear in all things (explaining covenants to the House of Israel)
Ether 2:5–12	Moroni discussed the "choice land"
Ether 12	Moroni discussed faith

HYPERBOLE

Hyperbole is a form of exaggeration or overstatement that involves carrying things to an extreme.[4] By emphasizing or overemphasizing a certain point, the writer or speaker makes it more conspicuous and prominent, so that the principle being discussed will work upon the minds and hearts of the readers.[5] The writers of the Book of Mormon seemed to use hyperbole less frequently than did the authors of the Bible.[6]

In the examples that follow, I will identify some of the passages of the Book of Mormon as hyperbole. I do not wish to be negative in any way or to minimize the commitment of the Book of Mormon people, especially in their desire to pray both day and night without ceasing. Likewise, in referring to the flames of the lake of fire and brimstone which burn people forever and ever, some people interpret these passages literally while others see them as a metaphor and as hyperbole. God's purpose, it seems, may best be achieved when a scriptural statement is emphasized or even overemphasized so that it can "work upon the hearts of the children of men, altogether for my name's glory" (D&C 19:6).

I did praise him all the day long (1 Ne. 18:16)

their torment is as a lake of fire and brimstone, whose flame ascendeth up forever and ever and has no end (2 Ne. 9:16)

> they fought like lions . . . like dragons did they fight (Mosiah 20:10, 11)
>
> prayeth continually without ceasing (Alma 26:22)
>
> there was not a living soul among all the people of the Nephites who did doubt in the least the words of all the holy prophets who had spoken (3 Ne. 5:1)
>
> to sing ceaseless praises with the choirs above (Morm. 7:7)
>
> and he did thank and praise the Lord all the day long; and when the night came, they did not cease to praise the Lord (Ether 6:9)

UNDERSTATEMENT

The opposite of hyperbole is understatement, in which the author purposely states things with a lack of emphasis or superlatives, often when superlatives are warranted and expected. Such statements may seem to contain a sort of dry humor. There are not many instances of understatement in either the Bible[7] or the Book of Mormon, but those that we have found are interesting and significant. For example, after many wars between the Nephites and Lamanites, the Lamanites achieved remarkable military victories in conquering the city of Zarahemla and many other cities of the Nephites. The military and political situation of the Nephites was indeed ominous and alarming. But the Lamanites were converted as a direct result of the remarkable manifestations to Nephi and Lehi in prison. Then in a classic understatement, the Book of Mormon simply says:

> And as many as were convinced did lay down their weapons of war, and also their hatred and the traditions of their fathers.
>
> And it came to pass that they did yield up unto the Nephites the lands of their possession. (Hel. 5:51–52)

Other instances of understatement are the following:

> I [Amulek] am a man of no small reputation (Alma 10:4)

> And he also knowing that it was the only desire of the Nephites to preserve their lands, and their liberty, and their church, therefore he thought it no sin that he should defend them by stratagem (Alma 43:30)

> Now Moroni thought it was not expedient that the Lamanites should have any more strength (Alma 46:30)

> Now behold, Helaman and his brethren were no less serviceable unto the people than was Moroni (Alma 48:19)

> and in these circumstances they found that it was not expedient that they should fight with the Nephites (Alma 55:23)

> But behold, the Nephites were not slow to remember the Lord their God in this their time of affliction (Alma 55:31)

> For if their wine should poison a Lamanite it would also poison a Nephite (Alma 55:32)

> and if it so be that ye believe in Christ, and are baptized, first with water, then with fire and with the Holy Ghost . . . it shall be well with you in the day of judgment (Morm. 7:10)

ANTENANTIOSIS

Antenantiosis is one of the most interesting literary forms found in the Book of Mormon and in the Bible. In some respects, it is similar to understatement, and in other respects it is related to antithesis. *Antenantiosis is "the practice of stating a proposition in terms of its opposite."*[8] According to Gail Call, the result of this figure of speech[9] "is to express the positive in a very high degree."[10]

Call gives the following examples:

"Despise not the revelations of God" (Jacob 4:8), which really emphasizes the importance of accepting and loving the revelations of God.

"If ye do this, and endure to the end, ye will in nowise be cast out" (Morm. 9:29), which emphasizes the blessings that will be received by those who endure to the end.

"It is not expedient that such abominations should come upon you" (Mosiah 29:24), which urges the people not to allow abominations in their midst.

"The devil awardeth you no good thing" (Alma 34:29), in which Amulek warns the Zoramites that Lucifer never rewards his followers, at least in the long run.

For me, the classic example of antenantiosis in the Book of Mormon is found in Moroni's promise regarding those who read the Book of Mormon:

> And when ye shall receive these things, I would exhort you that ye would ask God, the Eternal Father, in the name of Christ, if these things are not true. (Moro. 10:4)

I have frequently wondered why Moroni put the word "not" in that sentence. I just didn't understand that Moroni was using a figure of speech often used in the Bible. Both Isaiah and Malachi, who are frequently quoted in the Book of Mormon, use this figure of speech extensively (see 2 Ne. 20:8 and 3 Ne. 24:10). By putting the sentence quoted above in the negative, Moroni was really emphasizing the positive in a special way and causing the reader to think more deeply about the point he was making.

Some examples of antenantiosis used as a form of understatement may be found in the following scriptures:

> [Concerning Joseph, who was sold into Egypt:] And the prophecies which he wrote, there are not many greater (2 Ne. 4:2)

> and [Ammon] went forth and stood to contend with those who stood by the waters of Sebus; and they were in number not a few (Alma 17:34)

> Lehi [Nephi's brother] was not a whit behind him as to things pertaining to righteousness. (Hel. 11:19)

In a few cases, the use of antenantiosis results in a double negative, which may be understood to be a special case of emphasizing the positive.

> Yea, I know that God will give liberally to him that asketh. Yea, my God will give me, if I ask not amiss (2 Ne. 4:35)

> Thou shalt not take the name of the Lord thy God in vain; for the Lord will not hold him guiltless that taketh his name in vain. (Mosiah 13:15)

> Limhi was not ignorant of the iniquities of his father (Mosiah 19:17)

> And now, O king, if thou has not found me to be an unprofitable servant (Mosiah 22:4)

> And he doth not dwell in unholy temples (Alma 7:21)

> See that ye are not baptized unworthily (Morm. 9:28)

It would be difficult to overemphasize how frequently antenantiosis is used in the Book of Mormon. A few of these examples of antenantiosis may be found in the following scriptures.

> we lie not (Testimony of the Eight Witnesses)

> shall we not be diligent (1 Ne. 4:36)

> let us remember him, and lay aside our sins, and not hang down our heads (2 Ne. 10:20)

> Behold, hath the Lord commanded any that they should not partake of his goodness? (2 Ne. 26:28)

> I the Lord have not forgotten my people (2 Ne. 29:5)

> If they are not the words of Christ, judge ye (2 Ne. 33:11)

> take heed that ye do not transgress, that the name be not blotted out of your hearts (Mosiah 5:11)

> What have ye against being baptized in the name of the Lord (Mosiah 18:10)

> was he not a holy prophet? Did he not speak the words of God (Alma 5:11)

> bringeth not forth good fruit (Alma 5:36)

> if he had not been a prophet he could not have testified concerning these things (Hel. 8:9)

> they did not sin ignorantly (3 Ne. 6:18)

In many instances, the expressions of antenantiosis used in the Book of Mormon are similar to the antitheticals noted in chapter 15. A negative expression is made and then contrasted with a positive expression. This is often a comparison of righteous and unrighteous people, or of the plan of God as contrasted with the plan of Satan (see Hel. 10:12–15, and Morm. 9:1–10).

In conclusion, antenantiosis is a frequently used if also frequently unrecognized literary form found throughout the Book of Mormon. By contrasting the negative with the positive, the prophets are able to emphasize in a powerful way the significance of the positive principles of the gospel of Christ. The use of such expressions causes the reader to pause, to ponder, and to consider the principles being taught. Understanding such an often neglected figure of speech aids the reader to gain a better appreciation for the marvelous construction of the text of the Book of Mormon by the ancient prophets who labored to communicate to us today.

NOTES

1. Parry, *Book of Mormon Text Reformatted,* xxxi.
2. Bullinger, *Figures of Speech,* 399–400.
3. Parry, *Book of Mormon Text Reformatted.*
4. Bullinger, *Figures of Speech,* 423–28.
5. Ryken, *How to Read the Bible as Literature;* Sands, *Literary Genius of the Old Testament,* 59–61.
6. For the frequent use of hyperbole in the Bible, see Caird, *Language and Imagery of the Bible,* 133. See also Watson, *Classical Hebrew Poetry,* 316–21.
7. Caird, *Language and Imagery of the Bible,* 134.
8. Welch, "Antenantiosis in the Book of Mormon," *Reexploring the Book of Mormon,* 96.
9. Bullinger, *Figures of Speech,* 160–64.
10. Call, "Antenantiosis in the Book of Mormon," *Insights,* 6; Welch, "Antenantiosis in the Book of Mormon," *Reexploring the Book of Mormon,* 96.

CHAPTER TWENTY-ONE

EPANALEPSIS, EPIBOLE, POLYSYNDETON, AND PARADIASTOLE

Many of the literary forms to be discussed in this chapter are unusual and extraordinary. Many of these are unfamiliar to most readers of the Book of Mormon, as they were to me before I read Parry's book.[1] I admit that there are not many times when I can identify these myself, so I have drawn heavily from Parr's analysis in this chapter. However, I also have found that the more I have studied these literary forms, the more meaningful they have become to me, and the more easily I have been able to identify them myself.

EPANALEPSIS

When I first started reading the Book of Mormon, there were a few times when the wording seemed awkward, strained, and repetitive. The words didn't sound as I thought they should. These sentences were few, however, and the great majority of the book flowed in beautiful, poetic language.

How can we explain these awkward and repetitive sentences? Larry Childs has identified these as instances of what is called "epanalepsis."[2] *Epanalepsis is the repetition of a word or phrase after an intervening phrase.* This is done either for emphasis or clarity.[3] The phrase at the first part of a sentence is succeeded by the insertion of a new idea, often a whole phrase or sentence, even a whole paragraph. This is then followed by a restatement of the original phrase, either in the last part of the sentence or in the beginning of the next sentence. The inserted phrase typically gives contextual information or explains some other aspect of the situation. As Childs says, "the intervening material [is] parenthetical in nature and [is] inserted as background or supplementary information to the main thought expressed in the sentence."[4]

Childs has shown that epanalepsis is more frequently used in the narrative portions of the Book of Mormon than in the sermons. He also has shown that Mormon used epanalepsis much more frequently than other authors.[5] Epanalepsis is not just accidental repetition that is caused by poor writing and the need to clarify a statement that has been interrupted. Instead, epanalepsis represents a manner of parallelism that uses this type of expression in a literary way to allow for the insertion of important elements in the presentation of a narrative or discourse. The following instances of epanalepsis were identified by Childs and represent the more notable examples of this interesting form of poetic expression.[6]

> because of the many plain and precious things which have been taken out of the book, which were plain unto the understanding of the children of men, according to the plainness which is in the Lamb of God—because of these things which are taken away out of the gospel of the Lamb (1 Ne. 13:29).

> I say unto you that if ye should serve him who has created you from the beginning, and is preserving you from day to day, by lending you breath, that ye may live and move and do according to your own will, and even supporting you from one moment to another—I say, if ye should serve him with all your whole souls yet ye would be unprofitable servants (Mosiah 2:21)

> [Abinadi] began to prophesy among them, saying: Thus has the Lord commanded me, saying— (Mosiah 12:1)

For were it not for the redemption which he hath made for his people, which was prepared from the foundation of the world, I say unto you, were it not for this (Mosiah 15:19)

And it came to pass that while he was going about to destroy the church of God, for he did go about secretly with the sons of Mosiah seeking to destroy the church, and to lead astray the people of the Lord, contrary to the commandments of God, or even the king—And as I said unto you, as they were going about rebelling against God (Mosiah 27:10–11).

And it came to pass that the Nephites who were not slain by the weapons of war, after having buried those who had been slain—now the number of the slain were not numbered, because of the greatness of their number—after they had finished burying their dead they all returned to their lands (Alma 3:1)

and he came to a city which was called Ammonihah. Now it was the custom of the people of Nephi to call their lands, and their cities, and their villages, yea, even all their small villages, after the name of him who first possessed them; and thus it was with the land of Ammonihah. And it came to pass that when Alma had come to the city of Ammonihah (Alma 8:6–8).

while he was journeying thither, being weighed down with sorrow, wading through much tribulation and anguish of soul, because of the wickedness of the people who were in the city of Ammonihah, it came to pass while Alma was thus weighed down with sorrow (Alma 8:14)

Yea, well did Mosiah say, who was our last king, when he was about to deliver up the kingdom, having no one to confer it upon, causing that this people should be governed by their own voices—yea, well did he say that if the time should come (Alma 10:19) as he was with the Lamanitish servants going forth with their flocks to the place of water, which was called the water of Sebus, and all the Lamanites drive their flocks hither, that they may have water—Therefore, as Ammon and the servants of the king were driving forth their flocks to this place of water (Alma 17:26–27)

she having been converted unto the Lord for many years, on account of a remarkable vision of her father—Thus, having been converted to the Lord (Alma 19:16–17)

And as sure as the Lord liveth, so sure as many as believed, or as many as were brought to the knowledge of the truth, through the preaching of Ammon and his brethren, according to the spirit of revelation and of prophecy, and the power of God working miracles in them—yea, I say unto you, as the Lord liveth, as many of the Lamanites as believed in their preaching, and were converted unto the Lord, never did fall away. (Alma 23:6)

Now when the Lamanites saw that their brethren would not flee from the sword, neither would they turn aside to the right hand or to the left, but that they would lie down and perish, and praised God even in the very act of perishing under the sword—Now when the Lamanites saw this (Alma 24:23–24)

Now when Ammon and his brethren saw this work of destruction among those whom they so dearly beloved, and among those who had so dearly beloved them—for they were treated as though they were angels sent from God to save them from everlasting destruction—therefore, when Ammon and his brethren saw this great work of destruction (Alma 27:4)

and their dead were buried by the people of the land—Now their dead were not numbered because of the greatness of their numbers; neither were the dead of the Nephites numbered—but it came to pass after they had buried their dead (Alma 30:1–2) it was expedient that he should take his armies, who had gathered themselves together, and armed themselves, and entered into a covenant to keep the peace—and it came to pass that he took his army (Alma 46:31)

And it came to pass as he was thus pondering—being much cast down because of the wickedness of the people of the Nephites, their secret works of darkness, and their murderings, and their plunderings, and all manner of iniquities—and it came to pass as he was thus pondering (Hel. 10:3)

And thus, in the commencement of the thirtieth year—the people having been delivered up for the space of a long time to be carried about by the temptations of the devil whithersoever he desired to carry them, and to do whatsoever iniquity he desired they should—and thus in the commencement of this, the thirtieth year, they were in a state of awful wickedness. (3 Ne. 6:17).

when the words of Isaiah should be fulfilled—behold they are written, ye have them before you, therefore search them—And verily, verily, I say unto you, that when they shall be fulfilled (3 Ne. 20:11–12).

for verily I say unto you that when these things which I declare unto you, and which I shall declare unto you hereafter of myself, and by the power of the Holy Ghost which shall be given unto you of the Father, shall be made known unto the Gentiles that they may know concerning this people who are a remnant of the house of Jacob, and concerning this my people who shall be scattered by them; Verily, verily, I say unto you, when these things shall be made known unto them of the Father. (3 Ne. 21:2–3; see vv. 2–7)

And now it came to pass that when Jesus had said these words he said unto them again, after he had expounded all the scriptures unto them which they had received, he said unto them (3 Ne. 23:6)

> did hide up the records which were sacred—yea, even all the sacred records which had been handed down from generation to generation which were sacred—even until the three hundred and twentieth year from the coming of Christ. And he did hide them up unto the Lord. (4 Ne. 1:48–49)

In addition to these examples of epanalepsis given by Childs, I have found the following examples.

> Behold, saith the Lamb of God, after I have visited the remnant of the house of Israel—and this remnant of whom I speak is the seed of thy father—wherefore, after I have visited them in judgment. (1 Ne. 13:34)

> Behold, it came to pass that king Benjamin, with the assistance of the holy prophets who were among his people—
>
> For behold, king Benjamin was a holy man, and he did reign over his people in righteousness; and there were many holy men in the land, and they did speak the word of God with power and with authority; and they did use much sharpness because of the stiffneckedness of the people—
>
> Wherefore, with the help of these, king Benjamin, by laboring with all the might of his body and the faculty of his whole soul, and also the prophets, did once more establish peace in the land. (W of M 1:16–18)

> And because he said unto them that Christ was the God, the Father of all things, and said that he should take upon him the image of man, and it should be the image after which man was created in the beginning; or in other words, he said that man was created after the image of God, and that God should come down among the children of men, and take upon him flesh and blood, and go forth upon the face of the earth—
>
> And now, because he said this, they did put him to death. (Mosiah 7:27–28)

> And as sure as the Lord liveth, so sure as many as believed, or as many as were brought to the knowledge of

> the truth, through the preaching of Ammon and his brethren, according to the spirit of revelation and of prophecy, and the power of God working miracles in them—yea, I say unto you, as the Lord liveth (Alma 23:6)

> But behold, if a man shall come among you and shall say: Do this, and there is no iniquity; do that and ye shall not suffer; yea, he will say, Walk after the pride of your own hearts; yea, walk after the pride of your eyes, and do whatsoever your heart desireth—and if a man shall come among you and say this. (Hel. 13:27)

> O my beloved son, how can a people like this, that are without civilization—(And only a few years have passed away, and they were a civil and a delightsome people) But O my son, how can a people like this (Moro. 9:11–13)

See also the following passages of scripture:

Enos 1:23	Alma 1:1–2
Omni 1:6	Alma 56:3–5
Mosiah 1:3–5	Alma 57:26–27
Mosiah 15:11	Helaman 15:7–8
Mosiah 29:13	3 Nephi 8:1–2
Mosiah 29:40	Ether 6:4

EPIBOLE—RANDOM REPETITION

Epibole involves the repetition or reiteration of longer expressions or phrases in an irregular pattern.[7] This repetition ties together a series of sentences or thoughts. However, the placement of these repetitive words is relatively random and unpredictable. Yet they are still notable and fairly easy to identify. In modern English literature, the repetition of a single word over and over again in a few sentences is regarded as very poor style. Authors typically attempt to use a thesaurus to find other words that would convey the same meaning. Yet in other literary traditions, including the tradition from which the authors of the Book of Mormon came, such repetition is not only acceptable, but is used to aid the reader in focusing on the particular word and its meaning. The repetition is an aid to memory, perhaps also to memorization, and to help the reader concentrate on the meaning which the author is trying to convey.

We will not quote the entire passages of the Book of Mormon that contain these examples. The reader is urged to obtain the full text of the Book of Mormon as it is arranged in parallelistic passages by Donald Parry,[8] and to study the many examples of epibole found therein. As a starting point, you may wish to look up the following examples:

bear record (repeated eight times in 3 Ne. 11:32–36)

O House of Israel (repeated four times in 3 Ne. 16:12–16)

in the wilderness (repeated five times in 1 Ne. 4:38–5:6)

proceeding out of the mouth of the Jew (repeated three times in 1 Ne. 13:23–24, once in 1 Ne. 13:38, and another three times in 1 Ne. 14:23)

fruit of thy loins (repeated fourteen times in 2 Ne. 3:7–19, including five times in v. 12; in addition, "seed of thy loins" and "spokesman of thy loins" are both used once)

"order" appears thirteen times in Alma 13:1–16

"light" appears seven times in Alma 19:6

"joy" appears seven times in Alma 27:17–18

"rest" appears nine times in Alma 12–13.

"voice" appears five times in 3 Nephi 11:3

"desire" appears eight times in 3 Nephi 28:1–9

"time" is repeated seventeen times in Alma 40:4–10

"fallen" is repeated nine times in Mormon 6:13–15

"beheld" is used 57 times in 1 Nephi 11–14. In addition, "behold" appears 18 times, "behold" (as an interjection) is used 11 times, and "beholdest" appears six times, a total of 92 usages in four chapters.

POLYSYNDETON

Polysyndeton and paradiastole are two more literary forms that are closely related because they represent opposites. Polysyndeton is often referred to as "many ands."[9] *Polysyndeton is the presentation of a repetitive series of words or phrases that are introduced by the word "and."*

But behold, a hundredth part of the proceedings of this
people, yea, the account of the Lamanites
and of the Nephites,
and their wars,
and contentions,
and dissensions,
and their preaching
and their prophecies,
and their shipping
and their building of ships,
and their building of temples,
and of synagogues
and their sanctuaries,
and their righteousness,
and their wickedness,
and their murders,
and their robbings,
and their plundering,
and all manner of abominations
and whoredoms,
cannot be contained in this work. (Hel. 3:14)[10]

Turn, all ye Gentiles, from your wicked ways;
and repent of your evil doings, of your lyings and deceivings,

and of your whoredoms,
and of your secret abominations,
and your idolatries,
and of your murders,
and your priestcrafts,
and your envyings,
and your strifes,
and from all your wickedness
and abominations,
and come unto me,
and be baptized in my name (3 Ne. 30:2)[11]

We will discuss combinations of literary forms in the next section, but we need to note here that these two passages are classic examples of synonymia, or what I have called in chapter 13 "literary lists." Very frequently, polysyndeton is combined with synonymia, and indeed it would be difficult to separate the two literary forms in most instances.

There is a remarkable set of passages found in the ninth chapter of Ether. In Ether 9:17–19, the word *and* is used 17 times. In Ether 9:21–24, *and* is used 13 times, and in Ether 9:25–27, *and* is used 9 times, or a total of 39 usages of the word *and* in eleven verses.[12]

See also the following passages for notable instances of polysyndeton (the number of times "and" is used is in parentheses):

1 Nephi 8:13–20 (20)
1 Nephi 11:12–17 (12)
1 Nephi 11:30–32 (15)
1 Nephi 16:8–11 (12)
Enos 1:20–23 (24)
Mosiah 9:6–9 (15)
Mosiah 11:13–17 (12)
Alma 2:12–13 (10)
Alma 8:20–23 (11)
Alma 46:12–13 (15)
Alma 58:11–13 (10)
Helaman 5:31–34 (10)
3 Nephi 19:9–15 (16)
3 Nephi 28:19–24 (14)
4 Nephi 1:39–43 (10)
Ether 1:8–32 (25)
Ether 1:41–43 (14)
Ether 6:25–29 (14)
Ether 9:17–19 (17)
Ether 13:27–30 (12)

PARADIASTOLE

In contrast to polysyndeton, **paradiastole** involves a series of negatives, or what are called "disjunctives."[13] *Paradiastole is the presentation of a repetitive series of words or phrases introduced by disjunctives such as "neither," "nor," and "or."*

Have ye any that are lame,
or blind,
or halt,
or maimed,
or leprous,
or that are withered,
or that are deaf,
or that are afflicted in any manner? (3 Ne. 17:7)[14]

neither wickedness,
neither holiness,
nor misery,
neither good nor bad . . .
neither death,
nor corruption,
nor incorruption,
happiness
nor misery,
neither sense
nor insensibility. (2 Ne. 2:11)[15]

Other examples of paradiastole are found in the following passages, with the number of disjunctives noted in parentheses. The number of instances of paradiastole is much fewer than the instances of polysyndeton, and the lists of disjunctives are less extensive.

Mosiah 29:14 (6)
Alma 56:24–25 (3)
Helaman 1:31 (4)
3 Nephi 8:21–22 (9)

NOTES

1. Parry, *Book of Mormon Text Reformatted.*
2. Childs, "Epanalepsis"; see also Bullinger, *Figures of Speech,* 206–7.
3. Preminger, *Princeton Encyclopedia of Poetry and Poetics,* 242.
4. Childs, "Epanalepsis," 2.
5. Childs, "Epanalepsis," 5-9.
6. Childs, "Epanalepsis," 10.
7. Parry, *Book of Mormon Text Reformatted,* xli; This is also called *repetitio* by Bullinger, *Figures of Speech,* 263–66.
8. Parry, *Book of Mormon Text Reformatted,* xli.
9. Parry, *Book of Mormon Text Reformatted,* xxxviii–xxxix; see also Bullinger, *Figures of Speech,* 208–39.
10. Parry, *Book of Mormon Text Reformatted,* 344
11. Parry, *Book of Mormon Text Reformatted,* 432
12. Parry, *Book of Mormon Text Reformatted,* 466-467
13. Parry, *Book of Mormon Text Reformatted,* xxxix-xli; Bullinger, *Figures of Speech,* 238–40.
14. Parry, *Book of Mormon Text Reformatted,* 410
15. Parry, *Book of Mormon Text Reformatted,* 53-54. This verse is also the classic case of a dialectic found in the Book of Mormon. See chapter 15.

CHAPTER TWENTY-TWO

ANAPHORA, EPISTROPHE, AMOEBAEON, CYCLOIDES, GERUND PARALLELS, AND OTHER VERB FORMS

Among the many forms of parallelism that we have examined in this book, some of the most notable forms have yet to be addressed. These involve the specific structure of sentences, including "like sentence beginnings" and "like sentence endings," the structure of paragraphs, such as "like paragraph endings or refrains," and cyclical repetition. The first four literary forms I first learned about by reading Parry, and I have drawn examples liberally from him. One of my own discoveries was the use of gerund and other verb forms of parallelism. Again, we can discuss these only briefly, but hope that our readers will study these forms more fully in the text of the Book of Mormon and in other articles or books cited in the footnotes.

ANAPHORA—LIKE SENTENCE BEGINNINGS

In contrast to some of the other literary forms discussed here, anaphora is relatively easy for the average reader of the Book of Mormon to identify. Anaphora involves a series of identical words or phrases that begin two or more clauses.[1]

The classic example of anaphora in all the scriptures is the Beatitudes, given by the Savior in the Sermon on the Mount and in the land of Bountiful in the Sermon at the Temple.

Here the Savior begins a series of sentences with the word *blessed* (3 Ne. 12:3–11).

Another classic example of anaphora is the last part of the Ten Commandments, found in Exodus 20:1–17. Here each commandment begins with the statement "thou shalt not" (see Mosiah 13:21–24).

A wonderful example of anaphora is what is sometimes called the "ten wo's." We quote just the last part of this injunction.

> Wo unto the deaf that will not hear; for they shall perish.
> Wo unto the blind that will not see; for they shall perish also.
> Wo unto the uncircumcised of heart, for a knowledge of their iniquities shall smite them at the last day.
> Wo unto the liar, for he shall be thrust down to hell.
> Wo unto the murderer who deliberately killeth, for he shall die.
> Wo unto them who commit whoredoms, for they shall be thrust down to hell.
> Yea, wo unto those that worship idols, for the devil of all devils delighteth in them.
> And in fine, wo unto all those who die in their sins (2 Ne. 9:31–38)[2]

Other examples of anaphora include the following:

> O ye fair sons and daughters,
> ye fathers and mothers,
> ye husbands and wives,
> ye fair ones (Morm. 6:19)

> Who can deny his sayings?
> Who will rise up against the almighty power of the Lord?
> Who will despise the works of the Lord?
> Who will despise the children of Christ? (Morm. 9:26)[3]

> Why do ye go about perverting the ways of the Lord?
> Why do ye teach this people that there shall be no Christ, to interrupt their rejoicings?
> Why do ye speak against all the prophecies of the holy prophets? (Alma 30:22)

O that he would show you that he can pierce you, and with one
glance of his eye he can smite you to the dust!
O that he would rid you from this iniquity and abomination.
And, O that ye would listen unto the word of his commands,
and let not this pride of your hearts destroy your souls!
(Jacob 2:15–16)

Other examples of anaphora, or "like-sentence beginnings," that will not be quoted fully here are the following:

How is it (1 Ne. 6:9–12)

believe (Mosiah 4:9–10)

will ye (Alma 5:53–54)

ye are laying (Alma 10:17-18)

well did (Alma 10:19–21)

O Lord (Hel. 11:10–16)

it shall come (Morm. 8:26–32)

Why have ye (Morm. 8:33–40)

EPISTROPHE—LIKE SENTENCE ENDINGS

In contrast to anaphora, epistrophe involves "like-sentence endings."[4] Each sentence in a series ends with the same word or phrase. *Epistrophe is the repetition of a word or phrase at the end of successive sentences.* This literary form places special emphasis on a particular word. A notable example in the Bible is found in 1 Corinthians 13:11, in which "a child" is repeated four times. Examples in the Book of Mormon are the following:

And now it came to pass that all this was done in Mormon,
yea, by the waters of Mormon
in the forest that was near the waters of Mormon;
yea, the place of Mormon,
the waters of Mormon,
the forest of Mormon (Mosiah 18:30)[5]

beareth all things,
believeth all things,
hopeth all things,
endureth all things (Moro. 7:45; 1 Cor. 13:7)[6]

And they were built after a manner that they were exceeding tight,
even that they would hold water like unto a dish;
and the bottom thereof was tight like unto a dish;
and the side thereof were tight like unto a dish;
and the ends thereof were peaked; and the top thereof was tight like unto a dish;
and the length thereof was the length of a tree;
and the door thereof, when it was shut, was tight like unto a dish (Ether 2:17)[7]

AMOEBAEON—REFRAIN—LIKE PARAGRAPH ENDINGS

According to Donald Parry, *amoebaeon, or "refrain," features a recurring identical phrase or sentence found at intervals, always at the end of a paragraph.*[8] Parry suggests that Biblical scholars believe that many Biblical passages are liturgical in style, that is, they were created to be sung or chanted. Part of the passage might be chanted or sung by the priest or rabbi, while the conclusion of the passage would be joined by the congregation. Amoebaeon is rarely found in the Book of Mormon, perhaps because their mode of worship was different from that of the Jews. However, there are a few passages that demonstrate this literary style.

as never had been known in all the land (repeated twice in 3 Ne. 8:5–7)[9]

fight against the apostles of the Lamb (repeated twice in 1 Ne. 11:35–36)[10] to hide their wickedness and abominations from before my face, that the blood of the prophets and the saints should not come up any more unto me against them (repeated five times in 3 Ne. 9:3–11)[11]

CYCLOIDES—REGULAR REPETITION

The literary pattern known as *cycloides involves the "circular repetition" of a word or phrase in such a way that it is repeated at intervals.*[12] For example, Isaiah used the phrase "yet my hand is stretched out still" to illustrate God's willingness to forgive and help his children, even when they have seriously sinned and are far from doing his will. His hand is stretched out to them if they will be return to him and repent (2 Nephi 19:12, 17, 21; 20:4).

A beautiful series of cyclical parallels is found in Jacob's sermon in 2 Nephi 9 with the use of the word "O" as follows:

O the wisdom of God, his mercy and grace! (v. 8)
O how great the goodness of our God (v. 10)
O how great the plan of our God! (v. 13)
O the greatness and the justice of our God! (v. 17)
O the greatness of the mercy of our God, the Holy One of Israel! (v. 19)
O how great the holiness of our God! (v. 20)

These exclamations are contrasted with the following:

O that cunning plan of the evil one! (v. 28)
O the vainness and the frailties, and the foolishness of men! (v. 28)

I am greatly indebted to Parry for his analysis of this litereary form. It has enabled me to find the following instances:

"cast about your eyes" or "casting about your eyes" (Alma 33:21–22)

The phrases "fruit of my loins," "fruit of thy loins," and "fruit of his loins" are repeated three times in 2 Nephi 3:4–7, and then again the phrase "fruit of thy loins" is repeated three times in 2 Nephi 3:18–19.

The word "rest" is stated four times (Alma 12:34–37) prior to its serving as the turning point of the chiasm in Alma 13:2–9 (v. 6), and then is repeated again four more times afterward (Alma 13:12–16).

The words "humble" or "humblest" are repeated three times in the passage in Alma 32:13–16, and the phrase "compelled to be humble" is also found three times in the same passage in Alma.

In the Savior's Sermon at the Temple in the Book of Mormon, the phrase "they have their reward" is repeated twice, and the phrase "shall reward thee openly" is also found twice (3 Ne. 13:2–6).

Other examples found by Parry include:

partake of the fruit (1 Ne. 8:15–18)

after the manner of men (1 Ne. 18:2)

a fifth part (Mosiah 11:3)

have ye sufficiently retained in remembrance (Alma 5:6)

without beginning of days or end of years (Alma 13:7–9)

"not a few" (Alma 16:34–38)

fair sons and daughters (Ether 13:17)

The question "how is it" is repeated five times in 1 Nephi 7:8–12.

"that the blood of the prophets and the saints shall not come any more unto me against them" is repeated five times in 3 Nephi 9:5, 7, 8, 9, 11, with slight variations.

GERUND PARALLELS

An interesting type of parallelism that has received scant attention by Book of Mormon scholars is the form that I call *"gerund parallels," which are several parallel clauses that begin with a gerund form of a verb.* This is a notable manner of establishing parallels, using the verb of each sentence, specifically in its gerund or "ing" form. Among the many examples I have found are the following:

I, Nephi, having been born of goodly parents,
therefore I was taught somewhat in all the learning of my father;
and having seen many afflictions in the course of my days,
nevertheless, having been highly favored of the Lord in all my days;
yea, having had a great knowledge of the goodness and the mysteries of God,
therefore I make a record of my proceedings in my days. (1 Ne. 1:1)

the Lord their God, their Redeemer,
going before them,
leading them by day
and giving light unto them by night,
and doing all things for them which were expedient for men to receive (1 Ne. 17:30)

exhorting with all long-suffering the people to diligence;
teaching the law of Moses, and the intent for which it was given;
persuading them to look forward unto the Messiah (Jarom 1:11)

such as feeding the hungry,
clothing the naked,
visiting the sick
and administering to their relief (Mosiah 4:26)

And thus God breaketh the bands of death,
having gained the victory over death;
giving the Son power to make intercession for the children of men—
Having ascended into heaven,
having the bowels of mercy;
being filled with compassion towards the children of men;
standing betwixt them and justice;
having broken the bands of death, taken upon himself their iniquity and their transgressions,
having redeemed them, and satisfied the demands of justice (Mosiah 15:8–9)

walking in all diligence,
teaching the word of God in all things,
suffering all manner of afflictions,
being persecuted by all those who did not belong to the church of God (Mosiah 26:38).

stealing away the hearts of the people;
causing much dissension among the people;
giving a chance for the enemy of God to exercise his power over them (Mosiah 27:9)

zealously striving to repair all the injuries which they had done to the church,
confessing all their sins,
and publishing all the things which they had seen,
and explaining the prophecies and the scriptures to all who desired to hear them (Mosiah 27:35)

king Mosiah having gone the way of all the earth,
having warred a good warfare,
walking uprightly before God,
leaving none to reign in his stead (Alma 1:1)

preaching to them that which he termed to be the word of God,
bearing down against the church;
declaring unto the people that every priest and teacher ought to become popular (Alma 1:3)

wearing costly apparel;
being lifted up in the pride of their own eyes;
persecuting,
lying,
thieving,
robbing,
committing whoredoms,
and murdering (Alma 1:32)

while others were abasing themselves,
succoring those who stood in need of their succor,
such as imparting their substance to the poor and the needy,
feeding the hungry,
and suffering all manner of afflictions for Christ's sake,
who should come according to the spirit of prophecy;
Looking forward to that day,
thus retaining a remission of their sins;
being filled with great joy because of the resurrection of the dead (Alma 4:13–14)

having got the victory over the devil,
and the word of God being preached in its purity in all the land,
and the Lord pouring out his blessings upon the people (Alma 16:21)

And thus he did preach unto them,
leading away the hearts of many,
causing them to lift up their heads in their wickedness,
yea, leading away many women, and also men, to commit whoredoms—
telling them that when a man was dead, that was the end thereof (Alma 30:18)

he had been strengthening the armies of the Nephites,
and erecting small forts, or places of resort;
throwing up banks of earth round about to enclose his armies,
and also building walls of stone to encircle them about
(Alma 48:8)

withholding their food from the hungry,
withholding their clothing from the naked,
and smiting their humble brethren upon the cheek,
making a mock of that which was sacred,
denying the spirit of prophecy and of revelation,
murdering,
plundering,
lying,
stealing,
committing adultery,
rising up in great contentions,
and deserting away into the land of Nephi (Hel. 4:12)

sparing their lives,
and delivering them out of the hands of their enemies;
softening the hearts of their enemies that they should not
declare wars against them;
yea, and in fine, doing all things for the welfare and happiness
of his people (Hel. 12:2)

Nephi was baptizing,
and prophesying,
and preaching,
crying repentance unto the people,
showing signs and wonders,
working miracles among the people, that they might know that
the Christ must shortly come—
Telling them of things which must shortly come (Hel. 16:4–5)

Nephi—having been visited by angels and also the voice of the
Lord,
therefore having seen angels,

and being eye-witness,
and having had power given unto him that he might know concerning the ministry of Christ,
and also being eye-witness to their quick return from righteousness unto their wickedness and abominations;
Therefore, being grieved for the hardness of their hearts and the blindness of their minds (3 Ne. 7:15–16)

The verb "having" is frequently used to create such gerund parallels, as in 2 Nephi 1:10; Jacob 1:10; Mosiah 15:9–10; and Alma 13:29. An especially notable scriptural passage is found in Alma 9:19–22, in which the verb "having" is used thirteen times.

OTHER VERB FORMS OF PARALLELISM

There are a few other instances in which verb forms are used to create parallelistic expressions. Typically these are done using the past tense or the "eth" archaic ending, as follows:

which blindeth the eyes,
and hardeneth the hearts of the children of men,
and leadeth them away into broad roads (1 Ne. 12:17)

which slayeth the saints of God,
yea, and tortureth them
and bindeth them down,
and yoketh them with a yoke of iron,
and bringeth them down into captivity (1 Ne. 13:5)

Cursed is he that putteth his trust in man,
or maketh flesh his arm,
or shall hearken unto the precepts of men (2 Ne. 28:31)

for it persuadeth them to do good;
it maketh known unto them of their fathers;
and it speaketh of Jesus,

and persuadeth them to believe in him, and to endure to the
  end, which is life eternal.
And it speaketh harshly against sin (2 Ne. 33:4–5)

[a wicked king] keepeth his guards about him;
and he teareth up the laws of those who have reigned in right-
  eousness before him;
and he trampleth under his feet the commandments of God;
And he enacteth laws,
and sendeth them forth among his people (Mosiah 29:22–23)

Yea, he that repenteth
and exerciseth faith,
and bringeth forth good works,
and prayeth continually without ceasing (Alma 26:22)

then is the time that they do harden their hearts,
and do forget the Lord their God,
and do trample under their feet the Holy One (Hel. 12:2)

NOTES

1. Parry, *Book of Mormon Text Reformatted,* xxxvi–xxxvii; Bullinger, *Figures of Speech,* 199–205.
2. Parry, *Book of Mormon Text Reformatted,* 72.
3. Parry, *Book of Mormon Text Reformatted,* 451.
4. Parry, *Book of Mormon Text Reformatted,* xliii–xliv; Bullinger, *Figures of Speech,* 241–43.
5. Parry, *Book of Mormon Text Reformatted,* 175.
6. Parry, *Book of Mormon Text Reformatted,* 484.
7. Parry, *Book of Mormon Text Reformatted,* 456.
8. Parry, *Book of Mormon Text Reformatted,* xliv; Bullinger, *Figures of Speech,* 343–44.
9. Parry, *Book of Mormon Text Reformatted,* 392.
10. Parry, *Book of Mormon Text Reformatted,* 19.
11. Parry, *Book of Mormon Text Reformatted,* 394-5. Parry diagrams this as an extended alternate.
12. Parry, *Book of Mormon Text Reformatted,* xlii–xliii; Bullinger, *Figures of Speech,* 342.

CHAPTER TWENTY-THREE

FREE VERSE AND COMBINATIONS OF POETIC FORMS

Our discussion of the literary forms found in the Book of Mormon would be incomplete if we did not note the presence of both free verse and combinations of poetic forms. Those of us who read the book many times are often struck again and again with the beauty of expression of many of the passages. The words have a lilt to them, a pattern, an orderliness, and a beauty that are both remarkable and enthralling. This lyrical design helps us to remember the phraseology, so that as we read it again it becomes familiar and memorable.

FREE VERSE

Free verse involves *poetic expressions that have neither meter nor rhyme, but which have poetic style and phraseology.* Many passages have a phrasing that is poetic in style, and the whole is beautiful and remarkable. Some of the most beautiful poetry in the English language is written in free verse, and the same is true of the expressions found in the Book of Mormon. Below I have quoted some of the most significant passages that I personally have found and that have great meaning for me.

and if it so be that ye believe in Christ,
and are baptized, first with water,
then with fire and with the Holy Ghost,
following the example of the Savior,

according to that which he hath commanded us,
it shall be well with you in the day of judgment. Amen. (Morm. 7:10)

And because of the redemption of man, which came by Jesus Christ,
they are brought back into the presence of the Lord;
yea, this is wherein all men are redeemed,
because the death of Christ bringeth to pass the resurrection,
which bringeth to pass a redemption from an endless sleep,
from which sleep all men shall be awakened by the power of God
when the trump shall sound;
and they shall come forth, both small and great,
and all shall stand before his bar,
being redeemed and loosed from this eternal band of death,
which death is a temporal death. (Morm. 9:13)

may Christ lift thee up,
and may his suffering and death,
and the showing his body unto our fathers,
and his mercy and long-suffering,
and the hope of his glory and of eternal life,
rest in your mind forever.
And may the grace of God the Father,
whose throne is high in the heavens,
and our Lord Jesus Christ,
who sitteth on the right hand of his power,
until all things shall become subject unto him,
be, and abide with you forever. Amen. (Moro. 9:25–26)

Whatsoever thing ye shall ask the Father in my name,
which is good, in faith believing that ye shall receive,
behold, it shall be done unto you. (Moro. 7:26)

O have mercy, and apply the atoning blood of Christ
that we may receive forgiveness of our sins,
and our hearts may be purified;

for we believe in Jesus Christ, the Son of God,
who created heaven and earth, and all things;
who shall come down among the children of men (Mosiah 4:2)

O how marvelous are the works of the Lord,
and how long doth he suffer with his people;
yea, and how blind and impenetrable
are the understanding of the children of men;
for they will not seek wisdom,
neither do they desire that she should rule over them!
Yea, they are as a wild flock which fleeth from the shepherd,
and scattereth, and are driven,
and are devoured by the beasts of the forest (Mosiah 8:20–21)

Nevertheless, they did fast and pray oft,
and did wax stronger and stronger in their humility,
and firmer and firmer in the faith of Christ,
unto the filling their souls with joy and consolation,
yea, even to the purifying and the sanctification of their hearts
which sanctification cometh
because of their yielding their hearts unto God (Hel. 3:35)

And now I bid unto all, farewell.
I soon go to rest in the paradise of God,
until my spirit and body shall again reunite,
and I am brought forth triumphant through the air,
to meet you before the pleasing bar of the great Jehovah,
the Eternal Judge of both quick and dead. Amen (Moro. 10:34)

Think of your brethren like unto yourselves,
and be familiar with all
and free with your substance,
that they may be rich like unto you. (Jacob 2:17)

Such examples of free verse are comparable to the wonderful free verse found in Isaiah. One of the most notable passages from Isaiah is found in Isaiah 53, in which Isaiah gives a messianic prophecy concerning many of the notable characteristics of the Savior and his ministry on earth. This whole chapter was quoted by Abinadi to King Noah and his priests (Mosiah 14:1–12). There are parallelistic passages in this chapter, and it seems very poetic to me. While it is too long to quote completely here, let me note just two verses.

He is despised and rejected of men;
a man of sorrows,
and acquainted with grief;
and we hid as it were our face from him;
he was despised, and we esteemed him not.
Surely he has borne our griefs,
and carried our sorrows;
yet we did esteem him stricken,
smitten of God, and afflicted. (Mosiah 14:3–4)

COMBINATIONS OF POETIC FORMS

Many passages of scripture utilize two or more literary forms in their presentation. We have noted previously that there are many instances in which chiasmus is combined with alternates, including the classic case found in Alma 13:1–9, which we have outlined. The authors of the Book of Mormon have shown an undeniable tendency to combine literary forms, and a combination of forms probably indicates a more sophisticated and refined literary tradition than would be true if only single types of literary forms were used.

We illustrate this tendency to combine literary forms here with only two passages identified by Parry.

And we talk of Christ,
we rejoice in Christ,
we preach of Christ,
we prophesy of Christ,
and we write according to our prophecies [synonymia, anaphora, and epistrophe] (2 Ne. 25:26)[1]

And there could be no light,
because of the darkness,
neither candles,
neither torches;
neither could there be fire kindled with their fine and exceedingly dry wood,
so that there could not be any light at all;
And there was not any light seen,
neither fire,
nor glimmer,
neither the sun,
nor the moon,
nor the stars,
for so great were the mists of darkness which were upon the face of the land. [synonymia and paradiastole] (3 Ne. 8:21–22)[12]

Other combined forms may be found in the following scriptures:

Chiasmus, epibole, several antitheticals, several simple alternates, several extended alternates, and synonymia: Alma 36:1–30.

Chiasmus, alternates, synonymia, and anabasis: Alma 13:1–9

Chiasmas and alternates: 2 Nephi 11:2–8; Mosiah 3:11–16; Jacob 5:61–64

Anaphora and polysyndeton: 1 Nephi 12:4

Cycloides and synonymia: Mosiah 11:3

Synonymia and polysyndeton: Mosiah 9:6–9; Mosiah 29:36

Anaphora and simple alternate: Alma 34:18–25

CONCLUSION

In conclusion, the prophets who wrote the Book of Mormon were literary giants who made use of a remarkable number of literary forms and styles to express their prophetic messages. The Book of Mormon is a veritable literary masterpiece that has gone unrecognized because most of us do not understand the literary styles used by the Hebrew and Nephite people in their written works. The book is literary to its very core, and its beauty is beyond comparison.

NOTES

1. Parry, *Book of Mormon Text Reformatted,* 99.
2. Parry, *Book of Mormon Text Reformatted,* 393.

CHAPTER TWENTY-FOUR

ADDITIONAL LITERARY FORMS

We have thus far not been able to discuss a number of other literary expressions that are found in the Book of Mormon. These are all addressed well in other sources. Here, we will give only a quick definition and an example or two from the Book of Mormon, leaving it to the reader to explore the other sources that have identified and explored these literary types more fully. We draw on the work of three notable scholars of the Book of Mormon: Sidney Sperry, Donald Parry, and Hugh Pinnock.

SIDNEY B. SPERRY

Sidney B. Sperry was one of the first LDS scholars to make an analysis of the Book of Mormon from a literary perspective. His pioneering book *Our Book of Mormon* was devoted to an analysis of literary aspects of the Book of Mormon.[1] This was followed by his *Book of Mormon Compendium*, which dealt with some of the same literary questions.[2] Many of his most important essays and chapters have been reprinted in the *Journal of Book of Mormon Studies* 4 (spring 1995).

Sperry includes eighteen different literary forms in his analysis of the Book of Mormon. We have already noted Sperry's contribution to the study of 2 Nephi 4:16–35. Sperry is the first person to have named this passage "The Psalm of Nephi," and this seems to be the only psalm in the Book of Mormon. He also discussed in some detail the nature of allegories, with special reference to Jacob 5 (see chapter 6).

In this short summary of Sperry's work, we will discuss briefly each literary form and indicate the chapters and/or verses identified by Sperry as representative of each form. Those who desire a fuller discussion should go directly to the source and read Sperry's excellent analysis.

GOSPEL

Third Nephi, according to Sperry, is "the most outstanding selection of literature in the Book of Mormon."[3] "The American Gospel," as he calls it, includes 3 Nephi 1:4–21, which describes the birth of Christ, and chapters 8–28, which chronicle the visit of Christ to the American continent. Sperry's detailed analysis of this gospel emphasizes the Sermon on the Mount (e.g., the Sermon at the Temple), the blessing of the children, the calling of and instructions to the twelve disciples, and Christ's emphasis on Isaiah and Malachi.

PASTORAL EPISTLES

The Book of Mormon contains two pastoral epistles, Moroni 8:2–30, and Moroni 9:1–26. These are both letters by Mormon to his son Moroni, and are similar in some ways to several of Paul's epistles in the New Testament. They express the prophet's instructions to his son and to his followers.

PROPHETIC EPISTLE

According to Sperry, the one epistle of this type is found in Ether 5, and is Moroni's letter to the future translator of the Book of Mormon.

WAR EPISTLES

Warfare occupies a large place in the history of the Nephites and the Lamanites.[4] This is especially true of what are called the war chapters in Alma 43–62. There are six war epistles in the Book of Mormon:

Captain Moroni to Ammoron (Alma 54:5–14)
Ammoron's reply to Captain Moroni (Alma 55:16–24)
Helaman to Captain Moroni (Alma 56:2 to 58:41)
Captain Moroni to Chief Judge Pahoran (Alma 60)
Pahoran's reply to Captain Moroni (Alma 61:2–21)
Giddianhi to Lachoneus (3 Ne. 3:2–10)

LAMENTATION

"Mormon's Lamentation" is found in Mormon 6:17–22, in which Mormon mourns the destruction of his brethren, the Nephites. This lamentation is constructed by Mormon in a parallelistic style diagramed by Sperry.

HISTORICAL NARRATIVE

According to Sperry, perhaps half of the Book of Mormon is occupied with historical narrative. According to Sperry,

> The Nephite historians did not write history in the scientific, documented form that we do today. They wrote as intelligent, religious, and sincere laymen might write, telling the truth as they saw it . . . and they make few attempts at historical interpretation in the comprehensive and thoroughgoing manner common among first-rate historians of the present time.[5]

MEMOIR

Many of Nephi's writings may be classified as memoirs, in that they give details of his own life, but also emphasize the "personalities and actions" of other people. Sperry distinguishes between memoirs and autobiographies, which are longer narratives of the author's life. He also classifies as memoirs the book of Enos, Zeniff's account in Mosiah 9–10, and Mormon's writings in Mormon 1–7.

PROPHETIC DISCOURSE

As we noted in chapter 3, there are many sermons or prophetic discourses included in the Book of Mormon. Sperry distinguishes such sermons from "oratory," and notes that the prime example of oratory in the Book of Mormon is Benjamin's discourse to the people of Zarahemla in Mosiah 2:9–3:27, and Mosiah 4:4–30.

PATRIARCHAL BLESSINGS

Before his death, Lehi gave patriarchal blessings to his six sons, to Zoram, and, by inference, to the sons of Ishmael. He also bestowed blessings on the children of Laman and Lemuel. These are found in 2 Nephi 1–4, and are comparable in many ways to the blessings given by Jacob to his twelve sons in Genesis 49.

PROPHETIC PREDICTIONS

There are many instances in the Book of Mormon in which a prophet foresees the future and makes prophetic predictions concerning future events. Samuel the Lamanite's prophecies are notable (Hel. 13:5–15:17), as are the prophecies of the coming of Christ and of many of the events in the history of the Israelites and the Gentiles. The explanation of Lehi's dream by Nephi (1 Ne. 10–15) is notable in that the interpretation of the symbols contained in the dream is interwoven with prophecies concerning the future of various groups, including the House of Israel, present-day Jews, and the Gentiles.

PROPHETIC DIALOGUE

This involves a dialogue between the prophet and another person or group of people (see also chapter 19). According to Sperry, five such types of dialogues are found in the Book of Mormon:

with the Lord (1 Ne. 17:7–10; Mosiah 26:14–32)

with the Holy Ghost (1 Ne. 4:10–13; 1:1–13)

with angels (1 Ne. 11:14–14:27)

with inquirers (1 Ne. 15:6–16:5)

with the world (Mosiah 12:25–37)

PRAYERS

Many prayers of different types are included in the Book of Mormon. These include the Lord's Prayer (3 Ne. 13:9–13), the prayers on the sacrament (Moro. 4–5), the ordination of priests and teachers (Moro. 3), supplications to God by Jesus (3 Ne. 19:20–23), and by the brother of Jared (Ether 2:18–29, 22; 3:2–5), and many other prayers. Sperry also notes the "pagan prayer" by the Zoramites on top of the Rameumptom (Alma 31:15–18).

SONGS

"The Song of the Vineyard" from Isaiah and quoted by Nephi (2 Ne. 15:1–7) is the best example of a song in the Book of Mormon. According to Sperry, other songs are "incipient," or "almost" songs. These include Alma 26:8, 16, and some passages in Jacob's sermon in 2 Nephi 9.

GENEALOGIES

While the Nephites were concerned about their Hebrew heritage, only one true genealogy is found in the Book of Mormon. This is in Ether 1:6–32. Other genealogies are noted as being found in the plates of brass.

DONALD W. PARRY

Donald Parry's contributions to our understanding of the literary structure of the Book of Mormon are magnificent and extremely consequential. His influence on my own thinking has been very great and difficult to overestimate. Parry has discussed the following literary forms.[6]

SYNONYMIA

Synonymia involves two or more words or expressions that are synonymous with each other, the second matching or echoing the first.[7]

> Pray unto him continually by day,
> and give thanks unto his holy name by night (2 Ne. 9:52)[8]

What we have referred to as "literary lists" is really a series of synonymous words or phrases. Many of the parallels noted in chapter 12 are synonymous in nature.

SYNTHETIC

Two lines in which the second line explains or adds to the meaning of the first line. According to Parry,[9] the second line is neither synonymous nor antithetical to the first line.

> Adam fell that men might be,
> and men are, that they might have joy (2 Ne. 2:25)[10]

ANABASIS

Anabasis is also called "staircase parallelism" because in each succeeding line, the meaning "goes up" or is intensified.[11]

> And Melchizedek did establish peace in the land in his days;
> therefore he was called the prince of peace,
> for he was the king of Salem (Alma 13:18)[12]

CATABASIS

Catabasis is the opposite of anabasis, in that the meaning in each succeeding line is lower than or secondary to the meaning of previous lines.[13]

> if he have more abundantly, he should impart more abundantly;
> and of him that had but little, but little should be required;
> and to him that had not should be given (Mosiah 18:27)[14]

PARALLELISM OF NUMBERS

This type of parallelism involves a sequence of numbers that are either identical, or in which the second number is one unit higher than the first number (x / x+1).[15]

> he can command fifty,
> yea he can slay fifty (1 Ne. 3:31)[16]

> And in one year were thousands
> and tens of thousands of souls sent to the eternal world
> (Alma 3:26)[17]

PROSAPODOSIS

This is sometimes referred to "detailing," since the initial line is followed by one or more lines that add detail to what was said in the first line.[18]

> there was no contention in the land,
> because of the love of God which did dwell in the hearts of
> the people (4 Ne. 1:15)

Many of the literary types discussed in this book were first classified and discussed by Parry, and my indebtedness to his work is inestimable.

ELDER HUGH W. PINNOCK

In his wonderful analysis of Hebrew literary forms in the Bible and the Book of Mormon, Elder Hugh Pinnock added immeasurably to our understanding of these forms.[19] He discussed many of the forms noted in this book, especially those also discussed by Donald Parry. However, in addition, he discussed the following ancient Hebrew literary forms:

INCLUSIO[20]

With *inclusio, "the same word is repeated at both the beginning and at the end of a sentence."*[21] Within the repeated words is a message that the prophet author seeks to emphasize. One example given by Pinnock is:

> And now I, Nephi, do not make a full account
> of the things which my father hath written,
> for he hath written many things which he saw in visions and in
> dreams,
> and he also hath written many things which he prophesied and
> spake unto his children,
> of which I shall not make a full account.

ANTHROPOPATHEIA

In addition to the pattern of personification discussed in chapter 19, Pinnock adds this form, which involves *passages which "describe both God's and man's passions and physical attributes."*[22] These are characteristics that are attributes of both God and human beings. This form is found frequently in scripture, and gives us to believe that human beings are truly created in the very image of God, and that such usages are not merely metaphorical. Pinnock notes the physical attributes of both God and human beings include feet, body, arm, mouth, face, eye, hand, bowels or liver, voice, and finger; and the personal characteristics of love, comfort, mercy, favor, long-suffering, goodness, kindness, anger, and gives counsel.[23]

ELLIPSIS

Ellipsis involves an omission, or something being left out.[24]A gap is created by leaving out a previously used word. Thus, the passage is shortened, and the reader is left to fill in the gap. This is usually easily done and does not create a problem in interpreting the meaning of the passage.

> Turn, all ye Gentiles, from your wicked ways;
> and repent [all ye Gentiles] of your evil doings. (3 Ne. 30:2)

This form also involves what Hebrew scholars call "verb gapping," which is common in the Bible but uncommon in the Book of Mormon. *Verb gapping involves expressing a verb in the first sentence or clause, and then leaving out the verb in the second sentence or clause.* We noted this literary form briefly in chapter 5.

> For out of Zion shall go forth the law, and the word of the Lord [shall go forth] from Jerusalem. (2 Ne. 12:3; Isa. 2:3)

> There shall be no other name given nor any other way and means [given] whereby salvation can come unto the children of men (Mosiah 3:17)

> All mankind, yea, men and women, all nations, kindreds, tongues and people, must be born again; yea, [must be] born of God (Mosiah 27:25)

> But now that they may foresee that he will come, and [that they may foresee] that he remembereth every creature (Mosiah 27:30)

ELEUTHERIA

Eleutheria involves bold speech, in which a prophet or other leader speaks boldly and openly to his people, often either to exhort them to action or to reproach them for their sins.[25] Jacob spoke boldly to his people in Jacob 2, especially in verses 7–11. Nephi spoke boldly many times.

> And now behold, my people, ye are a stiffnecked people; wherefore, I have spoken plainly unto you, that ye cannot misunderstand. (2 Ne. 25:28)

Captain Moroni led his people with bold speech while carrying the Title of Liberty, and the later prophet also named Nephi spoke boldly from the garden tower. Samuel the Lamanite's preaching on the walls of Zarahemla is another good example. Mormon also interjected bold speech in many places in the Book of Mormon, as in Helaman 12:1–4, and his example was followed by his son Moroni (see Ether 8:20–26).

IRONY[26]

Irony involves a statement whose meaning is contrary to the typical meaning of the words used. As Elder Pinnock notes, "it is also used to communicate contrast or to reveal the foolishness" of the listeners.[27]

> And thus we see that the devil will not support his children at
> the last day,
> but doth speedily drag them down to hell (Alma 30:60).

Other examples of irony discussed by Elder Pinnock are the so-called "Dancing Princess" incident in Ether 12, and the execution of King Noah by fire (Mosiah 19:20) after he caused the execution of Abinadi by fire (Mosiah 17:13–20). Irony is closely related to the concept of paradox, which we discussed at some length in chapter 17.

SEVERAL OTHER FORMS

It might be possible to discuss many other aspects of Book of Mormon literary form, but we will need to limit our discussion. Here let us simply note two other forms discussed by other authors.

ENALLAGE

Enallage "refers to a syntactic device that is fairly common in the Old Testament, where an author intentionally shifts from the singular to the plural (or vice versa) for rhetorical effect."[28] Kevin Barney notes that several passages in the Book of Mormon, especially 1 Nephi 12:9; 2 Nephi 1:31–32; and 3:1–2, exhibit this form.

HEBRAIC CONDITIONALS

A fascinating discovery of another literary form in the Book of Mormon is the use of a conditional clause that is expressed differently in Hebrew than it is in English. Rather than an "if/then" conditional typically used in the English language, the Hebrews expressed a conditional with an "if/and" expression.[29] Research by Royal Skousen concerning the dictation by the Prophet Joseph Smith of some passages in the Book of Mormon demonstrated that he originally used the "if/and" expression, and that these passages were later changed to an "if/then" expression so that they would be grammatically correct in English. For example, the familiar passage in Moroni 10:4,

> if ye shall ask with a sincere heart with real intent having faith in Christ

> and he will manifest the truth of it unto you by the power of the Holy Ghost

was edited in later editions to express the "if/then" conditional. In this case, the word "and" was left out. Skousen has found at least thirteen other instances of the Hebrew conditional published in the first edition of the Book of Mormon and then later changed for grammatical purposes.

CONCLUSION

We have discussed in this chapter a number of different literary devices found in the Book of Mormon. Each is linked to Hebrew literary usage in the Old Testament. These add further testimony of the Hebrew origins of the prophets who wrote the Book of Mormon, and therefore to the ancient origins of this marvelous book.

NOTES

1. Sperry, *Our Book of Mormon.*
2. Sperry, *Book of Mormon Compendium.*
3. Sperry, *Types of Literature in the Book of Mormon: 'The American Gospel,'* 48.
4. Ricks and Hamblin, *Warfare in the Book of Mormon.*
5. Sperry, *Historical Narrative,* 81.
6. Parry, *Book of Mormon Text Reformatted.*
7. Parry, *Book of Mormon Text Reformatted,* iii–ix; Bullinger, *Figures of Speech,* 324–38.
8. Parry, *Book of Mormon Text Reformatted,* 74.
9. Parry, *Book of Mormon Text Reformatted,* xiv.
10. Parry, *Book of Mormon Text Reformatted,* 55.
11. Parry, *Book of Mormon Text Reformatted,* xxi–xxiii; see also Bullinger, *Figures of Speech,* 429–31.
12. Parry, *Book of Mormon Text Reformatted,* 228.
13. Parry, *Book of Mormon Text Reformatted,* xxiii–xxiv; see also Bullinger, *Figures of Speech,* 432–34.
14. Parry, *Book of Mormon Text Reformatted,* 175.

15. Parry, *Book of Mormon Text Reformatted,* xxiv–xxvii; see also Bullinger, *Figures of Speech,* 394–96.
16. Parry, *Book of Mormon Text Reformatted,* 6.
17. Parry, *Book of Mormon Text Reformatted,* 201.
18. Parry, *Book of Mormon Text Reformatted,* xxx–xxxi.
19. Pinnock, *Finding Biblical Hebrew and Other Ancient Literary Forms.*
20. Also called epanadiplosis.
21. Pinnock, *Finding Biblical Hebrew and Other Ancient Literary Forms,* 110. *Inclusio* is the Latin term, while *epanadiplosis* is the Greek term. See Bullinger, *Figures of Speech,* 245–49.
22. Pinnock, *Finding Biblical Hebrew and Other Ancient Literary Forms,* 119.
23. Pinnock, *Finding Biblical Hebrew and Other Ancient Literary Forms,* 119–30.
24. Pinnock, *Finding Biblical Hebrew and Other Ancient Literary Forms,* 141–45, and Bullinger, *Figures of Speech,* 3–130.
25. Pinnock, *Finding Biblical Hebrew and Other Ancient Literary Forms,* 145–50; see also Bullinger, *Figures of Speech,* 932–33.
26. Also called eironeia.
27. Pinnock, *Finding Biblical Hebrew and Other Ancient Literary Forms,* 150; see also Bullinger, *Figures of Speech,* 807–15.
28. Barney, "Further Light on Enallage," 43; Barney, "Enallage," 229–34; see also Bullinger, *Figures of Speech,* 490.
29. Skousen, "Hebraic Conditionals," 2; see also John W. Welch and Melvin J. Thorne, "Hebraic Conditionals in the Book of Mormon," *Pressing Forward with the Book of Mormon,* 201–3; and Peterson, "Not Joseph's, and Not Modern," 212–14.

CHAPTER TWENTY-FIVE

SUMMARY AND CONCLUSIONS

Our journey through the literary forms found in the Book of Mormon has been long and complex, but I have attempted to simplify our discussion as much as possible. I hope that this "journey" has also been informative and enlightening. Personally I am very grateful for and indebted to the many inspired scholars who have analyzed the literary forms we have discussed. They have inspired me to read and reread the Book of Mormon, and to look for the many ways that its prophetic authors have used literary forms to communicate with us the readers. It is my sincerest hope that we may all read the Book of Mormon with new eyes, to use a metaphor that seems appropriate to the book. As we read and ponder, I pray that the Spirit will testify to our hearts to the truthfulness of the messages of the book as well as the prophetic calling of its authors and translator.

The literary style of the scriptures is obviously very important to God and to the prophets whom he sends to carry his word to his people. It is obvious to me that God speaks to us, individually and collectively, in poetic and literary language. I make no claim that literary style is as important as the spiritual content of the prophetic messages. In a sense, literary style is fluff, or the frosting on the cake. Yet the scriptures are given for the purpose of helping God's children understand his message at a cognitive level, as well as to feel spiritual and emotional feelings that will motivate them to take actions that will lead them to salvation and exaltation.

Literary style helps people to pay attention to the message, remember it, and feel a sense of spirituality as well as beauty. So literary style is really not fluff after all, but an essential ingredient in communicating God's message to his children. To emphasize this point again, God speaks to us in poetic and literary language.

By my count, we have discussed ninety different forms, some with several permutations. Some of these we have discussed in great detail and others very briefly. The list is long but deserves to be included here as a summary of our investigation. The ninety literary forms discussed in this book are:

> stories, sermons, themes, poetry, imagery, figures of speech, parallelism, word pairs, psalms, allegories, types, metaphors, similes, simile curses, simile blessings, chiasms, alternates, half-line parallelism, couplets, tricolon, longer parallels, word pairs, triplets, quadruplets, literary lists, idioms, antitheticals, dialectic, aphorisms, memorable phrases, climax, universals, paradoxes, doctrinal terms, names of Christ, new words, duplication, colophons, allusions, apostrophe, personification, reverse reasoning, inductive inferences, dialogue, exergasia, exegesis, hyperbole, understatement, antenantiosis, epanalepsis, epibole, polysyndeton, paradiastole, anaphora, epistrophe, amoebon, cycloides, gerund parallels, other verb forms, free verse, combinations of forms, gospels, pastoral epistles, prophetic epistles, war epistles, lamentation, historical narrative, memoirs, prophetic discourse, patriarchal blessings, prophetic predictions, prophetic dialogue, prayers, songs, genealogies, synonymia, synthetic parallelism, anabasis, catabasis, parallelism of numbers, prosapodosis, inclusio, anthropopatheia, ellipsis, verb-gapping, eleutheria, irony, enallage, and Hebraic conditionals.

Throughout the book we have tried to make two major points, and to make them as explicitly as possible. These are, first, that the Book of Mormon is a monumental literary masterpiece that has long been unappreciated and underestimated by almost everyone, even those who have spent many years studying its text. The second point is that it would have been manifestly impossible for a young and uneducated person such as Joseph Smith to create such a literary work, and to do so in the very short time (less than three months) it took him to produce the manuscript of the Book of Mormon.

If the reader will pardon a personal comment, let me say that I have a doctor of philosophy degree from a major university, have taught university classes for more than forty years, and have written several books and many articles and papers. Yet none of my books, which often took as much as ten years to germinate in my mind and to be put on paper, match in any way the literary magnificence of the Book of Mormon. As the reader will acknowledge, my writing style is fairly simple, not very flowery, and not filled with many different literary styles and forms. I believe only a person who has attempted to write something with great literary value can appreciate what a monumental achievement is the Book of Mormon.

Joseph Smith produced a book of well over five hundred pages in just over sixty days, and this book contains at least ninety literary forms, most of which are closely linked to Hebrew traditions and poetic and literary styles. I challenge any critic or group of critics to produce any book of five hundred pages in sixty days, or ten or twenty years for that matter, that matches in any way the literary achievement of the Book of Mormon. I would be happy to see such critics produce five pages of text that equals the Book of Mormon in literary style and content. If a critic cannot do it, then I believe it behooves the critic to either accept the Book of Mormon for what it is, a majestic and sublime work of scripture, or to mute their criticism and acknowledge their inability to write in the same style or method as Joseph Smith.

I love the Book of Mormon with all my heart, and find

in it great inspiration and comfort. I testify that it is a true and living work of scripture given by God to His children through the instrumentality of His prophets. I commend it to anyone and everyone. I am assured that if a person reads it with a prayerful and sincere heart, with real intent, he or she will gain great enlightenment and edification, and will gain a testimony of its truthfulness.[1]

If we sincerely understand the beauty and significance of the literary style of the Book of Mormon, we will come to appreciate the book as one of the most beautiful and exceptional works of literature in any language. It truly is, to conclude with a familiar word pair, "a marvelous work and a wonder."

NOTE

1. Moroni 10:3–5.

BIBLIOGRAPHY

Alter, Robert. *The Art of Biblical Narrative.* New York: Basic Books, 1981.

———. *The Art of Biblical Poetry.* New York: Basic Books, 1985.

———. *The World of Biblical Literature.* New York: Basic Books, 1992.

Avishur, Yitzhak. *Stylistic Studies of Word-Pairs in Biblical and Ancient Semitic Literatures.* Alter Orient und Altes Testament, Bd. 210. Kevelaer: Verlag Butzon and Bercker; Neukirchen-Vluyn: Neukirchener Verlag, 1984.

Baker, Roger G. *The Bible as Literature: Out of the Best Book.* Ephraim, Utah: Snow College English Department, 1995.

Barney, Kevin J. "Enallage in the Book of Mormon." *Journal of Book of Mormon Studies* 3 (1994).

———. "Further Light on Enallage." In *Pressing Forward with the Book of Mormon: The FARMS Updates of the 1990's,* ed. John W. Welch and Melvin J. Thorne. Provo, Utah: F.A.R.M.S., 1999.

———. "Poetic Diction and Parallel Word Pairs in the Book of Mormon." *Journal of Book of Mormon Studies* 4, no. 2 (Fall 1995).

———. "Understanding Old Testament Poetry." *Ensign* 20 (June 1990).

Benson, Ezra Taft. "Beware of Pride." *Ensign* 29 (May 1989).

Berlin, Adele. *The Dynamics of Biblical Parallelism.* Bloomington: Indiana University Press, 1985.

———. "Introduction to Hebrew Poetry." In *The New*

Interpreter's Bible. vol. 4 Nashville: Abingdon Press, 1996: 301-315.

———. *Poetics and Interpretation of Biblical Narrative.* Sheffield, England: Almond Press, 1983.

Black, Susan Easton. *Finding Christ through the Book of Mormon.* Salt Lake City: Deseret Book, 1987.

Bullinger, E. W. *Figures of Speech Used in the Bible: Explained and Illustrated.* London: Eyre and Spottiswoode, 1898; Grand Rapids, Mich.: Baker Book House, 1968.

Bullock, C. Hassell. *An Introduction to the Old Testament Poetic Books.* Rev. ed. Chicago: Moody Press, 1988.

Bushman, Richard L. "The Book of Mormon and the American Revolution." In *Book of Mormon Authorship: New Light on Ancient Origins,* ed. Noel B. Reynolds. Provo, Utah: Religious Studies Center, Brigham Young University, 1982.

Caird, G. B. *The Language and Imagery of the Bible.* Philadelphia: Westminster Press, 1980.

Call, Gail. "Antenantiosis in the Book of Mormon." *FARMS Insights.* July 1991.

Childs, Larry G. "Epanalepsis in The Book of Mormon." Provo, Utah: F.A.R.M.S., 1986.

Church Education System. *Book of Mormon (Religion 121–122) Student Manual.* Salt Lake City: The Church of Jesus Christ of Latter-day Saints, 1979.

Dahood, Mitchell. "Ugaritic-Hebrew Parallel Pairs." In *Ras Shamra Parallels: The Texts from Ugarit and the Hebrew Bible,* ed. Loren R. Fisher, 1:71–382; 2:1–33; 3:1–178. 3 vols. Analecta orientalia vols. 49–51. Rome: Pontificium Institutum Biblicum, 1972–81.

Duke, James T. "The Literary Structure and Doctrinal Significance of Alma 13:1–9." *Journal of Book of Mormon Studies* 5 (Spring 1996).

———. "Word Pairs and Distinctive Word Combinations in the Book of Mormon," *Journal of Book of Mormon Studies (forthcoming).*

———. "The Traditions of Their Fathers." *Ensign* 2 (November 1972).

Fokkelman, J. P. *Reading Biblical Poetry.* Louisville, Ky.: Westminster John Knox Press, 2001.

Freedman, David Noel. "Another Look at Biblical Hebrew Poetry." In *Directions in Biblical Hebrew Poetry,* ed. Elaine R. Follis. Journal for the Study of the Old Testament, Supplement Series 40. Sheffield, England: JSOT Press, 1987.

Gorton, H. Clay. *A New Witness for Christ: Chiastic Structures in the Book of Mormon.* Bountiful, Utah: Horizon Publishers, 1997.

Hamblin, William J. "The Importance of Warfare in Book of Mormon Studies." In *Book of Mormon Authorship Revisited,* ed. Noel B. Reynolds. Provo, Utah: F.A.R.M.S., 1997.

Holland, Jeffrey R. "For a Wise Purpose." *Ensign* 26 (January 1996).

Jeep, John M. *Alliterating Word-Pairs in Old High German.* Bochum: Universitatsverlag Dr. N. Brockmeyer, 1995.

Koskenniemi, Inna. *Repetitive Word Pairs in Old and Early Middle English Prose: Expressions of the Type "Whole and Sound" and "Answered and Said", and Other Parallel Constructions.* Turku: Turun Yliopisto, 1968.

Kugel, James L. *The Idea of Biblical Poetry: Parallelism and Its History.* New Haven: Yale University Press, 1981.

Lamsa, George M. *Idioms in the Bible Explained.* Nashville: Holman Bible Publishers, 1985.

Lowth, Robert. *Lectures on the Sacred Poetry of the Hebrews.* 1753; New York: Garland Publishing, 1971.

Ludlow, Daniel H. *A Companion to Your Study of the Book of Mormon.* Salt Lake City: Deseret Book, 1977.

Morrise, Mark J. "Simile Curses in the Ancient Near East, Old Testament and Book of Mormon." Provo, Utah: F.A.R.M.S., 1982.

Nibley, Hugh. *Lehi in the Desert and The World of the Jaredites.* Salt Lake City: Bookcraft, 1952.

O'Connor, M. *Hebrew Verse Structure.* Winona Lake, Ind.: Eisenbrauns, 1980.

Parry, Donald W. *The Book of Mormon Text Reformatted according to Parallelistic Patterns.* Provo, Utah: F.A.R.M.S., 1992.

Peterson, Daniel C. "Not Joseph's, and Not Modern." In *Echoes and Evidences of the Book of Mormon,* ed. Donald W. Parry, Daniel C. Peterson, and John W. Welch. Provo, Utah: F.A.R.M.S., 2002.

Pinnock, Hugh W. *Finding Biblical Hebrew and Other Ancient Literary Forms in the Book of Mormon.* Provo, Utah: F.A.R.M.S., 1999.

Preminger, Alex, ed. *Princeton Encyclopedia of Poetry and Poetics.* Princeton, New Jersey: Princeton University Press, 1974.

Rasmussen, Ellis T. "Deuteronomy." In *Encyclopedia of Mormonism,* ed. Daniel H. Ludlow. 4 vols. New York: Macmillan, 1992.

Reynolds, Noel B. *Book of Mormon Authorship: New Light on Ancient Origins.* Provo, Utah: Religious Studies Center, Brigham Young University, 1982.

———. "Nephi's Outline." In *Book of Mormon Authorship: New Light on Ancient Origins,* ed. Noel B. Reynolds. Provo, Utah: Religious Studies Center, Brigham Young University, 1982.

Ricks, Stephen D., and William J. Hamblin, eds. *Warfare in the Book of Mormon.* Salt Lake City: Deseret Book; Provo, Utah: F.A.R.M.S., 1990.

Rust, Richard Dilworth. *Feasting on the Word: The Literary Testimony of the Book of Mormon.* Salt Lake City: Deseret Book, 1997.

Ryken, Leland. *How to Read the Bible as Literature.* Grand Rapids, Mich.: Academic Books, 1984.

Sabourin, Leopold. *The Names and Titles of Jesus: Themes of Biblical Theology.* New York Macmillan, 1967.

Sands, P. C. *Literary Genius of the New Testament.* 1932; Westport, Conn.: Greenwood Press, 1970.

———. *Literary Genius of the Old Testament.* Oxford: Clarendon Press, 1924.

Skousen, Royal. "Hebraic Conditionals in the Book of Mormon." *Insights* (December 1997).

Sperry, Sidney B. *Book of Mormon Compendium.* Salt Lake City: Bookcraft, 1968.

———. *Our Book of Mormon.* Salt Lake City: Bookcraft, 1947.

———. "Types of Literature in the Book of Mormon: Allegories, Prayers, Songs, Genealogies." *Journal of Book of Mormon Studies* 4 (Spring 1995).

———. "Types of Literature in the Book of Mormon: Epistles, Psalms, Lamentations." *Journal of Book of Mormon Studies* 4 (Spring 1995).

———. "What the Book of Mormon Is." *Journal of Book of Mormon Studies* 4 (Spring 1995).

———. "Types of Literature in the Book of Mormon: 'The American Gospel.'" *Journal of Book of Mormon Studies* 4 (Spring 1995).

———. "The Book of Mormon Writings of Sydney Sperry" *Journal of Book of Mormon Studies.* 4 (Spring 1995): 1-300.

Tanner, John S. "Responding to the Lord's Questions." *Ensign* 32 (April 2002).

Tvedtnes, John A. "Colophons in the Book of Mormon." In *Rediscovering the Book of Mormon,* ed. John L. Sorenson and Melvin J. Thorne. Salt Lake City: Deseret Book; Provo, Utah: F.A.R.M.S., 1991.

———. "Word Groups in the Book of Mormon." *Journal of Book of Mormon Studies* 6, no. 2 (1997).

Watkins, Calvert. *How to Kill a Dragon: Aspects of Indo-European Poetics.* New York: Oxford University Press, 1995.

Watson, Wilfred G. E. *Classical Hebrew Poetry: A Guide to Its Techniques.* Journal for the Study of the Old Testament, Supplement Series 26. Sheffield, England: JSOT, 1984.

———. *Traditional Techniques in Classical Hebrew Verse.* Journal for the Study of the Old Testament, Supplement Series 170. Sheffield, England: Sheffield Academic Press, 1994.

Webster's Third New International Unabridged Dictionary of the English Language, ed. Philip B. Gove. Springfield, Mass.: G. & C. Merriam Co., 1963.

Welch, John W. "Chiasmus in the Book of Mormon." *BYU Studies* 10 (autumn 1969).

———. "Colophons in the Book of Mormon." In *Reexploring the Book of Mormon: The F.A.R.M.S. Updates,* ed. John W. Welch. Salt Lake City: Deseret Book; Provo, Utah: F.A.R.M.S, 1992.

———. "Antenantiosis in the Book of Mormon." In *Reexploring the Book of Mormon: The F.A.R.M.S. Updates,* ed. John W. Welch. Salt Lake City: Deseret Book; Provo, Utah: F.A.R.M.S, 1992.

Welch, John W. and Melvin J. Thorne, "Hebraic Conditionals in the Book of Mormon," in *Pressing Forward with the Book of Mormon: The FARMS Updates of the 1990's,* ed. John W. Welch and Melvin J. Thorne. Provo, Utah: F.A.R.M.S., 1999.

Willis, John T. "Alternating (ABA'B') Parallelism in the Old Testament Psalms and Prophetic Literature." In *Directions in Biblical Hebrew Poetry,* ed. Elaine R. Follis, Journal for the Study of the Old Testament, Supplement Series 40. Sheffield, England: JSOT Press, 1987.

Yoder, Sanford C. *Poetry of the Old Testament.* Scottdale, Penn.: Herald Press, 1948.

INDEX

-A-

-B-

-C-

-D-

-E-

-F-

-G-

-H-

-I-

-J-

-K-

-L-

-M-

-N-

-O-

-P-

-V-

-W-

-Y-

ABOUT THE AUTHOR

James T. Duke taught at Brigham Young University from 1963 to 2003 in the Department of Sociology. He instructed both undergraduate and graduate classes in sociological theory, the sociology of religion, the sociological study of Mormon life, and the Book of Mormon. He received bachelor's and master's degrees from the University of Utah and a Ph.D. from the University of California at Los Angeles.

He is the author or editor of several books, including *Latter-day Saint Social Life,* which reviews recent research concerning LDS people. He has published articles in the *Ensign,* the *Journal of Book of Mormon Studies,* and the *Encyclopedia of Mormonism.* He has also authored many journal articles and is an internationally recognized scholar on Church growth.

Brother Duke has served all of his life in The Church of Jesus Christ of Latter-day Saints, including full-time missionary, bishop, branch president, high counselor, gospel doctrine teacher, ward and stake young men's president, ward and stake Sunday School president, counselor in a bishopric, and ward mission leader. He is currently serving (as of June 30, 2003) as a Church service missionary in the Research Information Division of the LDS Church in Salt Lake City.

He has been happily married to Ruth Sidwell Duke for the past forty-five years. They are the parents of nine children and twenty-two grandchildren. His hobbies are walking, music, reading, and spending time with his family.

0 26575 77115 2

IDENTICAL EXTENDED ALTERNATES

Three or more identical elements are repeated in an abc/abc pattern.

Identical extended alternates are composed of at least six lines. Lines one and four (the "a" lines) contain identical words or phrases, lines two and five (the "b" lines) contain identical words or phrases, and lines three and six (the "c" lines) also contain identical words or phrases.

a Therefore, ask
  b and ye shall receive;
    c knock,
      d and it shall be opened unto you;
a for he that asketh,
  b receiveth;
    c and unto him that knocketh,
      d it shall be opened (3 Ne. 27:29)[6]

a Ask,
  b and it shall be given unto you;
    c seek,
      d and ye shall find;
        e knock,
          f and it shall be opened unto you.
a For every one that asketh,
  b receiveth;
    c and he that seeketh,
      d findeth;
        e and to him that knocketh,
          f it shall be opened. (3 Ne. 14:7–8)[7]

a Thou art blessed
  b because of thy exceeding faith
    c in the words alone of my servant Abinadi
a And blessed are they
  b because of their exceeding faith
    c in the words alone which thou hast spoken unto them. (Mosiah 26:15–16)[8]